PLAYING WITH SOMETHING THAT RUNS

Playing with Something That Runs

TECHNOLOGY, IMPROVISATION, AND COMPOSITION IN DJ
AND LAPTOP PERFORMANCE

Mark J. Butler

OXFORD
UNIVERSITY PRESS

OXFORD
UNIVERSITY PRESS

Oxford University Press is a department of the
University of Oxford. It furthers the University's objective
of excellence in research, scholarship, and education
by publishing worldwide.

Oxford   New York
Auckland   Cape Town   Dar es Salaam   Hong Kong   Karachi
Kuala Lumpur   Madrid   Melbourne   Mexico City   Nairobi
New Delhi   Shanghai   Taipei   Toronto

With offices in
Argentina   Austria Brazil   Chile   Czech Republic   France   Greece
Guatemala   Hungary   Italy   Japan   Poland   Portugal   Singapore
South Korea   Switzerland   Thailand   Turkey   Ukraine   Vietnam

Oxford is a registered trade mark of Oxford University Press
in the UK and certain other countries.

Published in the United States of America by
Oxford University Press
198 Madison Avenue, New York, NY 10016

Library of Congress Cataloging-in-Publication Data
Butler, Mark J. (Mark Jonathan), 1970-, author.
Playing with something that runs : technology, improvisation, and
composition in DJ and laptop performance / Mark J. Butler.
        pages   cm
Includes bibliographical references and index.
ISBN 978-0-19-539361-3 (hardback : alk. paper)—ISBN 978-0-19-539362-0 (pbk.)
1. Underground dance music—History and criticism.
2. Underground dance music—Production and direction.   I. Title.
ML3540.5.B87   2014
786.7'6—dc23   2013043636

1 3 5 7 9 8 6 4 2
Printed in the United States of America
on acid-free paper

This volume is published with the generous support of the Gustave Reese Endowment of the American
Musicological Society.

To my parents, Jack and Carol

Contents

Acknowledgments

I WOULD FIRST like to thank the many musicians with whom I worked on this project. This book would not exist without you. I was amazed by the generosity that I encountered: performers with busy international touring schedules took the time to sit down with me and discuss their work, often in highly technical ways, for hours. They invited me into their homes and showed me their production studios and approaches. They put me on the guest list for clubs and allowed me to film their laptop screens. In many cases, they did these things on multiple occasions. For interviews and/or filmed performances, I wish to specifically acknowledge Apparat, Daniel Bell, Brian Crabtree, Kelli Cain, Dash, Deadbeat, Mijk van Dijk, DJane Aroma, DJ Mack, Thomas Fehlmann, Robert Henke, Bernhard Moosbauer, Pacou, Phon.o, Pole, Barbara Preisinger, Recyver Dogs, Henrik Schwarz, Stassy Litschko and Hendrik Vaak of Sender Berlin, Suop, and Stewart Walker. The innovation that you bring to the creation and performance of electronic dance music has had a major impact on the directions in which this book has evolved.

A number of institutions provided key financial support over the course of this project. A grant from the University of Pennsylvania Research Foundation funded my first fieldwork trip to Berlin as well as the purchase of a digital video camera, turntables, and other equipment. A Summer Stipend from the National Endowment for the Humanities enabled a second period of research in Berlin. Crucial periods of sabbatical were made possible by generous fellowships from the American Academy in Berlin (fall 2007) and the University of Texas at Austin (Donald D. Harrington Faculty Fellowship, fall 2009–spring 2010). The latter fellowship also supported a symposium centered around key research themes (this event is described further below). Finally, subvention grants from the Society for Music Theory and the Gustave Reese Endowment of the American Musicological Society provided funding for the production costs of the interactive online examples found in Chapters 1 and 3.

Feedback from scholars around the world has sparked the growth of my work in important ways. To the students and faculty members who responded to my ideas in colloquia and talks at Brown University, Indiana University, New York University, Princeton University, the University of Chicago, the University of Iowa, the University of Pennsylvania, the University of Texas at Austin, the University of Tübingen, and the University of Washington, thank you. Special thanks are also due to Anne Danielsen at the University of Oslo, Holger Schulze at the Humboldt University of Berlin, and Georgina Born at Oxford University for inviting me to participate in their symposia "Rhythm, Sound, and New Technologies," "New Technologies, New Sound Practices," and "Music, Digitisation, Mediation," respectively. I am also grateful to Georgina Born and Nicholas Cook for their comments on various chapters. Finally, I participated in informal writing groups with Luis-Manuel Garcia and Gregory Mitchell during several intensive periods of manuscript preparation; their support and feedback then and subsequently has been extremely helpful.

This book has had a lengthy gestation period, encompassing three institutional home bases: the University of Pennsylvania, the University of Texas at Austin, and Northwestern University. It is a much stronger document as a result of the many inspiring and thought-provoking ways in which colleagues at each of these universities engaged with my work. For their insightful commentary on various portions of this manuscript, special thanks are due to Emily Dolan, Guy Ramsey, Timothy Rommen, Eric Drott, and Sonia Seeman. Thanks as well to Emma Dillon for always reminding me to keep things gentle. I further wish to express my gratitude to all of the scholars who participated in the 2010 symposium "Discourses of Music, Sound, and Film" at the University of Texas at Austin. This event was an unparalleled opportunity to bring together a group of cutting-edge thinkers whose work had inspired my own, and the exchange of ideas that occurred was immensely stimulating. I co-organized this symposium with David Neumeyer, to whom I am extremely grateful for suggesting that we combine our (previously separate) events.

Ideas contained in this book also developed significantly during the course of several graduate seminars. The first was an introductory course, "Writing About Music," which I co-taught with Guy Ramsey at Penn in 2008. In this course I struggled with my students toward an analysis of "The Bells" by Jeff Mills, which now plays a central role in Chapter 3. My thinking benefited significantly from their contributions, and I have fond memories of sharing this experience with the students in that course:

Suzanne Bratt, Christine Thu Nhi Dang, Glenn Holtzmann, and Nina Ohman. Students in subsequent seminars—in 2009 at Penn, in the same year at UT-Austin, and in 2013 at Northwestern—also gave thought-provoking and informative interaction with my work. In addition, a number of graduate assistants provided invaluable help with various technical components; they include Christine Boone (who also did a great deal of the legwork for the UT symposium), Cora Palfy, Kristina Knowles, and Bruno Alcalde. Graphic designer Wil Lindsay (not a student) did an outstanding job preparing the online graphs that appear in Chapters 1 and 3.

My editor at Oxford University Press, Suzanne Ryan, has been a beacon of insight throughout this process. I thank her for believing in the project, for astutely shepherding it through the review and manuscript preparation processes, and for her wisdom and patience. Further thanks are due to Norm Hirschy, Madelyn Sutton, Adam Cohen, and the rest of the staff at OUP who have worked with me on this project. I also wish to express my appreciation to the anonymous reviewers; your insights have made this a stronger book, and I am grateful for your close and careful attention to my ideas.

Richard Herendeen and Babis Papachristou were key sources of emotional support during the writing process; thank you for your patience during what must have seemed like innumerable small neuroses. My stay at the American Academy in Berlin was greatly enriched by the friendships of Elizabeth Goodstein and Gary Shteyngart. In the electronic dance music communities of Berlin and Chicago I have been immensely fortunate to find not only a wide range of interesting musical experiences but also sustained friendship with an abundance of smart and remarkable individuals. And finally I wish to thank my parents, Jack and Carol Butler, who never questioned my desire to become a musician and a scholar, but instead gave me unconditional love and support. This book is dedicated to you.

About the Companion Website
www.oup.com/us/playingwithsomethingthatruns

PLAYING WITH SOMETHING THAT RUNS is an inherently multimedia project, involving in-depth analysis of performance technologies, sound recordings, and filmed performances. The website that Oxford University Press has created to accompany it is therefore a key component of the book. The website contains a large number of examples in a variety of formats: color images of the photographs, video stills, and screenshots that appear in the text in black and white; audio examples for Chapter 3; and video examples from my own fieldwork (and in one case, from a commercially produced DVD). In addition, certain figures in Chapters 1 and 3 appear as online-only graphs. Since the color images appear in the book as well, they are primarily supplemental in function (except in a few cases in which color is relevant to a point being made). All other online examples are essential components of my argument, however; in general, they are the focal points of detailed analytical discussion.

Materials that appear only on the website will have callouts placed in the text. For audio and video examples the relevant symbol is ◐; for the online-only graphs it is ▣. For figures that appear both within the book and online, the symbol ▣ will appear within each figure's printed caption.

Readers may access the site using username Music3 and password Book3234. Please note that these are case-sensitive.

PLAYING WITH SOMETHING THAT RUNS

Introduction

PICTURE AN ELECTRONIC musician in the process of creating sound. She works facing an array of electronic equipment, which surrounds her in a semicircular arc. Making up this assemblage of metal and plastic are racks of keyboards, drum machines, and sequencers, along with mixers, filters, and other black boxes whose function is hard to discern. A small computer, a laptop, is discreetly situated to one side. One sees a panoply of knobs, buttons, and blinking lights. The effect is not only functionally "techno"; it is aesthetically so as well.

The sounds that the musician sets in motion never stop. She turns rhythms into continuous cycles, generating repetitive riffs and loops that move away from and come back to their beginnings. Expectations are established and fulfilled in diverse and variegated ways. Constantly shifting textural and temporal configurations create a sense of ebb and flow. At times, the musician seems to be not so much producing as shaping or guiding the sound. She listens to it closely and makes constant adjustments: bringing in a new instrument here, changing the length of a loop there, emphasizing a particular frequency range, applying delay or reverb. These alterations are both spontaneous (they were not planned in advance) and instantaneous (she responds in real time, and we hear changes immediately). Connections between her actions and their results are noticeably direct as well: her hand touches something we can see, a piece of hardware, and a sound is transformed. Although her musical "instruments" are devices associated with sound production and recording, her gestures sometimes become so intense that she could just as well be playing a guitar or saxophone. We watch her turn a knob with her whole body, contorting her face with increasing expressivity as the sound distorts; we see her dance and gesticulate energetically.

The chain of events this musician has set in motion is unique. The timbres of the sounds are particular to this occasion; they arose through a sequence of slight adjustments, spontaneously chosen and large in number, and they would be virtually impossible to recreate in their exact form. Fortunately, however, they are being recorded. The ephemeral sounds of this dynamic improvisation are being inscribed into material, potentially permanent form. Broadening our view, we can see that the scene I have described is private, rarely witnessed. It is taking place not on stage but within the musician's home, in her personal recording studio. This musician is *composing*.

Scene two: a musician listening to a record. Although the year is 2008, the object of his attention is made of vinyl, a format that is still widespread within dance music. In a world in which the circulation of music is increasingly virtual, rendering even compact discs obsolete, electronic dance music (despite its strong associations with cutting-edge technology) maintains a stubbornly retrograde stance. The record plays back on an analog turntable, its continuous rotation tracing one long line, the spiral pathway of the groove. Aside from the digital file produced when the track was recorded, the composition he hears does not exist in any other material form; its only text is this slab of vinyl.

The musician is an avid consumer of such records; he seeks them out online and in specialist shops, choosing each record carefully with an ear sharply attuned to the fine gradations of style that distinguish particular musicians and subgenres. Right now, as he listens, he makes numerous small adjustments to the sound with his stereo equipment: placing more emphasis on the bass in this part, bringing out the mid-range in that part, and so on. A member of the iPod generation, he is fully enculturated in an era of increasingly customizable and private listening. But he is not alone in this act of consuming recorded music. He is on stage, where he has taken on the role of a DJ. He is *performing*.

Nor is he the only performer in the house. The large audience gathered before him also contributes to the unfolding event through their actions as listeners and dancers. Not only do they listen to and process the sounds they hear, they also formulate musically creative responses through movement. The DJ directs his performance toward them, seeking feedback in their reactions to his musical choices and actions. The variables guiding his performance are many: in addition to choosing which compositions are played and the order in which they appear, he also overlays records in ways that produce novel sound combinations, musical configurations arising only through his creative intervention. He transforms how each individual record is formally conveyed to the audience as well. He decides where it will begin and end; he sometimes moves backward or forward within its form to revisit or omit certain passages; and he emphasizes, diminishes, or completely eliminates certain parts of the texture. Recordings—objects that are strongly associated with musical fixity and permanence—become malleable and fluid in his hands.

The performances of both DJ and audience are improvisational. Decisions about music and rhythmic movement are made in the moment, generating and following a chain of choices that unfolds unpredictably. In addition to using their ears, the audience members especially pay attention to the DJ with their eyes. He moves in ways that locate him as the agent of the sounds they hear; through large and visible actions, he telegraphs "expressivity" to them. Through this collaborative performance a gathering of individuals listening to recorded music becomes a live musical event, a unique and irreproducible sequence of musical actions that is inextricably connected to a particular time and place.

Each of these examples involves an interplay between process and product. In the first example, an improvisational process led to the formation of a product (a recording). In the second case, recorded products served as bases for improvised performance. This book interrogates this play of process and product through the lenses of recording, performance, composition, and improvisation. Electronic dance music functions as a case study, one that illuminates the issues at stake while complicating reductive categorizations.

Tensions between process- and product-oriented perspectives are central to music scholarship more generally. Music theory is often said to focus on products, both literally (score analysis) and figuratively (the never-ending quest for musical "structure"). Similarly, positivist historical musicology gives pride of place to documentary evidence. More broadly, the ontological framework that underwrites the art-music canon, and a great deal of scholarship that centers on that canon, is based on an object-like conception of musical works (Goehr 1992). However, another kind of musical product—the recording—has aroused considerable suspicion from authors wary of music's circulation as a commodity within a mass-market economy.[1] A related antipathy to technological reproduction—now opposed to liveness, ephemerality, and co-presence—is discernible in the work of some performance studies scholars, as for instance when Peggy Phelan asserts, "To the degree that performance attempts to enter the economy of reproduction it betrays

---

[1] See especially Attali (1985 [1977]). The roots of this position lie with the work of Benjamin (1969 [1936]) and Adorno (2002 [1941]), although Benjamin does not discuss music and Adorno's essay does not speak to recording technology.

and lessens the promise of its own ontology."[2] Phelan further argues that "performance honors the idea that a limited number of people in a specific time/space frame can have an experience of value which leaves no visible trace afterward" (1993, 149). Exploring the work of philosopher Vladimir Jankélévitch, musicologist Carolyn Abbate expresses a related view, suggesting that "real music" inheres most purely in "an actual live performance (and not a recording, even of a live performance)."[3] In the field of ethnomusicology, meanwhile, there has been a strong tendency to frame music in processual terms, as a human activity. Although numerous examples might be cited, perhaps the most to the point is Christopher Small's notion of "musicking" (1998), a gerund referring to any form of human participation in music (e.g., listening to the radio, playing an instrument, dancing, conducting an orchestra). "Music is not a thing at all but rather an activity, something people do," writes Small (ibid., 2).

But music's existence is not so straightforward. The ways in which we know and make music are inextricably bound up with things. To define musical experience in opposition to products—and, more to the point with which we are concerned here, in opposition to recordings—is to deny the very materiality of the forms through which most people now encounter music. In today's world there are very few musical styles or cultures that recording has not touched in some manner, and a great many styles that have arisen entirely in conjunction with recording. If experiences of recorded music are not "real" musical experiences, then the majority of musical experiences in the world today are inauthentic.

This is not to say that critiques of product-oriented approaches are misdirected. To the extent that one wishes to account for musical *experience* (whether that experience is performing, listening, or something else), process must play a role. The concerns lie with the swing to the opposite pole and how it seems to exclude important material realities. Instead of choosing a side, this book argues that the technological mediation that characterizes contemporary musical performance leads to relationships between processes and products that are dialectical rather than dichotomous. Bringing recording, performance, composition, and improvisation into dialogue with each other reveals the complex and dynamic interaction of these modalities. Within these terms, the relationship between recording and performance has the shortest history of scholarly attention; the friction between these two particular forms of practice draws out older, already simmering tensions between performance and composition and composition/improvisation.

---

[2] Phelan (1993, 146). Auslander (1999, 41) documents the prevalence of this attitude within performance studies more generally.

[3] Abbate (2004, 505 and 506). I speak to Abbate's position in further detail in Chapter 1.

Though all four terms are central to the creative practices of electronic dance music (EDM), this book is not meant to function as a general explication of that style.[4] Rather, EDM serves as an exemplary instance of trends that are present to varying degrees in almost all music today. Considering the interplay of recording, performance, composition, and improvisation within EDM praxis exposes a number of related conceptual binaries that pervade the intellectual histories of these activities; these include fixed/fluid, prerecorded/live, work/performance, static/dynamic, material/immaterial, permanent/ephemeral, and even technological/human.[5]

Recording is often described as fixing, freezing, or preserving musical performances. In the vast majority of music-theoretical and musicological scholarship, meanwhile, performance is understood to be "of" something already composed. What is the nature and function of that something in a context in which performance may transform it radically? Moreover, what does it mean when the primary platform for such transformative performances is a recording? These questions are at the heart of Chapter 1, "Remixing One's Self: Ontologies of the Provisional Work." The chapter construes ontology broadly, as encompassing a wide range of ideas and practices involving the identity of musical entities. It also depicts the ontology of EDM as plural, as a site of many interconnected forms of musical existence. Among the relationships that DJ and laptop sets spin out are those between shorter elements (loops, samples, presets) and complete tracks, between previously recorded material and live performance, between tracks that are superimposed or juxtaposed within a mix, and between different versions of tracks.[6] Such relationships also emerge through the compositional activities that precede and follow performance. Musical identity is therefore not only multiple but also fluid; it changes over time. Drawing on recent critical work on technological mediation, I conceptualize this ontological assemblage as a *network*.

Much of the information presented in Chapter 1 derives from field research with EDM producers and performers; I highlight a broad range of representative practices. My account of ontology is deliberately anti-essentialist; it is not my goal to

---

[4] A more general introduction to the history and basic creative practices of electronic dance music can be found within my book *Unlocking the Groove* (2006). Here, as in that earlier text, I use *electronic dance music* (and the abbreviation *EDM*) as a broad term encompassing all genres that might be considered to fall within this category. This is in keeping with the way in which the term has been employed in both popular and academic writing since the late 1990s (and throughout my own work). In the past few years, EDM (and "Electronic Dance Music," often but not always capitalized) has also emerged as a label for recent, commercially popular genres such as dubstep. My own usage should not be confused with this narrower one.

[5] Whenever binary oppositions appear as terms in this text, a forward slash will be used as an abbreviation for "versus."

[6] As in my earlier work, I use *track* to refer to an individual recorded composition. The term can also refer to a single textural layer within a multitrack recording, but I avoid this usage for the sake of clarity.

define what (electronic dance) music "is" in some sort of absolute sense. Rather, I am interested in what people identify as the constitutive elements of an EDM performance or track and how producers and performers interact with these musical "things." A basic premise, then, is that abstractions about musical identity have a clear place in the discourse of fans and musicians. I posit a three-part conceptual scheme of work/text/performance, where "work" refers to a meaningfully formed musical entity (and not to the classical idealist "work-concept" documented by Goehr [1992] and others) and "text" to the physically or digitally encoded object that represents or transmits this work. The third term, performance, is understood as intrinsically creative rather than merely reproductive or interpretive.

The performances studied in this book are of two principal types: DJ sets and laptop sets (or "laptop performances"). The DJ set is the older and more familiar approach; it is performed with turntables, twelve-inch vinyl records, and a mixing board. EDM DJs do not simply play other people's records; rather, they select, combine, and manipulate parts of records to form new compositions that differ substantially from their source materials.[7] In recent years (particularly since 2000), the laptop set has become equally common; in this type of performance, musicians use computers, specialized software, and a variety of hardware to transform and reconfigure their own precomposed sounds in real time.[8]

This increasing technological mediation of performance has led to complex tensions between the expectations audience members bring to events, the technologies performers choose to use, and how they perform. I explore the ramifications of these tensions in Chapter 2, "Performing Performance: Interface Design, Liveness, and Listener Orientation." I begin by situating musical performance as inherently multisensorial. Recording problematizes this quality of performance by separating the act of listening from directly observable physical gestures. Consequently, performance is frequently described in opposition to recorded playback as "live." Indeed, the desire for liveness, and the very existence of such a concept, could not exist without its recorded Other, as Philip Auslander has demonstrated (1999).

For electronic dance musicians, who perform *with* recordings and their attendant technologies, the two modalities collide in a particularly intense way. The technologies involved are more strongly associated with functions of playback and recording than

---

[7] DJing may also be done with CD turntables, but that approach remains less common in EDM contexts and is not a focus here.

[8] Note that I do not use the term *laptop set* to describe DJing with laptop computers. Although this approach has also become common thanks to the proliferation of software such as Final Scratch and Traktor, my concern here is with a mode of performance that is distinct from DJing per se. Indeed, some laptop performers bristle if called "DJs," because they regard this as a misunderstanding of the fact that they are playing music that they themselves composed.

with performance; their interfaces and playing techniques are unfamiliar to the majority of clubbers; it is difficult to intuit how they are played from casual observation; and the actual technologies used can vary significantly from one performer to another. Nevertheless—indeed perhaps in part *because* of the highly mediated nature of the dancer-musician relationship within this tradition—liveness is a well-established value within EDM culture. A night in a club, and the musical performances that are central to that experience, is expected to be a unique and irreproducible event characterized by a collective energy that performers and audience members creatively coproduce. The dialectical relationship between technological mediation and liveness is perhaps most evident in the increasing prevalence of the term *live* within EDM's aesthetic lexicon: many performances are described as "live PAs" or "live sets," and the most commonly used software for laptop performance is a program called "Live."[9]

Chapter 2 situates the mediation of performance by sound recording practices and technologies along two axes: that between the performer and the sounds he or she creates, and that between the performer and the audience. For the first axis, "interface" is a key concept, indexing the actual site of mediation as materialized in a hardware or software surface. I discuss a wide range of commonly used interfaces, considering the kinds of interaction that they allow, suggest, or invite. I frame this sense of interactive possibility in terms of *affordance*, a concept originating within ecological psychology (Gibson 1977). I also consider the properties that musicians seek and value in their interactions with technology, as well as how they communicate liveness to their audiences. Finally, I explore the incursion of recording-based epistemologies into the domain of performance, delineating an attitude on the part of performers that I term *listener orientation*.

The relationship of improvisation to composition, performance, and recording in EDM is the subject of Chapter 3, "Making It Up and Breaking It Down." The process/product dichotomy mentioned earlier has been especially pervasive within scholarship on improvisation, with authors tending to locate the activity on one side or the other of the binary. For instance, some scholars have valorized jazz by finding the same sorts of properties in its improvisations that music theory typically prizes in notated compositions: structural coherence; hierarchy; complexity; and tight-knit, often hidden relationships between surface details and underlying design. More recently, trends have moved toward an emphasis on the ephemeral, processual nature of improvisations as experienced and performed. Sawyer, for instance, argues

---

[9] It is important to note that the sense of liveness described here is applicable to DJing as well as to laptop performance, and I apply the term *live* to both modes of performance. This is more inclusive than the common usage of the term within dance-music culture, where it most frequently refers to modes of performance other than DJing.

that the key aspect of improvisation is its *contingent* quality (1996). In other words, although it is possible to describe the structure of an improvisation after the fact, this structure is not predetermined but rather emerges during the process of performance and is subject to change at any moment.

In many respects, EDM performances are models of the processive, contingent approaches to musical creation discussed by Sawyer and others. Within performance, musicians frequently make spontaneous decisions about numerous variables, including such compositionally significant factors as which sounds they will play, when they will play them, and how they will be combined with other sounds. Yet the constituents of these improvisations are also *fixed* in certain fundamental ways. Performances are fashioned from patterns or tracks recorded beforehand, and in the case of DJ sets, these elements are also physical objects (vinyl records).

This gap between the fixed and the fluid, modulated through recording, forms the primary point of entry for Chapter 3. Rather than opposing improvisation and composition, this work frames them as related forms of musical creativity. It situates performances along a continuum that measures the relationship of musical specificity to time. At one end of the spectrum are musical outcomes that are specified fully ahead of time, while at the other lie those determined entirely within the time frame of performance. From this notion of gradated specificity emerges a set of analytical questions, involving factors such as which sonic outcomes are specified (and which are not), the level of detail involved, and the manner and means of specification.

I use these considerations to develop two extended musical analyses. These give particular attention to the interaction of elements composed and recorded prior to performance and the improvisational processes of performance itself. Each involves a group of interrelated examples. The first analysis focuses on three laptop performances by the Berlin-based duo Sender Berlin, and the second on the track "The Bells" as recorded and performed by producer and DJ Jeff Mills. My analytical method is multipronged, involving an overview of each performance under consideration, identification of its constituent elements (tracks), and close analysis of one or more tracks played within the performance. I consider these tracks both on their own terms as recorded prior to performance and as realized within the specific event. I also make comparisons across performances. Because one analysis focuses on laptop performance and the other on DJing, the two analyses together provide a detailed picture of musicians' approaches to performance in EDM. Furthermore, they function as additional examples of the networks of creative events theorized in Chapter 1. They also demonstrate several ways in which EDM performance connects improvisation to liveness. Another section, which precedes the two analyses, brings in a complementary perspective by exploring the improvisational dimensions of production and recording.

The central theme of Chapter 4, "Looking for the Perfect Loop," is technology. However, whereas Chapters 1–3 (and especially Chapter 2) address technology in a literal sense by considering the material technologies through which electronic music is created, recorded, and performed, this last chapter develops an expanded, critical sense of the word. Its orientation is more theoretical than analytical or field-based. I describe *musical* technologies, a term that I use here to refer not to software, drum machines, MIDI, and the like, but rather to principles of design that facilitate the kinds of actions that characterize improvised performance in EDM. Musical technologies are crucial to the coming unfixed of recordings within a live event. In all, I describe seven technologies, which I name *repeating, cycling, going, grooving, riding, transitioning,* and *flowing.* The use of the gerund form highlights the technologies as kinds of ongoing actions. They may also be understood in terms of affordance, a concept first introduced with respect to physical technologies in Chapter 2. Here, these musical technologies are shown to afford the improvisational interventions that transform recorded sound into dynamic performance.

As the technology with the most extensive literature addressing it, and one that is related to nearly all of the others, repetition receives the largest amount of space in the chapter. I seek to develop an account of repetition that is positive—showing what repeating does rather than what it fails to do—and that engages the subject directly rather than moving away from it in favor of difference. I also seek to theorize repetition in specifically *musical* terms. In order to do so, it is necessary to differentiate musical repetition from the more general sense of "repetition" as a stand-in for mechanical reproduction and the commodity system. In the latter capacity, repetition has been greeted with a great deal of suspicion. What authors such as Adorno and Attali failed to foresee, however, is how repetition as a musical technology can enable the transformation and release of prerecorded objects themselves within fluid, improvised performance.

In keeping with this objective, Chapter 4 seeks to differentiate the various musical phenomena indexed by the word *repetition* and to clarify the distinctions between cognate terms such as "repeating," "repetitive," and "recurrence." Among the questions that emerge are these: Why do some kinds of repetition attract attention and not others? Why does EDM in particular signify as "repetitive"? Also, how can we conceptualize or theorize literal or exact repetition? This last question is particularly pressing for technologically mediated styles such as EDM, as the exceptional degree of precision in repeating that they allow has often been a major source of anxiety. It is important to realize, however, that mechanically precise repetition in this style is not a technologically induced aftereffect but rather a deliberately cultivated aesthetic strategy.

This exploration of musical technologies further situates repetition as intrinsically *temporal.* To this end it considers its significance within phenomena such as duration, periodicity, pulse, and meter. How does repetition affect temporal attending and expectation, not only within listening but also in performance? How can an account of repetition vis-à-vis meter and time preserve the dynamism and particularity that people obviously value in this music? In order to answer these questions, it is necessary to stop equating repetition with stasis, and to tease apart notions of "activity" from those of "change."

Following from these emphases, the next section asks how musical cycles might be conceptualized in experiential, temporal terms rather than as atemporal, spatial entities. To do so, cycles must be differentiated from their most common geometrical representation, the circle. Spatial, circular conceptualizations of cycles have tended to exclude their temporal attributes, casting them as static, timeless, and devoid of clear points of origin. They have frequently positioned cyclical time as the Other of "linear" time, defining it in terms of what it is not (most commonly, simply "nonlinear"). I instead seek to uncover the kinetic properties of musical cycles, revealing the ways in which they possess clearly perceptible points of origin, movement toward goals, and distinct phases with particular qualities. Because they engage in-time attending, cycles involve a sense of past and future as well as "now."

The technology termed "going," which is treated in tandem with "cycling," indexes goal-directedness. The fact that EDM structures time cyclically does not mean that it lacks teleology. How can we account for the particular ways in which repetitive structures such as cycles configure energy? To what extent do repetitive musical constructs create a sense of forward motion, or of motion more generally? Furthermore, what are the implications of cyclical repetition for the in-time creativity of improvised performance?

The next technology, "grooving," might be understood as a more specific manifestation of tendencies seen in repeating, cycling, and going. The sense of groove in which I am interested is not about departures from regularity, as seen in a great deal of literature on the subject (e.g., Keil 1987; Danielsen 2006), but rather about how these musical entities are designed to function as technologies of mediated improvisation. Of particular interest is a notion of "autoteology"—that is, a kind of structuring that causes one to expect the end of a groove to lead back to its beginning.[10] The beginning of a groove thus serves as a point of both arrival *and* departure. To illustrate these principles at work, this section analyzes a particular set of grooves that were composed for use in improvised performances by the musicians Phon.o and Bernhard Moosbauer.

---

[10] Note the presence of expectation and leading as senses within this definition; grooving thus articulates a kind of tensional process. My discussion of autoteleology in relation to groove draws from and extends that found in Hughes (2003).

The remaining three technologies extend the concerns of the previous four onto new terrain: How does the fact of continuous, indefinite sound in EDM performances affect our sense of musical motion? To what extent does technology play a role in this? What is the relationship between technologically facilitated structuring of time and the time frames of human experience? The technology "riding" is a way of conceptualizing performance and listening—especially as regards teleology—as technologized process. Rather than a subject striving toward a goal, the teleology that riding articulates suggests a technologized force or conveyance that is marshaled or directed through human intervention. Sound itself, its continuous flow, is what is ridden. Related concepts that emerge in this discussion are automation and algorithm. The next technology, "transitioning," refers not to a kind of formal section but to a mode of actively and continuously transitioning: an ongoing musical strategy through which a sense of forward motion is constantly regenerated. The transitional state (described with terms such as the "third record" of DJ mixes) is unstable, but the performer seeks to sustain it; it is not merely a functional section that gets us from one point to another. Closely related to both riding and transitioning is "flowing." This technology denotes a quality of experience associated with certain kinds of performance, especially those that are improvised. In electronic dance music, flow is facilitated through and experienced in terms of technology. It develops from the fact that performance is indefinite in duration and unfolds continuously for hours without breaks, pauses, or rests.

Methodology and Disciplinary Orientations

The perspective adopted in this book is deliberately interdisciplinary. The research presented here has been driven by key questions that emerged from the object of study and not from the concerns of any one field of inquiry. The methodologies employed are interdisciplinary as well, involving field research, musical analysis, video analysis, and critical inquiry into a range of issues.

Field research took place primarily in Berlin, where I lived for three periods: July 2005, July–August 2006, and September–December 2007. Given this time frame, the information presented here should be understood as a snapshot of EDM performance as it was occurring in the latter part of the '00 decade.[11] During each research

---

[11] This comment may also be applied more specifically to the technologies used in EDM performance (discussed primarily but not exclusively in Chapter 2). Since the conclusion of field research, new models of certain interfaces, as well as a small number of entirely new devices, have been introduced, while others continue to be used in the same form. In spite of technological change, however, the materials and practices described here continue to be representative of EDM performance as practiced in subsequent years.

trip I interviewed EDM musicians and filmed their performances for analysis. All interviewees are active as recording artists and performers (in the latter capacity, as laptop performers and/or as DJs), and most are well known internationally. In addition, nearly all interview subjects live in Berlin.[12] Three-fourths of the individuals interviewed are German (of these, most moved to Berlin as adults); the remainder are American, Dutch, and Swiss. As is customary within EDM production more generally, these musicians compose and record in their own home studios. Whenever possible I held interviews there, as this allowed musicians to show me the tools with which they composed and to demonstrate their working method. Interviews were conducted in English. The topics discussed were quite wide-ranging, but they revolved around four main themes: performance, composition, improvisation, and technology. Discussion points ran the gamut from broad questions about method ("What is your basic approach to performance?" "Which parts of a performance are planned out ahead of time?") to technical questions about specific software and hardware. Most interviews were both filmed and recorded on audio.

The second major component of field research involved close analysis of specific performances by the same musicians. I observed many performances and, with the musician's permission, filmed them as well. During filming I was usually on stage, either behind or to the side of the musician. The camera was largely focused on the performer and his or her equipment, as the goal was to understand what he or she was doing. After filming I analyzed each performance, taking detailed notes. The beginning of fieldwork involved a steep learning curve, as laptop performances in particular involved technical software with which I was unfamiliar and a hardware configuration that was unique to each musician. With time and knowledge gained from interviews, however, I was able to understand not only the basics of what was happening but also the idiosyncrasies of each musician's approach and the degree to which improvisation was involved.

Whenever possible, I held a follow-up interview after the performance. In that conversation I asked each musician to assess his or her performance and sought verification or clarification of my own impressions. I also showed them approximately ten excerpts from the footage of their event and asked them to comment on or explain what was happening at that moment. These were chosen strategically: for example, they might be passages in which a technique discussed during the pre-performance interview seemed to be occurring, or moments where I had noticed something that I could not explain. Discussing the performances in this way allowed me to understand them much better, and the musicians were excited to have their work considered at this level of detail.

---

[12] The next section of this Introduction, "Contexts," provides detailed description of the subgenres and scenes with which these musicians are affiliated and explains why Berlin was an ideal site for research.

In *Unlocking the Groove* (Butler 2006), I defined three primary modes of creative interaction within electronic dance music: recording artist ("producer"), performing artist (DJ or laptop performer), and performing audience (dancers). Each of these roles is functionally distinct, although it is common for individuals to occupy different roles on different occasions; in particular, performing artists are often recording artists and vice versa (47–48). This tripartite division continues to inform the current work. My focus is first and foremost on the performing artist and secondarily on the recording artist. Due to the nature of my fieldwork and the focus of this book on the relationship between performance and composition, this is almost always a matter of studying the same individual embodying different roles.[13] My focus on the performer-producer is part of a larger, ongoing strategy in my research on EDM. Scholarship on this genre has given much more attention to clubbers and dancers than to those involved in creating the music, and there has been a tendency to frame the dance floor as "the" authentic social context of EDM.[14] Consequently, the creative contributions of performers and producers remain insufficiently theorized; there is a shortage of concrete information on their rich and complex practices. This book seeks to intervene in this regard. The third component in the productive web of club culture, the audience, is considered as well, but from the point of view of the producers and performers who participated in field research. Thus for instance I asked musicians questions about how they assessed the audience's reaction to their performance and the extent to which that response might affect the course of a developing improvisation. The most extensive consideration of the audience's role appears in Chapter 2, in relation to liveness and the communication of "performance." However, the question of how those witnessing a performance interact and communicate amongst themselves, while fascinating, is outside the scope of this project.

Close analysis of musical texts plays less of a role in this book than in my previous work on electronic dance music, which focused especially on questions of rhythm and meter. The most extended analyses appear in Chapter 3, where they constitute a large percentage of the discussion; shorter treatments appear throughout the text. I contend, however, that the whole of this work should be considered music-theoretical, even though much of the discussion engages with issues outside the boundaries of what professional music theorists have typically written about. The exploration of performance and composition that underlies this project (including the fieldwork described on the preceding pages) constitutes a poetics of how music is made.[15] To

---

[13] I did not work with any performers who were not also producers, or vice versa. In a few instances I did film a performer whom I was unable to formally interview.

[14] Cf. Butler (2006, 15–16).

[15] Krims uses the term *musical poetics* to index a similarly expanded notion of what music theory might encompass. See Krims (2000, esp. 27–31).

the extent that music theory is concerned with the design and creation of music, my treatment of this subject is self-evidently theoretical.

The emphasis on *making* music in the phrase "how music is made" has a further significance. Music theory conventionally involves an abstracting move; it strips away surfaces and reveals "underlying" structure. Here, however, I am equally interested in the concrete. This study takes the products involved in musical creativity seriously: not only recordings, but also the technologies and interfaces through which music is made. It can thus be understood as a *materially based* music theory. This orientation is part of the larger project of configuring the process/product relationship dialectically. I seek to reveal the social traces within objects, as well as the affordances that shape how they are used. This grounding in the material connects strongly to the inclusion of field research as a primary source of information: rather than speaking from the abstract perspective of "the listener" of analysis, the study engages with the specific practices of specific musicians, and particularly with how their music was realized on specific occasions.

The focus of this book on performance does suggest one possible connection to a branch of traditional music theory, that which concerns itself with "performance and analysis." This is a widely recognized area of research within the field, one that has led to numerous publications spanning the course of several decades.[16] As the author of a book on performance, I naturally considered what the literature on the subject in my primary field had to say about it. A thorough survey of publications in this area revealed that the ways in which authors configure "performance" is remarkably unified. First, they tend to assume a clear separation between a composition and its performances, treating the former as fixed and unchangeable and the latter as ephemeral and variable. Performance is understood to be "of" something—namely, an idealist, Romantic notion of the musical work.[17] Second, very rarely are actual performances taken as the primary objects of analysis. Thus a surprising majority of studies are hypothetically oriented, either suggesting how a performance *should* or *might* proceed in relation to an analytical insight, or addressing the relationship between performance and analysis in broad, speculative terms.[18] By and large, even

---

[16] A seminal work that marks a resurgence of interest in performance/analysis relationships is Cone 1968.

[17] This point is articulated clearly in Cook (1995a, 33 and 39).

[18] McClelland (2005) provides a useful survey and bibliography of the performance and analysis literature as it appears in music theory. He cites sixty-six sources; within that list, every publication that references a specific musical object in its title cites a work (or works) rather than a performance. (Nineteen sources focus on a single piece, and twelve focus either on two or more pieces or a specific subset of the classical repertory.) Twenty-seven works include both "analysis" (or "analyzing") and "performance" (or "performing") in the title. McClelland also makes the interesting observation that relatively few sources focus on recorded performances (ibid., 96). Recordings *have* received significant attention in the literature on performance by "empirical" or "systematic" musicologists, and within research on music perception and cognition. These areas are not usually focused on analysis, however, and are generally distinct from the discipline of music theory as it is currently practiced in North America.

those studies that do take actual performances as a significant focus of analysis or that speak to the analytical or structural implications of particular performance decisions do not attribute *ontological significance* to performances themselves. For this reason, the insights articulated in this body of research remain confined to a quite small portion of the world's music.

In this book, by contrast, analysis focuses on actual performances, which were filmed and studied in the manner described above.[19] Compositions are analyzed as well, but only insofar as they relate to performed events. In addition to the broader goal of bringing the processive dimensions of improvised performance into dialogue with the "products" composed prior to an event, this strategy serves as a continuation of work begun in *Unlocking the Groove*. In brief, that work mapped the musical design of electronic dance music through close analysis of individual recorded compositions. This was a crucial first step, as existing sources on EDM spoke of its musical properties only in the most general terms, if at all; methodologies and theoretical frameworks for discussing its sonic dimensions simply did not exist. In performance, however, composed tracks are not experienced in isolation, but rather are combined and transformed significantly. This project thus brings the analytical methodology and theoretical framework established in my earlier research to bear on this larger experiential context through detailed examination of specific events.

It is important to note that I do not deploy analysis in order to validate or otherwise prove the musical or aesthetic worth of EDM. I personally find EDM to be an endlessly fascinating style, and it is incontestable that it has served as a source of rich experience for millions of people around the world, but I find analysis as validation to be an ideologically suspect maneuver. As both a music theorist and a scholar of popular music, I have become keenly aware of how theory and analysis can collude in the formation and preservation of canons, and this is an outcome I wish to avoid in my own work. This music stands on its own. It is self-evidently valuable to those who immerse themselves in its sounds, and they are the ones who know it best (its stylistically competent listeners). My goal is therefore more neutral: put simply, to show how this music does what it does by providing specific examples.

Related to this point, even as this study seeks to reveal distinctive aspects of EDM's creative practices, it does not aim to position it as some kind of rare musical exception. Through more than a decade of researching this topic I have become keenly aware of a tendency, evident in certain reactions to EDM scholarship, to exoticize this music. It is, after all, a style with strong countercultural connections, one

---

[19] One music theorist who *has* repeatedly called for analysis of specific performances is Nicholas Cook (see Cook 1995a, 1995b, 1999a, and 1999b). Cook's work on this topic has generally adopted a more metatheoretical perspective, and the analyses he has chosen as examples have mainly been by other authors.

frequently associated with distinctive modes of dress, drug use, inverted sleep schedules, and novel instrumentation. However, EDM is many things. At this point in its history the range of EDM subgenres and attendant cultural manifestations is vast. If anything, it has shown itself to be remarkably fluid at moving through the world and forming musical and cultural alliances.[20] EDM is African American music, Latino/a music, European music, South Asian music. It is gay music and straight music. It is cerebral and physical. And more.[21] Instead of containing EDM by framing it as Other, this study treats it as an ultimate instance of trends that run through *all* of today's music: hypermediated, in flux, both product and process, both local and global.

Returning once more to questions of disciplinarity, there are at least two more intellectual traditions with which this project might be associated. The first is performance studies. This field is based on a broad, critically informed sense of "performance" as permeating every aspect of life and culture: in essence, as any social behavior or event. For instance, during the years in which the intellectual orientations that would characterize performance studies were beginning to emerge, scholar Richard Schechner defined performance as "a very inclusive notion of action" in which "theatre is only one node on a continuum that reaches from ritualization in animal behavior (including humans) through performances in everyday life-greetings, displays of emotion, family scenes and so on—to rites, ceremonies and performances: large-scale theatrical events" (Schechner 1977, 1). Performance studies is highly interdisciplinary, extending into fields as varied as literature, theater, philosophy, race/gender/sexuality studies, anthropology, and others. In taking performance itself as an object of analysis, the work presented here might be understood as a kind of performance studies. The connection is not strict, however. It arises mostly in a broad sense, through the common interest in performance, rather than through extensive engagement with performance-studies scholarship.[22]

The other relevant intellectual tradition is sound studies. This field of inquiry, which is also interdisciplinary, has been the site of much exciting work in recent years. Here I will cite Pinch and Bijsterveld's useful definition of sound studies as "an emerging interdisciplinary area that studies the material production and consumption of music, sound, noise, and silence, and how these have changed throughout history and within different societies, but…from a much broader perspective than standard disciplines such as ethnomusicology, history of music, and sociology of

---

[20] For a history of EDM's origins, see Chapter 1 of *Unlocking the Groove*.

[21] For a sense of the range of EDM's cultural and musical practices throughout its history and the diversity of the intellectual traditions that have sought to address it, see the essays contained in Butler 2012.

[22] The major exception to this point lies with the work of Philip Auslander, whose research on liveness is central to Chapter 2. The concept of "performativity" also makes an appearance in that chapter, where it is applied to a particular mode of performing.

music" (2004, 636). Because "sound studies" itself is a new term, there are a number of recent studies that might be taken as examples of this trend but do not use this label.[23] *Playing with Something That Runs*, with its pervasive interest in how technologies of recording, playback, and production relate to performance, composition, and improvisation, is a clear example of a sound-studies orientation.

Contexts

Nearly all of the musicians studied in this book have made Berlin their home, as well as the base of their creative activity.[24] Berlin has been a site of EDM activity since the acid-house days of the late 1980s, and in the 1990s it became famously associated with an annual summer event known as the Love Parade.[25] Since the turn of the millennium, however—and particularly since the middle of the '00 decade—it has gradually become *the* most active location in the world for both club culture and EDM record production. Finding an ideal combination of low rents, enthusiastic and knowledgeable audiences, and creative vibrancy, many electronic dance musicians have immigrated to Berlin. They include not only Germans from other parts of the country and recording artists from other countries in Europe but also a significant influx from North America and other parts of the world. In addition to these new long-term residents, the city has become a principal destination for techno tourists—EDM enthusiasts, primarily from other European cities, who visit Berlin on short trips for the sole purpose of going to its clubs. This trend has been aided greatly by the increasing availability of inexpensive commuter flights across the continent, and it has been part and parcel of a significant expansion in the scope and intensity of Berlin's already dynamic club culture.[26]

The musicians with whom I worked most closely have affiliated themselves with a diverse range of subgenres and scenes from Berlin's musical landscapes. These affiliations

---

[23] Some representative works that might be taken as instances of sound studies are Bull (2000), Chanan (1995), DeNora (2000), Katz (2004), Pinch and Trocco (2002), Schafer (1977), Sterne (2003), Taylor (2001), Théberge (1997), Thompson (2002), and Zak (2001). Note that this list includes only monographs.

[24] The one exception is Kelli Cain and Brian Crabtree, the designers and producers of the Monome interface discussed in Chapter 2. At the time of our interview they were based in Philadelphia. However, I learned of their work through a Berlin connection, when musician Robert Henke showed me a Monome device during an interview. Two other musicians whose work is discussed, Daniel Bell and Jeff Mills, do not live in Berlin now but have done so in the past and maintain strong ties to the city.

[25] For a historical and critical account of the Love Parade, see Nye (2009). I also discuss the Love Parade in my "(In)visible mediators: Interface design and the disappearing computer in Berlin-based laptop performances," forthcoming.

[26] The most thorough descriptions of these immigration and techno-tourism trends can be found in Rapp (2009), which has recently been published in an English translation.

are simultaneously musical (shaped by the kinds of music that each artist creates and performs), social (based on friendship and other interpersonal connections), and economic (involving monetary connections to entities such as record labels, clubs, and music technology companies). One significant group consists of artists drawn together by the record label and club Tresor. Both were founded during the immediate post-Wall era in 1991. The club was located in the very center of Berlin, less than a block away from the former site of the barrier and its accompanying "death strip." The music that came to exemplify the Tresor sound was strongly influenced by Detroit techno, which those most involved in the new scene generally regarded as *the* authentic source of electronic dance music. Detroit musicians had their tracks released on Tresor, were frequent performers at the club, and collaborated with German producers. Soundwise, however, the Tresor aesthetic was harder, faster, and rougher than its American predecessor. Tresor artists who participated in field research for this project include Pacou, Sender Berlin, Dash, DJ Mack, and Recyver Dogs. I have also closely studied the work of Jeff Mills (who is the subject of an in-depth analysis in Chapter 3), although I was not able to obtain an interview with him. One significant factor that brought many Tresor artists together was a highly popular amateur night at the club; called Headquarters, this weekly event became a kind of community gathering for the emergent DJs who participated in it and helped initiate the early careers of musicians such as Pacou, Sender Berlin, and Alexander Kowalski. Although real-estate pressures forced Tresor to shut down the club in 2005, it reopened in a new central-Berlin venue in 2007, and the label continues to operate as well. Leading Detroit artists still perform there regularly, although the energy that surrounded the club during its heyday in the 1990s has since shifted elsewhere.

In postmillennial Berlin, and particularly since the middle of the "zero years," subcultural capital has become strongly associated with the sound and scene known as minimal techno (or simply "minimal").[27] Originating in the 1990s, minimal techno was originally associated with a stark, back-to-basics aesthetic that greatly reduced the number of textural elements present in a track and expanded the length of its formal processes. Its more recent manifestation in Berlin has come to bear significant influence from styles such as tech-house, and especially microhouse. The latter style is characterized by a highly dense, microlevel approach to production that packs extremely short samples of voices, instruments, computer errors or "glitches," and other sounds into the roles normally occupied by bass drums, snares, hi-hats, and other percussive elements. In spite of this complexity, however, it remains strongly dance-floor-oriented.

---

[27] In the area of EDM research, Thornton (1996) was the first to connect Bourdieu's notion of cultural capital to subcultural theory.

In Berlin, minimal is as much a scene as a sound. The basis of the "techno tourism" described by Rapp (2009), it is strongly associated with ultrahip clubs such as Panorama Bar, Club der Visionäre, and Bar 25 (now closed), and with performers such as Richie Hawtin and Ricardo Villalobos. The musicians who participated in the field research for this book were generally less involved with the minimal scene as such; they are perceived as "minimal techno" artists more on the basis of their sonic aesthetics and production techniques. They include Daniel Bell, Stewart Walker, Robert Henke (Monolake), Pole, and Deadbeat.

Other musicians whom I studied affiliate less clearly with broad-based movements (although the ubiquitous presence of minimal makes it difficult for any highly active Berlin-based electronic musician to avoid at least having some sort of stance with regard to the style). These include Apparat and Phon.o, both of whom record for the label Shitkatapult; Henrik Schwarz, whose music combines up-to-the-minute production methods with many non-EDM sound sources; DJane Aroma/Discopunk, who brings a punk aesthetic to her interaction with electronic music; Thomas Fehlmann, a member of the influential early-techno group The Orb whose involvement with EDM dates to the 1980s; and Mijk van Dijk, most active in 1990s Berlin but still releasing recordings. All of these musicians can be described as "techno"; their musical outputs reflect various stylistic developments and influences available to Berlin EDM artists without fitting into one of the Tresor or minimal camps described above. Also drawing on trends outside of these categories are Robert Henke and Pole, whose work has been influenced in important ways by Jamaican dub.[28]

A final connective glue involving nearly all of the artists whom I studied is the software Live, which will be discussed extensively throughout this work. Live was developed by Gerhard Behles and Robert Henke, who recorded together under the name Monolake. Behles and Henke subsequently founded the company Ableton, which has released Live commercially since 2001.[29] Live has slowly but surely attained market dominance; the vast majority of EDM laptop musicians around the world now use it as the basis of their performances. In this respect it is no longer a distinctive feature of musical practice in Berlin, though it did originate there.

I chose Berlin as a site for field research because of its exceptional concentration of world-class electronic musicians, and because I felt I could learn a great deal from

---

[28] The dub-techno connection, which constitutes a distinct substream within Berlin EDM praxis, originates with the influential releases of Basic Channel in the 1990s. See Veal (2007: 235–39) for further information. Basic Channel member Moritz von Oswald also collaborated with Thomas Fehlmann and Detroit techno founder Eddie "Flashin" Fowlkes under the name 3MB.

[29] After the establishment of Ableton, Behles left Monolake and became CEO of the company. Henke has continued to record and perform—now solo—as Monolake, and he also remains quite active in the technical development and operation of Ableton.

the particular musicians who were there. I also selected it because I wanted to study live musical performances, and its nightlife proved to be without parallel in terms of both the quantity and quality of performances on offer. It soon became clear that there was further value in studying musicians in the city in which they lived, as this made it possible to track individual artists' performances across multiple occasions and contexts.

Nevertheless, this book is not about Berlin per se. It does present information on the city, its musical history, and its nightlife culture, but these are not principal areas of focus. Nor does it attempt to locate Berlin-specific elements in the work of the musicians described herein (such elements surely exist, although it would be highly problematic to reduce the globally informed soundscape of the city's many dance-music scenes to any monolithic category of "Berlin EDM"). Instead, I give primary attention to specific musical performances and to the compositional practices and choices that went into them. Questions of culture, performance reception, and other contexts do significantly inform my arguments, but they emerge in response to the rubrics delineated in the previous section rather than in relation to the place in which field research occurred.[30]

In addition to the criterion of having a base in Berlin, I selected the musicians who participated in field research on the basis of their prominence as recording artists and performers, their responsiveness to my inquiries and overall willingness or eagerness to talk,[31] the existence of connections that facilitated making contact with them, and the recommendations of other EDM musicians who suggested that I should talk with them. Therefore, they represent a cross-section of EDM in Berlin in the 2000s rather than a coherent group drawn from any one scene or subgenre. As noted above, the most consistently evident bases of affiliation among them are the Tresor club/label and the minimal techno subgenre/scene.

One further variable that warrants attention in contextualizing these musicians is the extent to which their work crosses over into "art-music" practices and institutions. Readers especially familiar with electronic art music may notice that certain issues that arise in the creation and performance of EDM (e.g., interface design; or the visibility and legibility of performance gestures) also surface in contemporary

---

[30] One fascinating question that a different study might explore is how race is inflected in Berlin's EDM scenes. With regard to the Detroit-Berlin connection mentioned above, it is significant that the music that the founders of Tresor looked to as authentic originated within African American cultural contexts, whereas all of the musicians living in Berlin whom I interviewed are Caucasian. For an interesting consideration of the African American roots of techno in Detroit and the racial politics of its subsequent dispersal and popularization in Europe, see Albiez (2005). Also relevant to questions of race in Berlin would be the role of the city's large Turkish population.

[31] On the whole I received clear, positive responses to interview requests, but a few musicians who might have been valuable contributors did not respond to inquiries or only replied to emails after I had left Berlin.

classical contexts. The computer-music literature has also explored such matters, particularly in recent years. In the work and careers of some EDM musicians whom I studied, elements of art-music practice are occasionally evident. These include isolated instances of institutional cross-pollination; for instance, the Montpelier National Orchestra of France performed a concert consisting entirely of arrangements of well-known tracks by Jeff Mills. (A recording of this concert was subsequently released on the Tresor label, thus moving the music back toward its popular-music base.) Robert Henke, meanwhile, has created sound installations and performed in venues such as the Centre Pompidou and the Tate Modern. In his *Mobiles* album, which claims sonic analogy to Alexander Calder's "stabiles," Stewart Walker adopts an experimental, concept-oriented approach to minimal techno. Jeff Mills' soundtracks to films such as Fritz Lang's *Metropolis* seek to establish links to other artistic genres.

These examples, more of which could certainly be cited, demonstrate that the borders between strains of electronic music have become increasingly porous in recent years. Many EDM musicians have become adept at fluidly negotiating complex artistic positions. Thus a figure such as Apparat, for instance, can be associated with genres such as ambient and IDM ("intelligent dance music") and make extensive use of the software Max (developed by Miller Puckette at IRCAM)—while simultaneously achieving marked popularity and commercial success and releasing albums with quasi-pop acts such as Ellen Allien.

Nevertheless, as within the world of music more generally, borders between "high" and "low" forms of electronic music still exist and continue to be actively maintained through institutional, socioeconomic, musical, and other means. The distinct but interdependent relationship between these cultural spheres has been theorized most clearly by Georgina Born in her pioneering ethnography of French electronic-music institution IRCAM (Born 1995). Dividing the post–World War II musical avant-garde (the context in which electronic music first flourished) into "postserialist modernism" and "experimental postmodernism" (62), she identifies how each tradition defined itself in relation to a popular "other." For modernism, an essential constitutive element has been an articulation—often implicit—of "absolute difference from the popular culture with which it coexists" (45). Expression of this position could take the form of complete disinterest, outright hostility, or even "the occasional surfacing of fascination, envy, and borrowing" (ibid.). Postmodern artistic movements, by contrast, have been much more likely to embrace popular culture. Experimental postmodern composers have drawn on popular music as a source of novel musical elements (rhythms, modes, etc.), as a means of articulating political positions, and as a way of problematizing high/low divides within art. Nevertheless, Born argues, these modes of relationality preserve a "certain distance" in which "popular and nonwestern musics retain the status of an 'other'" (61). Postmodern art music is still art music, no matter how arch its citationality may be.

Broadly speaking, all of the artists considered in this book are "popular" musicians. They learned their craft independently and through orally transmitted knowledge rather than through formal training. They make their livelihood through clubs, record labels, and the music-technology industry.[32] For the most part, they perform and record music with technologies that come from this industry, such as variable-speed turntables, samplers, drum machines, and the software Live. By contrast, electronic musicians working within art-music traditions have strongly favored unique, self-designed technologies and have not infrequently shunned or disdained commercially produced software and devices.[33] Reception contexts form another distinguishing criterion. EDM is defined through its association with dancing and with spaces that are explicitly designed for embodied musical experiences. Movement on the part of the audience is cultivated rather than proscribed; it is the foremost measure of a successful performance. Finally, the artists described in this book make music that is beat-based and deliberately repetitive. Groove and funk are important aesthetic criteria for them. The centrality of repetition and the bodily pleasures it can engender has been a particular magnet for criticism of EDM, as Chapter 4 will reveal. One especially telling example appears in a response by Karlheinz Stockhausen to recordings by EDM artists Aphex Twin, Scanner, Plastikman (Richie Hawtin), and Daniel Pemberton. His chief advice is, "I wish those musicians would not allow themselves any repetitions, and would go faster in developing their ideas or their findings" (Stockhausen et al. 2004, 382). Addressing each musician in turn, he admonishes Aphex Twin to listen to *Gesang der Jünglinge*, because "he would then

---

[32] One musician for whom this statement is more complicated is Robert Henke. Henke established his reputation and certainly earns his living through all of the means above; however, in 2009 he was also appointed as a professor of sound design and computer music performance at the University of the Arts in Berlin. This development in his career trajectory postdated the field research for this book. He was recruited for the position rather than seeking it out himself (pers. comm.). In general, Henke should be regarded as a popular musician with strong hybrid tendencies. His formal training is in engineering rather than music, and as noted earlier he is one of the creators of the wildly successful laptop performance software Ableton Live. Hybridity is evident in descriptions of his work, as for instance in this characterization from a press release for a 2011 Chicago concert: "Monolake is Robert Henke, a Berlin-based producer of sophisticated electronic dance music that represents the ideal synthesis of computer-driven musical experiments and dancefloor rhythms" (email from noaffiliation-chi, April 21, 2011).

[33] Born documents this attitude within IRCAM, although she also notes a moderate openness to mass-produced technologies in the period following her fieldwork (ibid., 310–12). In an article on laptop performance Nick Collins repeatedly expresses disdain for "ready-made software such as Traktor and Ableton Live" and claims that improperly educated audiences "tend to respond most often to gimmicky controllers, or to the tools they have had more exposure to—the (yawn) [sic] superstar DJs and their decks" (Collins 2003, 67).

immediately stop with all these post-African repetitions," while Plastikman is encouraged to listen to *Zyklus* in order to "get a taste for very interesting non-metric and non-periodic rhythms" (ibid.).[34] The EDM musicians had the last word, however. Among their various responses, Aphex Twin remarks, "You could dance to *Song of the Youth*, but it hasn't got a groove in it, there's no bass-line" (383).

---

[34] The question of race obviously surfaces in these critiques. The context for these remarks was a journalistic experiment of sorts initiated by British reporter Dick Witts. Recordings of the four EDM musicians were sent to Stockhausen and vice versa; remarks were solicited from all involved; and the results were published in *The Wire* in November 1995. In a more recent article on intersections between art and popular electronic music, Ben Neill identifies rhythm as the crux of the distinction, arguing that "it is the beat that draws the dividing line between serious and vernacular, visceral and intellectual" (2002, 3). In recent years a number of young art-music composers such as Mason Bates and Gabriel Prokofiev *have* begun to incorporate the aesthetics and practices of EDM into their music; however, they still have "high art" institutional groundings.

1 Remixing One's Self
ONTOLOGIES OF THE PROVISIONAL WORK

MUSICAL IDENTITY IS a principal arena of play for electronic dance music performance. Indeed, the very *modus operandi* of this style both invokes and problematizes questions of musical identity. On the one hand, performances of electronic dance music are consistently built on objects recorded prior to the event itself, such as vinyl records, digital files, loops, and samples. On the other hand—and in response—the work of the performer is to radically transform these objects through the disassembly and reconfiguration of musical structure. DJs and laptop musicians use their performance equipment to change and rearrange the textural and formal patterns of the material they play and to combine and juxtapose sounds from many diverse sources. The novel improvisations that they produce through these actions invoke and refract the creative music-making that takes place *before* performance (composition, production, recording), generating an elaborate web of distinct yet interconnected forms of musical existence.

These relationships between musical constituents become apparent, for instance, in an excerpt from an interview with recording artist and laptop performer Apparat (Sascha Ring):

MARK BUTLER: A question I have is how much is planned out in the performance....How much is planned out, [and] how much are you deciding then?

APPARAT: I have always eight loops made, which I take out of a song. I have a fully arranged song, normally, and then I take just eight short loops out of it, and sometimes I have variations of those loops. It's still very basic, so all I have to do is arrange the songs live using the eight loops or maybe a variation of the loop. And this is always a little bit different.

Notably, although I asked Apparat a question about improvisation, his answer focused instead on the musical entities involved in his performance approach. As he explains, each track that he plays in performance consists of eight basic loops drawn from a larger track that is recorded beforehand. Although he selects and extracts these loops ahead of time, storing them on his laptop, he creates the "arrangement" of each song—its formal organization as determined by changing combinations of textural patterns—in real time. The quantity of loops corresponds directly to the eight channels of his mixer, which he uses to bring patterns in and out of the mix. The arrangement that he creates in this way varies from one performance to the next, depending on factors such as audience response, the acoustics and design of the performance space, the sound system available, and his own preferences and reactions.

The basic approach that Apparat describes, in which a prerecorded, "fully arranged" track serves as a source for improvisational live performance, is common among laptop performers. The material that musicians draw on may derive from their own commercially released recordings, from works in progress that have not yet been released, or from material composed specifically for the live performance. In each case, the interplay of performance and composition generates many diverse forms of musical existence. In Apparat's description, for instance, at least five are evident: the "original" track arranged prior to performance, the loops extracted from it, variants of those loops, the arrangement, and the track as heard in performance. All of these elements have unique identities, yet in some sense they are all part of the same composition.

These distinct yet interrelated musical entities highlight the many questions, both fascinating and thorny, that EDM performance raises about musical ontology. What kinds of musical entities constitute the sonic fabric that one hears at an EDM event? How is musical identity manifested in EDM? This chapter explores such questions. Throughout I am particularly concerned with ontology in relation to recorded music; the ways in which recording practices and techniques have interacted with and affected musical ontologies are considered from multiple perspectives. Moreover, as the term *musical ontologies* suggests, I frame ontology as plural. I do not identify a singular "ontology of EDM," but rather a range of ontological practices and discourses. Other significant ontological phenomena that I seek to address include musical identity that changes over time and that encompasses multiple interrelated forms of existence (and in some cases, multiple creative agents as well). Another major area of concern involves relationships between elements of musical identity and their material instantiations.

In structural terms, my argument proceeds in four main sections. The first is theoretical: it addresses musical ontology in broad conceptual terms, considering the interaction of three related spheres that I call work, text, and performance. At the same time, it also moves through a range of styles toward an increasingly specific engagement with ontology in EDM. The second and third sections, which focus on DJ sets and laptop performances respectively, are based largely on ethnographic accounts of musical practice. The fourth and final section brings these theoretical and practical orientations into dialogue with each other, by developing a conceptual model for the multiple, fluid ontologies of EDM performance and applying this model through an extended analysis.

Works, Texts, and Performances

The term *ontology* references a branch of philosophy, that which concerns itself with the metaphysical nature of being or existence. Within musical scholarship more specifically, ontological inquiry has until recently involved a rather narrow set of idealist, "high-art" concerns (several of which I will detail shortly). For these reasons, it might seem curious to invoke the term in relation to electronic dance music, a populist, pragmatically oriented realm of musical practice. Certainly it is true that EDM musicians—as with any other musicians outside the realm of academia—are not in the habit of using the word *ontology* itself. Within everyday discourse and practice, however, they routinely articulate concerns about the nature of musical existence and formulate abstract conceptions of musical identity. In so doing, they operate fluently within what is clearly an ontological sphere.

Indeed, ontological concerns are neither as arcane nor as obscure as their scholarly gatekeepers might lead us to believe. In fact, claims about what music is or is not are a commonplace component of everyday musical discourse. As Philip Bohlman writes, "the ontologies of music do not occupy a philosophical realm of importance only to those who think about music."[1] At different stages in its creation and distribution, music may be conceptualized as a process (through activities such as singing together or invoking spirits, for instance) or as an object.[2] Ordinary words such as

---

[1] Bohlman 1999, 33; note the significant use of the plural ("ontolo*gies*"). To Bohlman's statement might be added a clarification: "those who think about music" *for a living*.

[2] Ibid., 34.

song, piece, tune, composition, and work point to just a few of the related but particular ways in which musical entities are referenced.

Within modern scholarship, accounts of musical ontology can be grouped into three broad phases according to the strategies used to define musical works. In the first phase the existence of the work is taken as given. Scholars aim to specify its properties through the exercise of logic, without significant reference to history or practice. Authors embodying this approach—well-known examples include Goodman (1968) and Levinson (1980)—address ontology only within Western high-art spheres.[3]

In the second phase, the work is framed as a historically and culturally situated concept. Its properties are thus understood to function within a particular interpretive context. The best example of this approach is *The Imaginary Museum of Musical Works* (Goehr 1992), a highly influential text that stakes out an explicitly historical position on the work. Note, however, that this historical position is also sharply delimited by musical style and culture: in spite of occasional brief references to jazz and popular music, Goehr's theory is based exclusively within Western classical music.

Scholars working in the third phase adopt a pluralistic approach in which work-like constructs are understood to exist within a variety of musical styles. They accordingly seek to identify many "work-*concepts*" instead of a single, dominant "work-concept." These scholars have also sought to theorize the role of modern media practices such as recording in relation to the abstractions about musical identity that humans use, and they have been concerned with how works change and interrelate over time as well. Authors working in this vein include Bohlman (1999), Born (2005), and myself. A related group of scholars (Gracyk 1996, Théberge 1997, Zak 2001) offer accounts that are less focused on general models of ontology and more specifically on the ramifications of recording practices; I discuss their work further shortly.

Certain criteria have repeatedly emerged as significant within scholarly definitions of works. These include authority (who brings the work into being?), originality in relation to other works, relationships between the general and the particular (is the work unique?), wholeness, boundedness (the extent to which a work might overlap or share material with other works), relationships to time (is the work considered permanent after its creation?), and relationships to change (is work changeable after its creation?). Goehr, for instance, defines the European work-concept of

---

[3] Goehr locates this approach to the work within analytic philosophy. Within this area she gives closest attention to the work of Goodman and Levinson, but also cites a number of other authors such as Peter Kivy and Kendall Walton (see Goehr 1992, 5 n. 6).

Beethoven's time as an original, unique, structurally integrated whole that, once created, is imagined as a permanent and unchangeable artifact akin to a museum piece (1992, 2).

A tension emerges in Goehr's account with regard to its frame of reference. Is the work-concept that she describes one of many, or is it *the* work-concept? In situating the argument as historically and socially specific, she opens up the former as a possibility. But in the absence of serious consideration of other musical contexts, the reader ends up with a discussion of this particular work-concept to the exclusion of others. Indeed, it eventually becomes clear that Goehr regards "the work-concept" as a product of this specific time and place, and that other musical traditions, in her view, have functioned or continue to function without a work-concept.[4] This stance is a problem for scholarship, because it preserves classical music's position of authority and leaves us without a means of discussing work-like constructs in other styles. The principal ontological elements of jazz, popular music, and other styles are left undefined; they are simply "without a work-concept."[5] Moreover, if one uses "work" to describe such a style, one risks being charged with inappropriately imposing a concept derived from a classical context.

Increasingly, however, authors have begun to recognize that works exist and are variously inflected in a range of musical styles. The present chapter adopts such a perspective. Because abstractions about musical identity are common to many musical contexts (even though the terms with which they are conceptualized vary), thinking about music broadly in terms of works remains useful for understanding ontology in a variety of styles. Conceptions of works are not unique to nineteenth-century art music; nor does "work" necessarily invoke the classic aestheticist formulation of the work-concept. When I use the term *work*, therefore, I mean to invoke ontology at a general level to suggest a construct of musical identity. I do this with an awareness of the particular conditions associated with the "work-concept" in Western classical contexts, but without implying those conditions in my use of the more general term. A similar caveat is in order with respect to the term *ontology*. The sense in which I use it and its cognates is not one that seeks to define "what things are," but rather to identify what people *say* things are, and how people's musical practices construct, disassemble, and rearrange musical "things." It is thus socially and

---

[4] See, for instance, pp. ix–x (on jazz and popular music) and 8 (on Bach).

[5] I write this with full awareness that one of Goehr's main objectives in situating the work-concept as she does is to dislodge its ostensibly "natural" status. However, her historicization still operates within a sphere in which art music sets the terms for other discourses. Goehr addresses some of these issues in the introduction to the revised edition of *The Imaginary Museum* (see esp. xxx–xxxiv). She maintains a speculative tone, at times seeming to embrace pluralism, more often cautioning that an overly inclusive concept of the work would lose meaning, and ultimately avoiding a definitive answer.

historically contingent. It is also a present-tense version: it looks at works "in the making," not just as "made."

One of Goehr's most important observations is that the "work-concept" configures music as an enduring object whose ontology is more like that of a sculpture or painting than a process unfolding in time. This point connects suggestively to my own interest in the play of process/product and fluid/fixed within the musical practices I describe. However, objects under Goehr's work-concept are fixed and untouchable, whereas the present study aims to show not only how musical objects can be formed but also how they can be broken down and reconfigured. Moreover, Goehr refers to metaphorical objects, whereas I describe real ones. And here a final critique emerges: accounts such as Goehr's fail to address the very significant role of recording and affiliated practices on musical ontology. This critique has been voiced most recently by Georgina Born, who contends that Goehr does not pursue the full implications of her thesis of historical contingency, in no small part because of "her reluctance to pursue the significance of technologies of music production and reproduction for the shifting ontology of contemporary music," and this despite "the ubiquity and prominence of technological mediation in each element of contemporary musical experience—creation, performance and reception" (Born 2005, 10). A similar avoidance or even antipathy toward mediation is evident in other ontologically inflected accounts, as for instance when Carolyn Abbate (citing philosopher Vladimir Jankélévitch) contends that "real music" is "music that exists in time, the material acoustic phenomenon"—namely, an "actual live performance (and not a recording even of a live performance)."[6]

Recording, Abbate suggests, "alter[s] a basic alchemy, making the event an artifact, handheld and under control, encouraging distance and reflection"—a "pale" remnant of real music.[7] However, recordings are a central component—in many cases *the* central component—of the very real musical experiences of millions of people. Moreover, they are also essential constituents of live musical performance in widely followed styles such as EDM and rap. This chapter accordingly frames ontology in relation to these pervasive recording practices. I do so first by considering works in relation to the material objects or inscriptions with which they are frequently associated. Depending on the style, these may include items such as scores,

---

[6] Abbate 2004, 505 and 506. Dichotomies between "live" performance and recording will be problematized extensively in Chapter 2.

[7] Ibid., 534. Note that this statement assumes that recording comes after performance and documents it. However, this applies only to small and historically/stylistically delimited portions of the world's recording practices, as subsequent discussion of the ontology of recording in rock reveals.

lead sheets, records, compact discs, or digital files.[8] These objects represent the work and certainly affect our understanding of what kind of entity it is, but they are not co-terminous with it. If we encounter "My Funny Valentine" by playing the printed score, for example, we experience an entity—a "song," in this case—that lies at a more abstract level than the material object. Whereas I call these abstract entities "works," I describe the objects or inscriptions that represent them as "texts."

The term *text* is commonly used in contemporary literary theory and cultural studies to refer to anything that can be "read." The thing in question is some kind of cultural object or performance—a film, a Madonna video, a poem, an Elvis impersonation—and the reading involved is obviously metaphorical, an approximate synonym for "interpretation" (even when the text is written). The value of this metaphorical extension is clear, for it allows theories of writing and performance to be extended beyond their original, canonical domains to many diverse forms of cultural expression. In the present context, however, I use "text" in a narrower sense—one that does not necessarily imply the written word, but does invoke some sort of "inscribed" entity. In order to call attention to the presence of such elements within otherwise fluid performances, it is useful to reinvigorate the literal qualities of the term.

Traditions of music making articulate relationships between works, texts, and performances in a variety of ways. In Western art music, for instance, performance has typically been construed as ephemeral in relation to the fixity of the work; as a result, variations between performances have not been seen as ontologically significant. Within this discursive tradition, the work is understood to lie at a deeper level than any possible realization, whether score or performance; it transcends its material and textual instantiations. The score, however, as the most concrete representative of the work, is accorded special privilege; performers are expected to be faithful to its instructions (Goehr 1992).

Scores were also central to the popular music that developed around Tin Pan Alley in New York City in the early twentieth century. For instance, songs were popularized (and their popularity measured) through the sale and distribution of sheet music. Scores, however, were less detailed than those within the classical tradition; they provided basic information about pitches, rhythm, and lyrics, but gifted performers could alter a song greatly to make it "their own." Because fidelity to the score was not necessary, and because vaudeville circuits were essential to the popularization of a song before commercial recordings and radio were widely available,

---

[8] I consider the digital file to be a kind of "inscription"; it is recorded with a material object (such as a computer), and it requires a material object for implementation. Therefore, the intangible properties of digital music—although clearly important to the ways in which it has been received, transformed, and transmitted—should not be overemphasized. I return to this topic in greater detail subsequently.

performers played a more important role in the musical hierarchy than composers, as a number of scholars have noted. Richard Crawford, for instance, has described the Tin Pan Alley tradition as an example of "performer's music," in which musical notation serves "not as a finished statement but an outline to be filled in, to be 'realized,' by performers in any way they choose" (Crawford 1993, 65). Notions of the "work" were still in play, however, although individual works were not seen as highly unique (hence the initial lack of copyright protection for songwriters). Nevertheless, a song was still a song, and performance was still fleeting in relation to the permanence of the mass-produced, printed score.

As these examples reveal, texts vary in their specificity. This variability may inhere in several domains: in the level of detail conveyed to the performer or listener, in the parameters that are specified, and in the *ways* the text specifies. The effects of these differences are especially evident in jazz, in which several kinds of texts function simultaneously. First, although musicological scholarship has generally (and correctly) emphasized jazz as an oral tradition, many jazz musicians do make use of written texts. These include the collections of lead sheets found in "fake books" (which are neither very specific nor prescriptive in their indication of musical detail) as well as written-out arrangements for larger ensembles (which can approach classical scores in their level of precision). Second, and more importantly for my concerns here, jazz traditions incorporate *recorded* texts to a significant extent. As Zak notes (Zak 2001, 2), "while spontaneous performance is central to the idiom [of jazz], preservation of performances on records has been essential to its influence, its pedagogy, and the development of its historiography." Because of their portability (one of the principal "phonograph effects" described in Katz 2004), recordings have played key roles in the spread of jazz styles across large geographical distances. Within jazz education, the added effect of repeatability has been essential; students make a habit of studying recorded solos very carefully, sometimes slowing them down in order to learn to sing them, and learning to play them note-by-note either in part or *in totum* (Berliner 1994, 96–97).[9] Processes of textual fixation are therefore pervasive within the "oral tradition" of jazz; as Katz notes (2004, 79), "a recorded improvisation is…music of the moment made timeless, the one-of-a-kind rendered reproducible, the spontaneous turned inevitable."

Ultimately, however, these materials feed into and facilitate new improvisations. A cycle emerges: a fluid musical process crystallizes into a fixed product, and then becomes fluid again. Recorded solos, therefore, function ontologically as constructive elements within performance, along with a variety of other musical entities:

---

[9] These processes may also incorporate or generate additional written texts, either in the form of published solos that may be treated as etudes or through students producing their own transcriptions (ibid., 98).

basic riffs or licks learned in practice, quotations from other songs, and ultimately, entire composed pieces or tunes, which, as Berliner notes, "have provided the structure for improvisations throughout most of the history of jazz" (Berliner 1994, 63).

Although jazz traditions, unlike classical ones, developed in association with recordings, overly simple contrasts between the two styles should be avoided. As a number of scholars have revealed, the advent of recording technologies has also had significant effects on practices of classical music making and appreciation, even if the prevalence of purist ideologies might conceal their impact. Moreover, despite their differences both traditions share a view of recording as reflecting a single uninterrupted performance; Gracyk describes this ontological prioritization of performance over recording as "recording realism" or simply "realism" (1996, 39ff). At times, the realist aesthetic may be more nominal than functional. As Katz (2004, 26–27) has noted, the possibility of note-perfect recorded performances has surely affected the expectations with which both audiences and performers now approach concerts. Furthermore, although studio manipulation is certainly less prevalent in classical traditions than in popular ones, many recordings nevertheless represent an amalgam of spliced-together takes rather than a single, uninterrupted rendition. Performers' interactions with the recording process may even affect how the notes of a composition are rendered; Katz, for instance, argues that a "constant and strong vibrato" emerged along with recording as performers adjusted to the technical limitations of early equipment, sought ways to conceal less-than-perfect intonation (which was more evident in recorded form), and learned to create a sense of "presence" in the absence of live appearances on stage.[10]

In rock, recorded texts come to play an even more defining role, while written texts become scarcer, to the point that they are rarities in composition and performance.[11] As with jazz, rock spread and became popular through recordings. Gracyk links this historical emergence to musical innovations as well, writing that "rock is popular music of the second half of the twentieth century which is essentially dependent on recording technology for its inception and dissemination. Its major *musical* developments have almost always occurred in recording studios" (ibid., 13; original emphasis). Perhaps more importantly, he connects these musical developments to an *ontological* basis in recording: "rock embraces a host of performance styles, but most have *some* basis in African American popular music, are rooted in song, and paradigmatically exist as *recorded* music" (ibid., 7; original emphases). Other scholars

---

[10] Ibid., 93. These examples represent only a very small portion of what might be said about the impact of recording technologies on classical music making; full consideration of this topic would take us well beyond the scope of the present work. See also Clarke 2007, 54.

[11] I use "rock" to refer to a broad category of Western popular music that emerged from a more specific style, rock 'n' roll; Gracyk defines the former term usefully as "guitar-heavy music with a debt to rock 'n' roll" (1996, 2).

concur: Zak, for instance (2001, 12), notes that rock 'n' roll was "first and foremost a recorded music," while Toynbee writes that the site of "ideal performance" shifted from live performance to the recorded work in the 1950s, and that there was consequently less need for an "authentic moment behind the record" (2000, 87). In contrast to jazz and classical approaches, in which recordings have conventionally been understood as "snapshots of live performances" (ibid.), these scholars position rock as the first style in which records were conceived of as *goals* rather than by-products of artistic endeavors.

Not surprisingly, a number of scholars writing about recording practices in rock have taken up issues of musical ontology. The relationship between the recording and the work has been an area of particular concern, with many arguments centering on contrasts between scores and recordings. Obviously, both kinds of text inscribe musical sound into material form (whether it be with the pen or the needle), yet they do so rather differently. A recording conveys the sounds in question more specifically and seems to offer much less flexibility in terms of altering the sounds involved. Furthermore, a recording does not require a conscious translation across media, whereas a score requires a deliberate move from writing to sound. Zak frames the distinction in terms of presentation versus existence: "A rock recording is not an 'acoustic presentation' of a written text. It is itself a text, a sonic one; 'what it *sounds* like' is precisely 'what it *is*'" (Zak 2001, 41; original emphasis).[12]

Theodore Gracyk describes the differences between recordings and scores using aesthetician Nelson Goodman's categories of "autographic" and "allographic" works (Goodman 1968, 113–16). An autographic artwork—for instance, a painting—is unique; any duplication would not be authentic. By contrast, any reasonable duplication of an allographic work is a genuine instantiation. According to Gracyk, music realized from a score is allographic, but recorded rock compositions are autographic (Gracyk 1996, 31–35). After making this general claim, he modifies his definition in a way that allows for the influence of style-specific historical practice; drawing on an adjustment to Goodman's formulation suggested by Jerrold Levinson (1990, 101), he paraphrases: "a work is allographic if a historically indicated structure is presented and autographic if notational determination plays *no* role in its genuineness" (ibid., 33–34; original emphasis).

To describe a work as "autographic" is to claim, in a metaphorical application of the word's literal roots, that it *writes itself*. However, in a rock context (and possibly in others as well), the circularity of this formulation is problematic. Notice, for

---

12. The internal quotations within this excerpt derive from Charles Ives' "Essay before a Sonata," in which the composer argues, "That music must be heard is not essential—what it *sounds* like may not be what it *is*" (Ives 1970, 84; original emphasis). Zak presents it within a larger discussion of the "silent musical text" in which several composers' aesthetic claims are cited.

instance, how Zak uses "text" in the quotation above. The "written text" to which he refers is a score (and thus a "text" in the sense in which I have been using the term), while the "sonic" text is a *work*. This slippage reveals a failure to distinguish between texts and works, as well as a conflation of works and recordings that both Gracyk and Zak articulate rather forcefully. Zak (2001, 42–43) writes that "it is clear that records are musical works," while Gracyk (1996, 1) argues that "in rock the musical work is less typically a song than an arrangement of recorded sounds" and "the musical works [of rock] do not exist apart from the recording process itself" (ibid., 13). Gracyk also writes that "recordings are the 'primary texts' of this music" (ibid., 21), a statement that reflects and supports a larger tendency within rock scholarship; in the absence of notated scores for analytical study, scholars have often been concerned with the identification of other kinds of definitive texts, which they have generally located in the recording, the most permanent material object of rock's compositional practice. The phrase "primary text" appears in numerous sources in conjunction with recording, with the most likely definitive usage appearing in Allan F. Moore's textbook *Rock: The Primary Text*.[13]

To say that record making is a creative process, that recordings deserve critical attention, that aspects of a recording are important to the interpretation of a work, or that nontraditional "sound" aspects can be part of the work—all of these are important claims, but none of them require that the record *be* the work. The crucial distinction, again, is between abstract conceptualizations of musical identity ("works") and material instantiations of ontic entities ("texts"). The problems that emerge when works and texts are conflated become evident in Gracyk and Zak's discussions of *related* ontological constructs in rock, such as "songs," "arrangements," and "versions." Zak, for instance, posits a threefold taxonomy of song, arrangement, and track. By using terms derived from musical practice, Zak highlights the important role that abstractions about musical identity play in the discourse of musicians and average listeners (and not just that of musicologists and aestheticians). A "track" in Zak's formulation is a recorded work; his use of the term thus evokes a particular association between recording and ontology. A song is something more abstract, which "is easily separated from any particular recorded rendering" (2001, 25). The arrangement, meanwhile, lies somewhere in between: it is "a particular musical setting of the song. It provides a more detailed prescriptive plan: instrumentation, musical parts, rhythmic groove, and so forth" (ibid., 24). All of these categories are

---

[13] Ironically, however, Moore uses the phrase in a somewhat more general sense, to refer to the text "constituted by the sounds themselves," as opposed to the "secondary" text of discourse about the sounds (Moore 2001, 1). It is clear, however, that Moore sees the sounds as inhering definitively in recordings; for instance, he later refers to the primary text as "what is heard" in a section contrasting recordings with classical scores (35).

certainly pertinent to Zak's focus on the compositional dimensions of the recording studio. Their appearance here, however, raises several difficult questions: If a "song" is a kind of abstraction about musical identity, but the recording is the work, what kind of "work" is the song? Is it the same work as that represented by the recording? Perhaps a subset of it, or a different version? And what is the ontological status of an "arrangement"? If it is a concrete realization of something else, as Zak's definition seems to suggest, then the abstract nature of the underlying entity (in Zak's formulation, a "song") comes into sharper focus, returning us to the first of the questions above.

Gracyk favors a view in which the "song" is its own kind of work, distinct from the recording. He allows that rock "retains some allegiance to established dichotomies of song/performance and composer/performer" (Gracyk 1996, 43) and notes that "the relevant work (the recording) frequently manifests another work, usually a song, without being a performance of that song" (ibid., 18). What is confusing here, however, is the claim that both the song and the recording are "works." If this is the case, we are still left wondering how, exactly, the two are related (if at all). Later in his book, in chapter 2, Gracyk offers a comment that clarifies this concern: "recordings," he writes, "simultaneously exemplify two different sorts of musical works: the autographic recording and the allographic song" (ibid., 43). Elsewhere, Gracyk introduces terms for other varieties of musical existence, such as "versions," "instantiations," and "remixes." In some cases, he claims these as distinct works and in other cases not. He remarks, for instance, that "many different versions of a work" may circulate simultaneously in popular culture (ibid., 22). He then mentions "multiple instantiations of a work" that are often dissimilar enough to be different works; as examples, he cites translations of poems and revised symphonies (ibid., 23–24). The practices of the relevant tradition, he argues quite reasonably, are most important in deciding whether these are separate works or not. In either case, however, it remains unclear how the ontological relationships between these entities—whether "versions" or separate works—should be described; even if a revised work is treated as distinct, it is obviously more closely related to its predecessor than another work by the same composer, for instance.

One useful theoretical formulation within these scholars' work addresses the specificity with which the features of a work are indicated. Gracyk posits a notion of ontological "thickness" or "thinness" pertaining to the level of detail involved. Performances are ontologically thicker than compositions, for instance.[14] In rock, songs are ontologically thin, while recordings are thick. Zak develops this distinction in a useful way, writing, "The important functional difference between a popular song

---

[14] Gracyk 1996, 19–21, citing Davies 1991, 37.

and a classical work lies not so much in aesthetic or stylistic matters but in relative degrees of specification. A song has a built-in fluidity. It is 'ontologically thin'" (Zak 2001, 42). Cook, in turn, argues that because representations of compositions always fail to specify some of their parameters fully, performance is a "negotiation" between composer and performer.[15]

One of the major projects in which Gracyk and Zak are engaged is the validation of the recording studio as a site of creative activity. This goal is both important and challenging for musicology, which has traditionally approached music making in terms of single compositions written by individual authors. In contrast, the studio is a site of collaborative creativity, in which songwriters, producers, engineers, and performers all contribute to the emergence of a work. Furthermore, emphases on timbral and spatial effects (echo, reverb, delay, etc.) challenge traditional foci on pitch and rhythm as carriers of musical identity. Gracyk and Zak place all of these qualities as realized through recording technologies within the broad category of "sound."

Paul Théberge also comments on the ontological ramifications of "sound" in a chapter entitled "The New 'Sound' of Music: Technology and Changing Concepts of Music." His basic claim is as follows:

> Although there are certainly valid distinctions to be made between "songs" and their realization in sound, for much popular music such distinctions have become increasingly difficult to make.... The term "sound" has taken on a peculiar material character that cannot be separated either from the "music" or, more importantly, from the sound recording as the dominant medium of reproduction.
>
> (Théberge 1997, 190–97)

Because of its ever-increasing electronic mediation, the creation of popular music has moved toward an increasing "fusion of instrument and recording device" (ibid., 194). One consequence of this trend has been a blurring of the boundaries between electronic effects and the sounds on which they operate. Tracing the emergence of "chorusing" effects—which were initially a technique for making sounds "fatter," but became part of the sound itself—Théberge describes how these and other effects have become integral to certain sonic identities. They are "no longer seen as a separate operation applied *to* a sound," he argues; "rather, the effect becomes an inherent characteristic *of* the sound itself" (ibid., 210; original emphases). This process

---

[15] Cook 1995a, 35–36. Cook is speaking at a general level in which "representations" include various kinds of texts (scores as well as recordings).

of ontological consolidation clearly exemplifies a significant way in which "the possibility of sound *re*production reorients the practices of sound production," as Jonathan Sterne has written (2003, 221; emphasis mine). Moreover, as we have shifted toward a paradigm in which the entire universe of sound is available for music making, musical creation has increasingly become a process "of simultaneous production and consumption" (Théberge 1997, 213). Théberge emphasizes this simultaneity within composition, but its role within performance will also become evident within subsequent analytical discussions.

Research on the compositional and ontological dimensions of recorded texts has focused largely on rock styles. Although this emphasis is certainly relevant given rock's historical significance as the first widely dispersed style based in recording practices, it is also rather out of date. Since the 1970s, recorded texts have served as the very material *of* performance in a variety of newer, mostly dance-based styles. These emerging traditions of musical practice include disco, rap, dub, and electronic dance music.

EDM performance, considered in terms of the style as a whole, involves many kinds of recorded texts. Artists may use CDs, vinyl records, preset sounds from drum machines or synthesizers (both analog and digital), self-composed loops and tracks stored on their computers, and audio files of other artists' music. Some of these texts involve analog signals, others digital ones. Some are permanently encoded into a fixed physical product; others are not. Although it is easy to categorize an object such as a record as a text, understanding entities such as digital files in these terms can present some conceptual challenges, especially in relation to certain emphases of scholarship on recording practices.

Scholars have repeatedly focused on certain qualities or potentials as essential characteristics of recordings. Katz, for instance, mentions tangibility, portability, (in)visibility, repeatability, and manipulability.[16] In addition, scholars have stressed the *materiality* of recorded texts more than any other feature. Purely electronic texts heighten some of these traits while diminishing others. Digital files, for instance, are more portable and manipulable than vinyl records, but they are not directly visible or tangible. Nevertheless, they are not out of place within a materially oriented conceptual framework. In order to have the permanence associated with other recorded texts, digital information must be stored mechanically. Although it can move between users and platforms and be transformed very easily and rapidly, it must rematerialize in some way to have any utility for humans. In this regard it is similar to

---

[16] See Katz 2004. Katz structures much of his book around these "phonograph effects"; the initial citations for each of the qualities above begin on pp. 9, 12, 18, 24, and 41, respectively. Two other traits that he mentions are "temporality" (31) and "receptivity" (37); these complete his list but are less relevant to my concerns here.

sound itself, a phenomenon that requires matter to have an effect. Because of these properties, the digital file can be understood as a kind of "inscription."[17]

Whether digital or analog, then, recordings function as a kind of text within the threefold schema of works, texts, and performances. Relationships between recorded texts and *performances* form another area with significant ontological implications. Performance theorist Philip Auslander, who addresses these relationships at length in his book *Liveness: Performance in a Mediatized Culture*, writes that "live performances and recordings are *not* treated as fully separable artworks in rock culture" (Auslander 1999, 82; original emphasis). Whereas recordings initially served as documents of complete live performances, almost all rock recordings are now mediated so extensively by techniques such as overdubbing (through which a single musician may produce multiple simultaneous iterations of the same part) and multitrack recording (in which the members of an ensemble record their individual parts separately) that the "performances" they represent do not exist. This does not mean, however, that we cease to experience these texts through the lens of performance. Simon Frith describes the mental transformation involved:

> I listen to records in the full knowledge that what I hear is something that never existed, that never could exist, as a "performance," something happening in a single time and space; nevertheless, it is now happening, in a single time and space: it is thus a performance and I hear it as one.
>
> (Frith 1996, 211)

Gracyk effectively captures the qualities of this imagined performance using philosophically oriented terms. Rock recordings, he argues, "represent" rather than transmit performances (1996, 43); they create "virtual" spaces and times of performance (53).

Auslander also highlights the extent to which live performances of popular music now imitate recordings and other media forms.[18] In concert, for example, many rock musicians perform in a way that is, in Auslander's terms, "videated"—that is,

---

[17] In an account of the materialities of the hard drive, Matthew Kirschenbaum develops the idea of digital inscription in significant detail. "As a written trace digital inscription is invisible to the eye, but it is not instrumentally undetectable or physically immaterial," he writes (2004, 92). At several points in his essay he makes interesting comparisons between the properties of hard drives and vinyl records, noting for instance that both technologies afford "(essentially) instantaneous access to any portion of the physical media, without the need to fast-forward or rewind a sequence" (101).

[18] It also seems clear (although Auslander does not make this point) that performances that do *not* imitate recordings are still, quite frequently, construed in relation to them. Performances that are marked as especially "live"—such as the improvisational "jams" of the Grateful Dead, for instance—are defined as such in opposition to a recording.

performed and perceived in relation to a previously released music video, through close imitation or reference to its choreography, narrative, or imagery (1999, 35). As a result, no live performance is the "authentic original" anymore; instead, each performance is experienced as one instantiation of a given, reproducible text (50).[19] At the same time, performance may serve other kinds of authenticating functions, especially in rock contexts, in which notions of traditional performance skill often still hold sway. Although live performance imitates the recording, the mediated nature of the latter stimulates a desire or need for authentication through live performance. Ultimately, then, the two outlets of musical expression exist in a dialectical relationship (82–84).

Having explored work/text/performance relationships from a range of theoretical and stylistic perspectives, I now turn my attention to musical practice. The next two sections offer accounts, largely ethnographically based, of a range of performance practices and their ontological implications within the recording-centric style of EDM. The first section focuses on EDM's foundational mode of performance, DJing, while a second, longer section addresses musical identity within the laptop set.

Creating the "Third Record": Works and Texts in DJ Performances

Despite the futuristic, high-tech aesthetic often associated with EDM, DJs performing in this style continue to use twelve-inch vinyl records. As material instantiations, records function as texts, while the more abstract objects they represent can be understood as works. The practice of disassembling, rearranging, and combining preexistent compositions within DJ performances subverts conventional perceptions of material texts and the works they instantiate as fixed or permanent objects. Significantly, they work against what Born has described as the tendency of "material artifacts" to "stop the flow of re-creation" (Born 2005, 26). More specifically, they bring tensions between "fixed" products and fluid processes into sharp relief, destabilizing this dichotomy in the process.

I developed a particular awareness of these tensions within DJ performance while learning to beat-match. As I worked on acquiring this basic technical skill, I often wrote about my experiences in my journal. The passages below are excerpts from written descriptions of my thoughts after a practice session on September 16, 2006; I have paraphrased some of the sentences slightly in order to create a smoother flow. At first, I wrote about how I was struck—indeed, overwhelmed—by the fixity and discreteness of the two tracks I was trying to mix:

---

[19] Here Auslander uses "text" to connote a kind of work.

As I was playing, the problem I was having (besides all the basic technical problems) was combining these two tracks in my head. I was listening, and there were two totally separate things going on. I couldn't hear both at the same time, at least not with independent meters. I tried to find a way to put them together. But this was hard too. I would ignore one at the expense of the other, which led to disastrous mixes. Or I would try to hear the other but fail.

Eventually, I managed to match the tracks successfully. "I was looking for this moment where the two records would combine in my head," I wrote. "When it happened, a new track formed." More specifically, the formation of the "new track" occurred in a remarkable way. When I found the precise alignment between the records, they suddenly and dramatically merged. I no longer heard them as two separate entities—indeed, I found it difficult to do so even when I tried. Instead, this combination of texts produced something that did not exist in material form. DJs describe this chimeric entity as the "third record."[20]

It is difficult to envision a more succinctly ontological phrase than this term, which is widely used within dance-music communities. The incursion of ontological discourse into this realm also highlights the curious status of the original works that constitute DJ performances. What happens to these works when they become part of a set? Can they still be understood as "works"? How do the transformations they undergo affect any conventional qualities of the work that might be associated with them?

The works contained in the recordings that constitute a DJ set are rarely presented in their entirety; instead, they are truncated, altered, and combined with other works. The borders and seams of the original work dissolve; it no longer functions as a unitary, bounded entity. The stability, fixity, or permanence that is classically associated with the work slips away, and any authorial value that might have accrued to the work is seriously weakened. At the same time, aspects of the original work's essence remain, and its former identity is not irrelevant. These ontic elements, however, become part of new, larger entities—the third record, and ultimately the set.

In addition to the works behind the original records and the ontological phenomenon of the third record, other constructs of musical identity may come into play within DJ sets. One common possibility is the sample, which presents a brief chunk of material—often recognizable—from a preexistent recording. Katz describes these kinds of samples as "performative quotation," because of the highly specific way in which they point back to the unique "aura" of the original recording (Katz 2004, 140).[21]

---

[20] For an introduction to this term, see Butler 2006, 94 and 243.

[21] I address the ontology of sampling in greater detail in the next section of this chapter.

A further ontological construct is the set itself. Within EDM contexts, sets are clearly understood as bearers of musical identity. They grow and develop in certain clearly definable ways and are understood as musically unified totalities. At the same time, they do not possess many of the features most commonly associated with works.[22] Instead of elaborating a single underlying identity, most sets develop processually and contingently. In an earlier work I described the unity of the set as follows:

> In a set, the emphasis is on logical flow—on making a continuous musical progression—rather than on unifying devices (themes, motives, keys) that persist throughout an entire work. Form is not derived from an object-like model, in which coherence can be viewed within a complete musical structure just as one would perceive the unity of a sculpture (all at once), but rather on a sense of a continuous development through time. This approach to form is more perceptually than structurally based: it is like a journey on a train in which the destination is unknown to the rider, but one can see out the window the whole time. We end up in a completely different place than we started, but our route made sense; the coherence is that of the trip itself, not its components.
>
> (Butler 2006, 242)

The narrative thread that unifies a set is therefore specific to a particular event. It creates something coherent, but the end result is not necessarily defined at the outset, and it might develop quite differently on another occasion. Another kind of formal contingence pertains to how sets conclude: they stop when the DJ's time slot is over, and they often end with a fadeout rather than a clearly defined point of closure. As a result, their borders are defined contextually rather than essentially; boundedness is not an important aspect of their unity.

Composing Performance in the Laptop Set

The kinds of identity play that occur within DJ sets are rich, having developed over the course of the art form as practiced within club and dance music cultures since the 1970s. All the same, EDM DJing involves a relatively consistent set of practices,

---

[22] Robert Fink (2005, 182), describing the "faux-unity" that arose when listeners would play hours of Baroque concerti using stacks of long-playing records, coins the term *Überwerk*. The word has potential as a descriptor for the ontology of the set (particularly as no such term exists), yet I resist applying it: primarily because of its synoptic overtones, and secondarily because the German term may linguistically connote a particular aesthetic context. Furthermore, the unity of the set is not artificial, though it differs from a classical idealist unity as described above.

even as individual styles of performance vary tremendously. By contrast, the approaches and techniques found within laptop sets are considerably less uniform, as this mode of performance developed much more recently and is still changing rapidly. This section, based primarily on my fieldwork with Berlin-based musicians, reveals many diverse forms of musical identity and identity play arising within their laptop performances. Discussion begins with various shorter elements (samples, preset patterns, and the like)—which are treated as bearers of musical identity no less significant than tracks themselves—and proceeds toward increasingly expansive designs. Relationships that emerge as significant include those occurring between shorter elements and full tracks, between preexistent recordings and performances, between versions of a track (whether performed and recorded), between tracks within a musician's *oeuvre*, and between his or her own tracks and those of other artists (including non-EDM artists as well as those within the style).

Presets

The manufacturers of drum machines and synthesizers frequently preload banks of short rhythms, typically one to four measures in length, into the memory of the machines. These "presets" may consist of individual patterns (e.g., a conga riff) or of several instrumental patterns in combination (which together form a basic "groove"). One might expect musicians to shun these patterns, since EDM musicians and fans typically frown on simply using machines as their makers intended.[23] The realities of performance and compositional practice, however, turn out to be more complex. Some musicians *do* make use of presets, but in ways that are very much in keeping with the creative approaches favored within EDM as a whole. First, they do not use them without significant modification. The transformations that they introduce may be textural, rhythmic, or timbral.[24] Second, they do not form entire tracks from presets, but instead incorporate them into larger compositional designs. Third, they use presets as vehicles for *live improvisation*. Modifications—for instance, muting or unmuting instrumental parts within the patterns, or changing their rhythmic values—almost always take place during real time and are generally unplanned. In this way, presets serve as tools with which to improvise. Such improvisation is

---

[23] For further discussion, see Butler 2006, 67–70.

[24] With regard to the last of these parameters, many devices (especially digital synthesizers) include huge quantities of preset instrumental sounds. However, any EDM musician who uses one of these timbres in an unmodified way would be regarded as unoriginal and lacking in creativity. This aesthetic is in direct contrast to the practices described by Théberge (1997, 75 and 89), who describes musicians selecting digital instruments precisely *for* the preset timbres they include. However, his focus (though not explicitly stated) is on musicians working in "mainstream" styles, and mostly during the 1980s.

common both within performance and during the compositional process as a track is being recorded.

Pacou touches on several of these themes in an explanation of how he uses preset rhythms on the Korg Electribe-R mkII drum machine:

> PACOU: What I'm using is mainly the things that are in there [*in the machine's memory*], because they have almost three hundred or something. So you can use all those patterns that are in there, and you can mute certain parts that are playing. Like, you can take out the bass drum, take out the hi-hat, the claps, or whatever elements. And it will just play the rest of the elements along with the other machines.
>
> MARK BUTLER: Right.
>
> PACOU: So that's the way I'm using it.
>
> MB: So you mainly use the preset rhythm patterns that are in that machine?
>
> PACOU: Yeah. But I'm changing them around while I'm playing live. That means every time, every live act will sound different.

Pacou also incorporates preset rhythm patterns into recorded tracks in a transformational manner. He explained, for instance, that he often discovers preset grooves that are generally "cheesy" but feature one or more interesting sounds. In such cases, he often mutes all the parts except the preferred sound; for instance, a hi-hat. From a traditional compositional perspective (by which I mean, in this case, one less mediated by electronic technology), his approach seems indirect: Why not just *compose* a hi-hat pattern? After all, such patterns are rarely longer than four bars (and frequently shorter), and Pacou is certainly not lacking in the ability to devise them. Instead of constructing a sound that wasn't there before, however, he takes prerecorded sounds as his starting point—as elements that must be muted, taken apart, and otherwise transformed in order to form the fabric of a new work. In treating these elements as basic musical materials, Pacou's approach reveals the degree to which conceptions of musical sound as recorded object have permeated the creative process itself.

When presets are operative, the actual musical units—the things that we think of as unique, as needing to be imagined and "composed"—function as "readymades" within a larger composition. From an ontological perspective, these entities are provocative. Just what kind of musical object are they? In conventional analytic terms they are most like motives, yet their status as immediately accessible, mass-manufactured products challenges the unique status and germinative power that this label typically connotes. In EDM terms they are similar to loops, yet they lack the authorial value of those patterns, which are composed by the creator of a track rather than programmed by an anonymous figure. They are also less specific: a loop is a unique combination of timbre and rhythm, whereas a preset may or may not have defined timbral qualities.

At the same time, presets do have some of the qualities associated with stable musical identity. Indeed, their very name points to something that is fixed, permanent, and closed. Yet these seemingly "preset" patterns are subject to considerable transformation. They may also reconfigure the values through which musical identity is assigned in surprising ways. This possibility first became evident to me in a follow-up interview with Pacou, when I asked him to demonstrate each of the machines he had used in a recent performance. He began with the Future Retro 777, a modern "emulator" of a vintage machine, the Roland TB-303 Bass Line. The latter, manufactured in 1982, is one of the most famous machines in the history of electronic dance music; the former, manufactured in 1998, is a monophonic analog synthesizer that features the classic "acid" sound of the 303 along with various improvements (a digital sequencer; more solid hardware). After switching the 777 on, Pacou selected a sixteen-step rhythm (equal to four quarter-note beats, with the "steps" having been assigned the default value of a sixteenth note) and demonstrated its sonic similarities to the 303. Then, after telling me that "what you can do with the Future Retro is, you can completely turn it into something completely different," he did just that: namely, he applied a filter and adjusted the resonance of the sound, effectively changing its timbre from a bass line to that of a kick drum (video example 1.1 🔊). After I checked with him to verify that the sound he was using was a preset, he took care to show me several ways in which the sound could instantly be changed: for instance, by applying portamento (he called this "gluing the notes together with glide") or by shortening the length of the loop. As he made these alterations, the sound gradually returned to a 303-like bass-line sound (video example 1.2 🔊).

Pacou next proceeded to demonstrate the Roland SH-101, an analog synthesizer made in 1983. He connected it to the 777, in such a way that the MIDI information provided by the 777 controlled the output signal of the SH-101. As a result, the bass line heard previously changed instantly to a much higher synth loop. After about thirty seconds, however, Pacou transformed the pattern quite dramatically into a kick-drum sound—"authentic" in the sense that it closely mimicked the timbral qualities of a classic EDM drum-machine kick—which he allowed to play for about one minute before reinstating the synth sound (video example 1.3 🔊).

To summarize, Pacou began by setting up the 777 to imitate the sound of a 303, changing this sound into a "kick drum," and then returning to a 303-like sound. He subsequently used the 777 to control the output of the SH-101, thereby creating a synth loop and a kick-drum sound before returning to the synth loop. Only one constant underlay all these transformations: the "preset" rhythm pattern with which they began. The actual rhythms of the pattern—presumably the bearers of its identity—remained the same, the only exception being the shortening of the overall loop length. On several occasions, however, the overall sound changed so thoroughly and suddenly that any listener not privy to the methods of production would be hard-pressed to identify the various instances as related. On the one hand, then, we have a physical phenomenon, an electrical signal, that never changes; on the other, a rapidly shifting series of percepts. The ontology of this process is *slippery*: the preset projects an identity that is constantly in flux; its instrumental connotations migrate unexpectedly.

Aside from its very evanescence, several aspects of this process are noteworthy. First, it neatly reverses the ontological weight that music theory conventionally ascribes to particular musical parameters. Pitch, typically the most important marker of a motive or theme, is completely ancillary here; it becomes more or less definite as the "instrument" changes from a "synthesizer" to a "drum machine," and raises or lowers as it migrates between bass line and synth loop. Rhythm, the second most important carrier of motivic identity (and the other main parameter presented in discrete values by Western notational systems) is the originator of all the sounds we hear, but it is not particularly recognizable as such; in fact, several of the transformations obscure the underlying rhythmic connection. Instead, timbre is the focus of musical development in Pacou's demonstration. He changes the sound so as to suggest the tone colors of several quite different electronic "instruments."

A number of scholars have argued that "sound" is essential to the identity of recorded popular compositions. Zak, for instance, writes of the rock musical work, "Every single detail of its sound [is] a fixed element of its identity." "The essential and irreducible element [of a record] is sound" (2001, 22 and 23). Gracyk, in turn, argues that rock "unifies an interpretation with a specific sound medium as inseparable parts of a single work; each listener who learns these songs through these recordings grasps every aspect as properties of a *total* musical work" (1996, 14; original emphasis). These connections between "sound" and musical identity certainly hold for the examples I have presented; what is remarkable, however, is that the "grain of the voice" (Barthes 1977) is not consistently associated with any particular stable identity; instead, it is continually shifting. The two physical instruments heard in this passage (the 777 and the SH-101) are used mainly as vessels for these connoted kinds of identity.

Video example 1.4 shows Pacou manipulating the sound of the SH-101 in a similar manner during live performance. ◉ This passage began forty-two minutes and fifty seconds into his live set at SO36 in Berlin on July 15, 2006. During our follow-up interview after the performance (July 25, 2006), Pacou identified the source of sonic change as a low-frequency oscillator (LFO). A single rhythm pattern is clearly audible throughout the entire passage. Nevertheless, as in the previous example, the preset rhythm functions not so much as an established motive but as raw material for timbral development.

Samples

Another kind of formative musical entity within performances of electronic dance music is the sample. Scholars have written widely about the practice of sampling in both EDM and rap; they have highlighted its role as a significant technique of recording and production as well as a specifically *digital* phenomenon (see, for example, Born 2005). More than anything, however, they have emphasized sampling as a source of musical borrowing and intertextuality; as a result, most of the literature assumes that samples are derived from sources external to the work. This is certainly often the case, and such sampling practices do occur in EDM performances, but many musicians also use sampling as a more general constructive technique.

Apparat, for instance, frequently uses the KAOSS Pad to sample some part of his performance, thereby turning it into a loop (or, into a different kind of loop than it was before, since most of the tracks he plays consist of loops to begin with). He especially uses this approach at transitions: he will capture a musically striking moment as a sample and loop it, prepare several new instrumental parts (which the audience cannot hear) while it runs, and then cut the sample off and instantaneously bring the other parts in. Pacou uses the Future Retro 777 in a similar manner, as he explains in this passage:

> You can record one program that is in there, like one little pattern, you know, like a certain bass line, like *dd-dd-dd-dd/DE-dd-dd/dd-dd-dd-dd/DE-dd-dd/dd-dd-dd-dd/DE.*[25] And you can have that playing, and you can adjust the sound, and then you bring it into the mix. And then you can see each step while it's running, and you can select each individual step and make a higher or lower note, or add more resonant sound, or ...[26]

Each musician's description emphasizes the familiar idea of recording technology as a way to "capture" sound. What is new here is the way in which the techniques and potentials associated with recording begin to penetrate live performance. Both

---

[25] Slashes indicate my perception of quarter-note beats in Pacou's imitation of the bass-line sound. Each "dd" lasts one sixteenth note, while the "DEs" last for an eighth note each (except for the last syllable, which does not have a precise cutoff point).

[26] In quotations I use "..." with no spaces between the periods for instances when a speaker trails off mid-sentence. I use "..." with spaces to indicate an ellipsis.

Apparat and Pacou describe a technique in which a sample is recorded and looped in real time, thereby enabling some other action to be undertaken while the sampled loop runs. These approaches draw circles around the linear unfolding of time, in this way generating and deploying new kinds of musical modules. Ontologically speaking, there are multiple layers of recorded objects involved, and multiple kinds of musical things.

Sampling, like popular music more generally, is often associated with multiple authorship, a phenomenon that raises its own set of issues for theories of ontology (see Cook 1995a for further discussion). In the instances I have cited, however, producers consistently sample their own music. In some cases, this process may stretch across *multiple* performances, as in the next example, from a 2006 performance by Henrik Schwarz at the Mutek Festival in Montreal (video example 1.5 ⬤). According to Schwarz, the aqua-colored loops that appear in the sixth column from the left are all variants of each other. More specifically, they are variants of the topmost loop, which was the first clip that he recorded. As Schwarz played different versions of this set over time, he would sometimes spontaneously vary this loop during performance. Each time he did so, he saved the results for possible incorporation into future performances. This process—in which recording technology is once again central—shows a particular accumulative cycle of musical creation: composition forms the basis of improvisation, which in turns feeds back into composition, and so on. Along the way, multiple forms of musical existence are generated.

From Loops to Tracks

Presets, loops, and samples are the shortest constructive elements in EDM performances, with average lengths of one to four measures (less commonly extending up to thirty-two). The ways in which laptop performers use these building blocks to form larger entities varies considerably. Three optics provide useful criteria with which to apprehend the distinctions involved. The first is the extent to which a formal relationship adheres between the shorter constituents of a performance and prearranged tracks.[27] In some performances the arrangement of loops, samples, and other building blocks may be completely extemporaneous, bearing no relationship to previously composed tracks. At the opposite end of the spectrum are performances that imitate a preexistent recording closely. In between, many musicians construct distinct but loose formal relationships to their recorded tracks.

Within track-based performances a second optic emerges, one that involves potential relationships between the performance and the artist's publicly released

---

[27] In all cases keep in mind that we are speaking of the artist's own tracks, in accordance with the conventions of laptop performance.

recordings. A performance (or part of a performance) may be based on tracks that an artist has already released, on works in progress (in effect, potential future releases), or on tracks composed specifically for the set. None of these options are mutually exclusive, of course. As an additional creative resource, the first of these possibilities offers a potential interplay between audience members' familiarity with the tracks and the way in which they are realized in performance.[28] Moreover, the extent to which a track is recognizable as a discrete entity is itself a question of musical identity; I develop this theme in greater detail in subsequent portions of this chapter.

Finally, a third optic entails the degree to which performances actually consist of discrete tracks in general (regardless of whether these tracks have been previously recorded). At one extreme, musicians such as Pole create fully realized tracks with clear beginnings and endings. At the other, Pacou (like many "hard techno" artists) employs a loop-based approach in which "tracks" are rarely perceptible.

Apparat's method provides a fairly typical example, falling in the middle of the various continua I have described. He plays full tracks, but mixes them together in the manner of a DJ set. The sounds he plays are drawn from a preexisting recording, but his arrangement is not identical to it. He draws on tracks from his albums occasionally; when he does, he needs to alter them to make them suitable for the dance floor, as his albums tend to feature ambient tracks with slower tempi. For the most part, however, the tracks he plays are written specifically for his live set; he uses these tracks as the core of his live sets without ever releasing them to the record-buying public. As a result, although his originals are fully arranged, self-standing compositions, they are never heard by anyone other than himself. Here he explains this aspect of his method:

> MARK BUTLER: So, some of them [the tracks used in performance] come from your albums but they're sort of modified so that they're more up-tempo and more like a dance-club kind of feel.
>
> APPARAT: Yeah.
>
> MB: But then some of them basically you're just composing for the live set.
>
> APP: That's true, yeah.
>
> MB: And then it's kind of interesting because you're saying that you take loops from it, so there's this fuller track that people don't actually hear in a way, right? Do you think about that as a track, or is it sort of like material you're drawing from?

---

[28] Most performers who play versions of commercially released tracks expect *some* audience members to recognize them, although the level of recognition expected is a great deal lower than that of a rock or pop audience. This type of performance can also serve a promotional function, in that some performers go on tour with new live sets in conjunction with the release of a new album.

APP: It's kind of a remix, you know, if you remix yourself. So that's what I ended up doing to be able to use that stuff live. Because it's very hard if you have to do a complete new live set, different from your material. A lot of those mellow songs I used in my live set really developed through various versions. If you hear the same song on a recording two years ago, it might sound totally different. So sometimes I decide "Oh, maybe that loop fits better" and then I figure out "Oh that's great" and I keep on playing it that way. This usually happens live. You have an idea—"Oh, wow, that could fit pretty well"—and sometimes it's *the* idea.

As described in the introduction to this chapter, Apparat constructs each track that he plays by selecting eight loops from a fully arranged track. In performance, he departs flexibly from the preexistent arrangement while following its overall shape. Overall, this manner of performing features the eight basic loops and their variants as building blocks and the arrangement, the original track, and the track as performed as larger musical constructs. The interaction of these elements raises intriguing ontological questions. What sort of entity is the original, unheard track? What is the point of arranging a track fully if no one is going to hear it that way? What is special about the eight loops? Why does Apparat choose them? Do they have any kind of privileged ontological status?

The unheard tracks that form the bases of Apparat's performances fall somewhere between fully independent tracks and the loose collections of source materials favored by loop-oriented performers. In some respects, these tracks are work-like; for instance, they are both originary (they serve as the basis for all subsequent performances) and structural (they guide the formal organization of the performed tracks). Their identities are not strictly bounded or stable, however, since they are taken apart and rearranged during performance (indeed, the extraction of loops is actually a *precondition* for Apparat's sets). At the same time, they stand as exemplars of "finished" works in certain ways: this role is evident in Apparat's description of them as "fully arranged" tracks as well as in the way the performed tracks mimic their arrangements without copying them exactly. In contrast to more loop-based musicians, Apparat clearly imagines his tracks as needing a particular formal structure in order to be "finished." His approach is less improvised than that of someone like Pacou; because of the prerecorded version, he has a more definite idea of how a track might "go" than if he had only loops to work with.

The eight loops that Apparat extracts from each track also have special roles to play in the ontology of each performance. Most obviously, they are the most important sounds in the track, "importance" being a matter of identity as well as formal weight. When they are all sounding at once, Apparat notes, they should create the effect of the "full song." As all other sounds are cut from the track prior to performance, these are the only ones that are allowed to exist. Consequently, they are the sounds with which Apparat has to work; they are not really changeable except through omission or the application of effects.

"Reduced" Tracks

Preset rhythms and loops generally consist of single musical lines. Samples, by contrast, are "total" recordings, in which all elements fed into the recording device are combined into one signal. In this respect samples index not only the specific recording from which they are taken, but also the technical act of recording itself. Within DJ sets, vinyl tracks also function as total recordings; they cannot be precisely separated into the discrete textural components that formed the track. Although laptop performance makes it easier to preserve distinctions between recorded elements, musicians working in this style sometimes use total recordings as well. At two points in the performances I observed by Apparat, for instance, he played what he called a "backing track" from his hard drive. He uses this approach when a track is too complex to be created live in the usual manner. In such cases, instead of extracting eight loops, he makes a "reduced" version of the overall track and plays it from his hard drive. On top of this reduced version, he adds new loops extemporaneously. As he explained when we spoke in 2006, he used this technique at the end of his performance at the 2005 Movement Festival in Detroit, which he concluded with breakbeat-based music in an extremely fast tempo.[29] Throughout this passage, Apparat uses the KAOSS Pad to make the sound "explode" or split; he employs this technique with increasing frequency until the set climaxes and ends. Video example 1.6 shows the first half of this passage. ◐ The use of a backing track is evident from the fact that all the sliders on the Tascam mixer (the blue device in front of the laptop) are lowered, except for the one channel from which the main sound is coming (and occasionally a second channel that appears when Apparat "cuts" back and forth with another sound). The moment when the track begins is also clearly audible. Apparat explained that the use of a backing track in this case stemmed partly from a technical dimension relating to its origin: because the track began as a "jam session" in the studio, it was recorded in real time as a single soundsource, and there was no way to extract its loops.

A similar phenomenon occurred at one point in Henrik Schwarz's Mutek performance. This passage consisted of a series of striking diminutions applied to the overall tempo: first one-half, then one-fourth, then one-third (as indicated by

---

[29] For an explanation of the musical qualities of breakbeats, see Butler 2006, 78–80.

Schwarz during our interview). These changes were recorded earlier, during *another* performance; here, Schwarz allows them to play as recorded, while adding new sounds (e.g., bass drums, hi-hats, shaker) with the program Live and effects with his MIDI controller (video example 1.7 🔊).[30] Notably, both this instance and that described by Apparat involve multiple refractions of liveness: a performance (in Apparat's case, that which occurred in the studio) is distilled into a recording and then made live again. Although playing back recordings during a set might seem to confirm certain misperceptions of laptop sets (i.e., that they are not performances at all), here the musicians continue to transform and recontextualize the original texts; in fact, the ways in which they manipulate these recorded objects are not dissimilar to the techniques of the DJ set.

Versions

More often that not, electronic dance music tracks exist in multiple versions.[31] The phenomenon of the "remix," for instance, originated and proliferated within club culture. Paradigmatically, a remix occurs when a musician is asked to create an alternate version of another musician's track. The record company associated with the original recording sends the remixer a copy of the multitrack recording to work with (in earlier days tapes were sent, but the recording transfer now occurs through digital files). She can keep, cut, or alter any of this material, while also adding material of her own; in relation to the original, the sonic configuration of the remix ranges from quite similar to radically different. EDM musicians also frequently produce multiple versions of their own tracks, called either "mixes" or "remixes," which are often released simultaneously.[32]

---

[30] Schwarz also plays this passage in another live mix, contained on a demo CD entitled *Sunday Music Live*. On that recording, the passage with tempo alterations has the same duration (1'21"), but the effects and instrumental supplementations are different.

[31] This is true for many other styles of popular music too, of course, and truer for art music than its ideologies would have us believe. However, many of the alternate "versions" of both popular and classical styles (for instance, studio recordings, bootlegs, or first drafts) are not readily available to the public. Instead, a particular version is frequently put forth as "definitive." In the case of dance music, by contrast, multiple versions not only exist but also are simultaneously available to anyone who can buy a commercial release.

[32] Although certainly interesting from an ontological perspective, the remix will not be a principal focus of this chapter: its history is well documented in other sources, and it is primarily a studio phenomenon. Gracyk briefly addresses the ontology of the remix, although his comments clearly pertain to rock traditions rather than EDM. He argues that "there are…many remixes that constitute distinct works," provided that "there has been an intention to produce something that is to be treated as a distinct work, usually signaled by the fact that the remix is given a separate title" (1996, 28). In dance music, remixes usually carry the original title, but with a parenthetical addition that identifies the remixer and possibly some affective qualities of the mix as well (e.g., "Tenaglia's Underground Mix").

In addition to remixes, multiple versions of tracks arise within or through performance. One interesting example occurred during the last twelve minutes of Apparat's July 2005 performance at Maria in Berlin; here, he ended his set by playing two versions of a track in succession. In interviews Apparat had told me that his performances drew on previously created tracks, and that he would usually play nine to ten tracks within an hour-long set. In analyzing his performances, I sought to identify where individual tracks began and ended. In this set, as in the majority of laptop performances, junctures between tracks were not apparent from casual listening. Sets frequently involve tracks that are not commercially available, and laptop performers often mix tracks together in the manner of a DJ, creating an unbroken flow of sound as well as significant periods of overlap that obscure the location of beginnings and endings. Apparat's performance, for instance, consisted of fifty-four minutes of continuous sound. After analyzing it closely and discussing some of my choices with him, I felt confident in my identification of seven distinct track beginnings, but I was unsure about a possible eighth track that seemed to begin around the forty-eighth minute. At this point, the entrance of a new sound seemed to signal a significant change, but the harmonies underlying the loops and their overall timbre were very similar to those heard during the previous six minutes. Was this really a new track, or just a new section within the previous one?

When I asked Apparat these questions, he told me that this portion of his set consisted of more than one version of an individual track. The original version was entitled "Bang," and he subsequently created increasingly dance-floor friendly versions, which he nicknamed "Bang Rave" and "Bang Megarave."[33] In 2005, when this performance was recorded, he would often end his set in a way that was both climactic and unified by playing all three versions in succession. In this particular set, he played only "Bang" and "Bang Rave," each of which lasts for approximately six minutes. Video example 1.8 presents the transition between "Bang" and "Bang Rave." ◑

Apprehended collectively, the various versions of "Bang" reveal a diversification of the ontological multiplicity evident in previous examples. As in other performances (Henrik Schwarz's variant loops, for instance), there is a web of short patterns, some directly related and some linked through association. Here, in addition, there is a group of interconnected track versions. As with loops and other shorter elements, how tracks interrelate varies. For instance, although "Bang" is clearly the key source of existence for "Bang Rave," the musical patterns within each version are distinct. One significant exception occurs near the end of "Bang Rave," when

---

[33] These are all working titles, for Apparat's use only; like most of the tracks in his live set, "Bang" was not released commercially on a single or album. The name of the track may refer to the "bang" command in the program Max, which Apparat uses as his primary performance software. Probably the single most important command in Max, "bang" tells elements within the program to carry out their functions. I describe Max in further detail in Chapter 2.

Apparat reintroduces loop 1 from "Bang." He thus links the two versions explicitly as the performance draws to a close. In so doing he connects these two versions from the Berlin performance by chaining the loop level to that of the track, through a technique that might be understood as a kind of self-sampling. Loop 1, in other words, becomes a signifier of not just a simple eight-bar pattern but also "Bang" in its entirety. Lurking silently within this play of identity, moreover, is the unheard original "Bang." This efflorescence of multiplicity raises challenging questions concerning musical identity. Are these musical entities better understood as variants of a single composition or as distinct tracks? How should we conceptualize the relationships between them? In the final section of this chapter I suggest that a *network* model of ontology is the most effective means of addressing these issues. I also revisit "Bang" in greater detail in that context. First, however, I discuss two more instances in which multiple versions arise.

Reflexivity and Reflectivity

The multiplicity of tracks often spills over the boundaries of the set, creating intertextual connections that extend across diverse recordings and performances. In interviews, I always asked producers to explain the origins of the material they played live. Most obviously and most commonly, their own compositions serve as sources; in performance, they "remix" themselves. I describe this strategy as *reflexive*, in that the performance points inward by alluding to or incorporating an artist's own recordings. In the examples already discussed, reflexive techniques include sampling one's own performances (mentioned in reference to Henrik Schwarz), the practice of "reduced" versions, and Apparat's technique of extracting loops for performance from an original, private recording. Reflexivity is the most common approach to intertextuality among the laptop musicians whom I studied. Much less frequently, these musicians may also borrow from the work of other artists. Because this strategy points outward, calling our attention to externally produced works, I describe it as *reflective*.

At the level of the track, reflexive approaches entail three main possibilities: material composed specifically for the live set, material based on previously released recordings, and material drawn from works in progress.[34] An interesting example of the second type of reflexivity occurred in Pole's performance at the Mutek Festival on June 2, 2006. This live set was a special case; instead of playing solo as he typically does, Pole performed with a live drummer and electric bassist. As I learned in a pre-performance interview, the performance recreated tracks that Pole had previously

---

[34] I previously introduced these strategies within a discussion of three optics describing the formation of performances from shorter elements; see optic no. 2.

written and recorded. The other musicians learned their parts by listening to a recording, which they recreated relatively closely without being required to follow its every detail. After this stage, Pole (as the leader of the process) encouraged a fair degree of spontaneity and flexibility. He arranged relatively few rehearsals; prior to the performance, the musicians met once or twice in the studio in order to develop a fluid interaction with each other and get to know each other as musicians, but Pole noted that he specifically wanted to avoid predictability or boredom within the performance. When playing live, all three performers were free to vary their parts, although Pole clearly took on the main improvisatory role. He compared their setup to that of a dub band, in which a rhythm section consisting of bass and drums provided an underpinning for improvisational vocal performance and overdubbing; in this case, his work with the computer and effects fulfilled the roles of "voice" and overdubbing alike.

At the same time, certain elements of the performance were controlled so as to support fluent group interaction as well as relatively clear, compositionally oriented arrangements. At several moments Pole used countoffs or other kinds of hand gestures to cue elements such as fadeouts. In analyzing the performance, I also noticed several passages in which all three performers began to change their parts at regularly recurring intervals. One such excerpt appears in video example 1.9. ◑ As you watch and listen, begin counting measures with the crash cymbal that occurs about seven seconds into the example. You will notice a clearly articulated change every eight bars (as well as at most of the four-bar subdivisions). Changes are audible in particular through the recurrence of the crash cymbal, and visible on the computer screen when Pole shifts from one row to the next. Particularly striking is the moment four bars after the first crash, where Pole gesticulates in a way that seems to anticipate and animate the cymbal attack with his body, even though he does nothing to produce this sound. When I asked him about this passage, he told me that he and the other performers had decided ahead of time to count in eight-bar units, in order to create regular articulations with a track that is mainly about a "steady groove that doesn't change much." The passage thus reveals the interpenetration of recording techniques and consciousness into live performance: in effect, these performers are playing in a sequenced manner, even though their timing is "live."[35]

When performers adopt a *reflective* strategy, they allude to or incorporate portions of tracks by other musicians. This kind of musical borrowing is less common in laptop sets than one might expect given the large amount of attention that

---

[35] For discussion of the sequence as a formal element within the sonic organization of EDM, see Butler 2006, 206–16.

the practice of explicitly referential sampling has received in scholarly literature on dance music. Of the musicians I studied, the only one who regularly draws on external source materials is Henrik Schwarz. Schwarz is especially fond of incorporating music in non-EDM styles. In the Montreal performance I observed in June 2006, for instance, he played excerpts from "He's Got the Whole World in His Hands" as well as a track by the experimental American musician Moondog. The majority of his set draws on his own tracks, however, and he expects his audience to recognize both these compositions and the external ones he quotes. As he explains, he considers the inclusion of recognizable elements to serve an important part of making his performances accessible: "Because if you play with a laptop, nobody really knows what you're doing there, because it's just a screen. But if you play a sample that everybody knows, and then you start tweaking it, it's quite easy for everybody to follow what's happening." In a further statement, he relates this emphasis on recognizable process to the way in which the audience might comprehend a musician's performance gestures: "I like if it's possible to follow. I mean, if you see somebody else on stage playing guitar, you see that he's really touching the strings, and you see what he's doing. But you can't do that on a computer, so I'm trying to give some hints of what's happening."[36] Schwarz also likes to use nondance materials in particular because the combination of a straightforward bass-drum pattern with diverse source materials allows him to play "very difficult" music within a dance context (he mentions Sun Ra as an example). Video example 1.10 presents a portion of the Moondog-based track, which was the final number of the Mutek performance.

Research on sampling in dance music has typically emphasized how borrowed materials are de- and recontextualized. Though certainly not irrelevant here, what is perhaps most striking about this and other passages in which obviously nondance sources appear is how *they* reorient EDM. The inclusion of the Moondog track illuminates the electronic dance music that forms the substance of the set, revealing its abstractness in a strikingly concrete fashion. I have previously noted a number of ways in which the practices and listening techniques of recording have permeated live performance. Here, however, recognizable tracks stand out not only as examples of recording-based practices, but also *as recordings* themselves. They call attention to the kind of media play that Schwarz is accomplishing. In comparison to their concrete presence, the sounds of electronic dance music seem almost like a gel or ether in which more fully formed media objects float.

---

[36] Given these emphases, it is surprising how little gear Schwarz uses, since most artists with strong interests in "hands-on" performance (e.g., Pacou) tend to use more hardware.

Conclusion: Mapping the Astronomy of the Provisional Work

Many of the abstractions used to conceptualize electronic dance music, including terms such as "loop," "track," "remix," "version," and "third record," are clearly ontological but not fully work-like in the most conventional sense. Some of them, such as presets, locked grooves, loops, and samples, are fragmentary in nature. Some of them reference larger entities synecdochically, as when a sample references the track from which it is excerpted (regardless of whether that track was composed by the artist or another musician). Some of them involve kinds of sonic identity that are crucial to understanding a style yet do not involve compositional identity per se; an example would be changing the sonic identity of certain "instruments," as when Pacou transforms an SH-101 synthesizer sound into a "bass drum." Broad debates about "sound" and its position vis-à-vis musical identity (and in relation to "effects") are clearly connected to this issue as well.

Larger entities such as tracks also complicate attempts at simple taxonomies of musical existence, not only on their own but also in relation to the smaller elements that form them and the larger entities that they themselves make up. Sets, for instance, emerge from series of "third records," yet as a whole they do not typically project a single abstract musical identity. At a more local level, performances based loosely on loops extracted from a previously recorded track are obviously less predetermined than those that imitate a recorded work closely. In between these two poles, many performances follow a preexistent "arrangement" to a certain extent without copying a particular recording exactly. Other tracks may be "reduced," which suggests a process of distillation, of boiling down to an ontological essence. In many other performances (such as those of loop-oriented, hard-techno musicians such as Pacou), tracks scarcely exist, if at all. The contrasts that musicians and listeners make between loop-based and track-based structures is related to a higher-level distinction between "songs" and "tracks," in which the former are understood to possess discernible sections such as verses and choruses, and to contain vocals more frequently, while the latter are more repetitive, more rhythmic than pitch-based, and more open-ended structurally.[37] These differences also resonate in the reflective sampling practices of musicians such as Henrik Schwarz. The external tracks that Schwarz references typically contain some combination of vocals or traditional instruments; in their recognizability, they contrast with the generic, purely electronic sounds that surround them. Emphasizing the epistemological presence of the non-EDM tracks—specifically, how they stand out as recordings—I described them as "fully formed media objects." In relation to the present discussion, they can also be understood as more ontologically individuated

---

[37] See Butler 2006, 41, for further discussion.

than the EDM tracks in which they are embedded. Musical identity, it seems, is something that sonic configurations can accrue to varying degrees.

Perhaps the most difficult question posed by the ontology of EDM performance, however, is the multiplicity of musical identities it proffers. As the examples I have presented illustrate, complex configurations of related yet distinct musical entities challenge attempts to identify individual definitive works. Georgina Born, in an essay on the "new music ontologies that became ascendant over the course of the twentieth century" (Born 2005, 8)—particularly those prompted by increasing technological mediation—proposes several conceptual frameworks that might be used to theorize this multiplicity. She describes "music's many simultaneous forms of existence" as a kind of constellation; specifically, she refers to a "constellatory conception of music's multiple mediations" (13). Bohlman articulates a similar perspective when he argues that none of the "metaphysical conditions" associated with musical ontology "stands out as isolated when we examine music's ontologies as a complex" (Bohlman 1999, 33–34).

These approaches, which might also be described as "network" models, offer useful ways of thinking about *relationships* between musical entities in a network rather than simply highlighting ontological multiplicity as a condition unto itself. Further insights into these relationships are revealed in the theoretical roots of some of Born's ideas, especially in her exposition of Alfred Gell's anthropological model of artistic creation (Gell 1998).[38] In explaining his theory, Gell considers examples that range from anthropological objects (such as Congolese nail fetishes) to canonical Western artworks (such as Velázquez' *Rokeby Venus*) and that include both individually and collectively produced works. As such, his approach suggests one way of freeing accounts of musical ontology from the paralyses that multiply related versions and multiple authorship seem to induce.[39] In particular, he argues that a corpus of artworks may be understood as a kind of "population" in which individual artworks within the system function as part of a larger object distributed across space and time (Gell 1998, 220–22). As examples of these "distributed objects," he cites the body of Marquesan art known as *Tiki* as well as the *oeuvre* of Marcel Duchamp from 1913 onward (220 and 245). Authorship in the former case is the product of an "'extended mind'—that is, externalized and collectivized cognitive processes" within the culture (Born 2005, 20, quoting Gell 1998, 221–22)—while in the latter case agency is individually produced but still extends across time.

---

[38] See also Zbikowski 2002, chap. 5, in which the author theorizes ontological relationships between various versions of "Bye Bye Blackbird" and "I Got Rhythm." Zbikowski's approach draws primarily from an area of cognitive science focused on "conceptual models" and is not explicitly structured around notions of network, constellation, or complex. His schematic diagrams of elements within a category present a kind of visual network, however, and he twice describes conceptual models as functioning within a "network of knowledge" (218–19).

[39] Nicholas Cook in particular has frequently criticized conventional aesthetic accounts of the work-concept for their inability to address multiple authorship in rock and other contexts; see esp. Cook 1995a.

The concept of "distributed objects"—and more broadly, constructions of musical ontology as networks or constellations of related entities—provides a suggestive optic for conceptualizing the diverse forms of musical existence that populate EDM performances. Consider, for instance, the various versions of the Apparat track "Bang" described above. The total musical identity of "Bang" encompasses the original studio version, the eight loops extracted for performance, the intensified mixes "Bang Rave" and "Bang Megarave," and the new realizations of "Bang" and "Bang Rave" from the Berlin performance. These last two entities were subsequently textualized in my field recording.[40]

In addition to the two mixes I recorded in Berlin, another version of "Bang Rave," from a set recorded in Tel Aviv, was released commercially in 2005 as part of an EP entitled *Strike 69*. The three performed versions have a complex interrelation. All three share a tempo of 130 bpm as well as a generic snare-drum backbeat. Their overall textural construction is similar too. It is based on three types of materials: one or more midrange synth patterns (loops, or shorter "riffs"), a bass line, and a drum groove. See Figure 1.1, in which I have transcribed the patterns found in all three tracks. Some of these elements form families of sound. For instance, loops 1, 2, and 4, although distinct, have similar tone colors, and each oscillates between four-bar harmonies while midrange melodic tones fluctuate above. The two bass lines, however, are quite distinct, and riff 1 is a distorted, raucous sound that stands out individually.

The individual versions of the track draw from these potential elements in varied ways. "Bang" Berlin contains six identifiable patterns, "Bang Rave" Berlin nine, and "Bang Rave" Tel Aviv eight. Here are the configurations involved:

Patterns in "Bang," Berlin performance	Patterns in "Bang Rave," Berlin performance	Patterns in "Bang Rave," Tel Aviv performance
Loop 1	Loop 1	Loop 3
Loop 2	Loop 3	Loop 4
Bass Line 1	Loop 4	Riff 1
Hi-Hat 1	Riff 1	Bass Line 2
Snare Drum 1	Bass Line 2	Hi-Hat 2
Bass Drum 1	Hi-Hat 2	Snare Drum 2
	Snare Drum 2	Tom-Toms
	Tom-Toms	Bass Drum
	Bass Drum 2	

---

[40] The source for all these transformations—the original studio version—must be understood as both a work ("Bang") and a text (a recording).

FIGURE I.I Musical materials employed in performances of "Bang" and "Bang Rave" (transcription by Mark J. Butler)

The two mixes of "Bang Rave" share the most material, eight patterns in all. However, the patterns are presented in different orders and in varying textural configurations. At the opposite end of the spectrum, the Berlin version of "Bang" and the Tel Aviv version of "Bang Rave" share no patterns. Between the two Berlin versions, the most interesting commonality is how loop 1 from "Bang" returns near the end of "Bang Rave."

In order to illuminate more vividly the musical environment that Apparat navigates, Figures 1.2a–c present each of the three realizations in a graphical format. (These figures are online; please open each in a separate window and arrange side-by-side if possible. 🔘 a. Graphic animation of Apparat, "Bang," Berlin, 🔘 b. Graphic animation of Apparat, "Bang Rave," Berlin, 🔘 c. Graphic animation of Apparat, "Bang Rave," Tel Aviv) The overall field—the twenty-five rectangles common to each figure—constitutes a network of possibilities. Each rectangle within the network represents a unique configuration of the musical elements shown in Figure 1.1, arranged in order from the thinnest texture that occurs (one pattern by itself) to the thickest (seven patterns at once). Color indicates the specific set of configurations actually chosen by Apparat. Each realization is further conceptualized as a unique path through the network: clicking "begin" will animate the figure, revealing the order of textural configurations as well as the duration of each (each blink represents one measure). Pausing the animation will illuminate the complete path once more. The information tabulated below, which summarizes the order and duration of configurations, may be used as a guide while viewing the animation. Configurations are labeled according to the number of elements present (one to seven) and with a letter corresponding to the top right corner of each rectangle.

"Bang" Berlin (192 mm.)	*"Bang Rave" Berlin (204 mm.)*	*"Bang Rave" Tel Aviv (180 mm.)*
3a • 8	3f • 8	3h • 4
3b • 4	4d • 16	4f • 4
4a • 4	4e • 12	5b • 16
3c • 6	5a • 8	6a • 32
2a • 10	6a • 16	7a • 32
3a • 8	6b • 12	5c • 8
4b • 32	7a • 32	5a • 32
3a • 16	3g • 16	7a • 32
3d • 16	7a • 16	5d • 16
4c • 40	5b • 16	
3e • 32	6c • 52	
2b • 8		
1a • 8		

In light of this analysis, answers begin to emerge in response to the questions posed earlier: specifically, whether these musical entities are better understood as variants of a single composition or as distinct tracks, and how the relationships between them might be effectively conceptualized. First, describing the alternate mixes and performances as "variants" of the originally recorded "Bang" does not accurately represent the kind of identity play involved. This terminology privileges the original version, whereas its function in Apparat's musical context shows that no particular version is favored. (This absence of privilege is most strikingly evident in the fact that the original version is kept private.) Instead, the creative plane on which Apparat operates involves a constellation of "Bang" elements: in short, a distributed object. This object constitutes all of its compositionally formed and recorded constituents, as well as all of its performed instantiations. It is not bounded but rather fluid, capable of growth and expansion. Furthermore, as the language of the preceding section suggests, it is best imagined as a network of possibilities, one that the musician both creates and navigates.

The ontological constellation "Bang" was composed and recorded on an individual basis, as is the norm for EDM. Within this tradition, most recordings are made by one person: in contrast to the majority of contemporary rock and pop, a single individual generally assumes the roles of engineer, producer, and performer. Bandmates are rare. Performances are usually solo as well. Laptop sets, which are generally the province of producer-performers, maintain this single authorship.

In spite of this individually oriented approach to composition, however, there are certain senses in which the musical constituents of entities such as "Bang" may be understood as socially inflected. First, Apparat produced them—particularly the alternate mixes—in response to experienced social contexts. This is most apparent in his nicknames for the mixes, which reference social and musical environments quite familiar to him (the rave and the "megarave"). As noted in the introduction to this book, the dance floor is not absent from the recording studio. In terms of actual dance floors, meanwhile, each of the three performed versions arose in a particular place, at a particular time. At the same time, each had a distinct relationship to recorded entities, and those relationships inflected their instantiations within performance.

It is also important to develop approaches capable of handling works that are multiply authored in a straightforward sense. Within electronic dance music, the most important of these is the DJ set, which is a paradigmatic example of a multiply authored form. The set can also be understood as a distributed object, consisting of a network in which musicians are the agents and records the constitutive elements. In Gell's formulation, such networks are inherently social; even the objects within them index the individuals involved in their creation. A producer creates each record within the set; a DJ then selects and combines two records so that they overlap, creating a virtual "third record"; series of records mixed in this way over a time span of an hour or more form a set. From a synoptic perspective, the set itself embeds all of these relationships. This way of explaining the set reveals the logic of its unity, which organicist conceptions of the work seem to call into question.

If creativity is inherently social, then the material objects produced by creative acts also *embed* social relations. Accordingly, Born's theorization of the provisional work emphasizes relations between the social and the material. Whereas the hierarchical organization of the idealist work-concept, with the composer at the top and the listener at the bottom, denies the creative significance of music's material and social instantiations (Born 2005, 26–27), a recuperation of these realities can reveal the "construction by the musical work of a 'we,' of communicative relatedness, across chasms of time and space" (25). This elegant formulation captures the social dimensions of a network or constellatory model very effectively.

In further contrast to the hierarchical orientation of idealist or transcendentalist accounts, Born describes what she calls a "lateral assemblage."[41] As an initial example, she cites jazz: "Jazz entertains no split between ideal musical object and mere instantiation, no hierarchy between composer as Creator and performer as interpreter of the Word. There is no final, untouchable work that stands outside history" (27). The jazz assemblage may also be described as "processual," in that its ontology moves or oscillates between "two phases, two crucibles of creative practice"—namely, performance and recording (ibid.). Born describes the "cumulative movement" between these two dimensions across the development of jazz, representing the process schematically as $P^1 \rightarrow R^1 \rightarrow P^2 \rightarrow R^2 \rightarrow P^3 \rightarrow$ et cetera, where P stands for performance and R for recording.

If, as I have argued, an interplay between music as process and as product is fundamental to EDM performance, then it becomes clear that conventional philosophical accounts of musical ontology have not effectively addressed the processual dimensions of this and other technologically mediated styles. By contrast, and crucially, models that map ontological relationships as networks, assemblages, or constellations can also chart the development of interconnections across time.

In conclusion, the work of electronic dance music is not fixed, but rather always in flux, developing from and into related versions in a potentially endless series of connections. Musicians remix and sample themselves, both within single performances and across *multiple* events. Conglomerations of related sounds recorded during performance engender cumulative cycles of musical creation; composition leads to improvised performances, which in turn congeal in the form of recordings that feed into subsequent events. The migrating or slippery ontology that makes itself known when the identity of an instrumental sound changes or a chimeric "third record" emerges through the combination of two actual records are also instances of musical identity in flux. It is in this sense that the work is "provisional"; as Born has written,

---

[41] I interpret the term *assemblage* in the context of her argument as an approximate synonym for "constellation."

"its finitude or openness" becomes "a matter of pragmatics" (Born 2005, 28). Notably, both finitude and openness remain possible. The tension between them motivates musical creation and discourse, and scholarship should explore and reveal the mechanisms of this dialectic rather than seeking to resolve it. In sum, the ontological extravagance of DJ and laptop performances reveals, ultimately, that the essence of this improvised music is not a matter of *whether* it is a process or a product, but rather *how* its mutually implicated capacities as both process *and* product coexist and interact.

2 Performing Performance
INTERFACE DESIGN, LIVENESS, AND LISTENER ORIENTATION

Introduction: When Recording Meets Performance

It seems almost self-evident that sound is the principal medium through which music communicates. In contemporary culture, in which the primary means of preserving and distributing music is recording, it is particularly easy to conceptualize music as *purely* sonic, for it is possible to experience recorded sound in isolation through exclusively aural means. When we experience music in performance, however, we encounter a complex signal that involves multiple senses. In particular, attending to performance significantly engages our visual and kinesthetic faculties. With regard to the former, for instance, the design of performance spaces usually promotes the clear display of instruments and performers, especially performers' faces and the parts of their bodies in direct contact with their instruments. In many performance contexts, it is equally important for the musicians to be able to see the audience.

What do we see when we look at a performer's actions? Above all else, *movement*. On the basis of the movements that we see, we might interpret the performance along lines such as the following: the performer is the person creating the sounds that we hear; the performer is producing and shaping sound through movements such as x, y, and z (imagine various sound-producing actions); the performer is responding to the music physically; the performer is expressing emotional involvement, the character of the composition, virtuosity, grace, or other affects that are valued in the relevant musical and cultural context; and finally, the ways in which the performer moves reflect both a gestural vocabulary common to his or her instrument and a uniquely personal set of characteristic motions. The extent to which performers themselves attend to these criteria, and which criteria matter to them, will depend on the musical tradition in which they are involved, their own personal histories and inclinations, and the particulars of the performance situation.

Our perception of musical performance in kinesthetic terms thus involves a coupling of aural and visual signals through the medium of movement. In the simplest form of this phenomenon, we perceive a sound that we hear as produced by a movement we see. Above and beyond this, however, an increasing amount of research has begun to explore how we identify kinesthetically with the movements we observe. One can sense—indeed, one may know—how it would feel to make those movements, how they would connect to the sounds one hears. Observable tension, relaxation, and breathing offer more fundamental and deeply physical opportunities for identification. It is important to realize that in cognitive terms this identification is not detached or contemplative, but rather embodied.[1] In particular, recent research has described the function of specialized "mirror" neurons—nerve cells that fire not only when an individual performs a certain action but also when he or she observes that action performed by someone else.[2] Additionally, there is a rapidly expanding body of research that conceptualizes patterns of sound as gestures in their own right.[3]

Recording complicates these matters. One of its most fundamental attributes is the way in which it separates sounds from their observable sources. This property, which has come to be known as "acousmatic," has been treated most extensively in the literature on electroacoustic music, particularly that emanating from the *musique concrète* tradition in France.[4] The term derives from the Greek word *akusmatikoi*, an epithet for certain pupils of Pythagoras, who would teach from behind a

---

[1] Foster (2010) traces the intellectual history of kinesthetic identification with particular attention to dance. Among the formulations she cites are John Martin's notion of "kinesthetic sympathy" (1936) and Deidre Sklar's term "kinesthetic empathy" (1994), which she appropriates and broadens in her own work.

[2] For the first published account of mirror neurons, see di Pellegrino et al. (1992). For a recent exploration of mirror neurons in relation to music, see Overy and Molnar-Szakacs (2009).

[3] Work on musical gesture encompasses many fields, but two distinct streams of inquiry are particularly evident. The first examines actual physical gestures made in performance; see for instance the essays collected in Godøy and Leman (2010). The second, which draws heavily from semiotics, considers how music as sonic signal may be understood in gestural terms; see for instance Hatten (2004). A recent monograph by Leman (2007) bridges the two perspectives. Another accomplishment of Leman's work is to bring embodied-cognition perspectives on performance into dialogue with theories of technological mediation.

[4] Emmerson and Smalley (2007) cite uses by the French writer Jérôme Peignot (1955), composer Pierre Schaeffer (*Traité des objets musicaux*, 1966), and composer François Bayle (1974).

screen in order to keep attention focused on content rather than delivery.[5] In the electroacoustic literature, "acousmatic music" has most conventionally referred to tape music (and subsequently to computer music), in which concert presentation involved listening to the music through loudspeakers with no performer present at all. However, the concept is also applicable to recorded music more generally. As Eric Clarke has noted, when one cannot observe a performer's actions, vision is left "'unattached' and uncomfortably redundant" (Clarke 2007, 63). In the popular-music contexts with which I am concerned, the separation of sounds from their sources through recording first becomes a major issue in rock. The prevalence of recorded texts in rock and subsequent popular styles has led to complex and often oblique relationships between recordings and performance. As described in the preceding chapter, there is a strong tendency to imagine recordings as representing a single coherent performance, in spite of multitrack recording, engineering, and other interventions. Nevertheless, their acousmatic nature stimulates a desire for authentication through live performance (Auslander 1999).

Modern forms of club music intensify these dialectical relationships between performance and recording. The principal means of experiencing styles such as techno and house—as encapsulated in the etymologically transparent term *discotheque*—is through dancing to recorded music. Considered individually, an EDM record cannot be said to imply some sort of "virtual" performance underlying it; one does not imagine musicians producing its sounds by playing instruments. Nor is re-creation through performance implied or expected *after* the recording process. Instead, the recording itself is the end result of composition.

The experiential gaps that recordings open for listeners intensify when that music is also electronic. For example, the task of imagining or understanding *how* the sounds one hears were produced becomes even more difficult with synthesized sounds that cannot be traced to any single familiar instrument. Furthermore, in club situations where the person manipulating recordings is visible, she or he needs to prove to the audience that something other than playback is involved. In response to these vacuums, performance rises to the fore. The DJ takes records and performs with them, while the audience members perform their role as listeners by enacting the music through dance. Paradoxically, through the very primacy of recordings, liveness becomes a crucial aesthetic value within the club experience.

---

[5] A related concept is R. Murray Schafer's concept of "schizophonia," which he defines as "the split between an original sound and its electroacoustical transmission or reproduction" (1977, 90). The principal difference seems to inhere in the key role that visual observation plays in defining the acousmatic; Schafer's schizophonic, by contrast, emphasizes aspects of location and space.

An enhanced awareness of the here and now has long been an experiential goal of clubbing. Especially important to an effective EDM event is the development of a particular kind of collective energy or "vibe" between a performing musician and dancers.[6] For vibe to emerge, one must feel part of a unique, one-time occasion; a technically proficient performance is not enough. At the same time, as the extent and variety of technology within EDM performance has increased with the advent of laptop sets and other novel approaches to performance, so too has the mediation of this dancer-musician relationship.

In a tendency that may at first seem paradoxical, this technological diversification has been accompanied by an increasing emphasis on the erstwhile "liveness" of EDM performances. Although the roots of this development date back to the emergence of the "live PA" in the mid-1990s, framing EDM performances as "live" has become especially common since the advent of the laptop set. And this proliferation of laptop sets has in part been facilitated by new kinds of software that support flexible, real-time control of musical parameters; the most widely used of these programs, produced by the software company Ableton, is named—appropriately enough—Live. First released in 2001, Live's distinctive characteristic is its performance orientation: it is a software sequencing program that allows users to change any of its parameters instantaneously.

But what does it mean for a performance to be "live"? The term is now so commonplace that it seems transparent. Yet our perceptions of performances as "live" are by-products of the distinctly modern phenomenon of producing and distributing music in recorded form. When we experience a performance in this way, we are experiencing it as "im-mediate" in a literal sense—that is, unmediated by the technologies of sound reproduction. Indeed, it is only as we become aware of the opposing possibility—that musical performances can be played back without human intervention—that certain kinds of performances begin to seem live.

This point has been made most thoroughly by Philip Auslander, who, in his book entitled *Liveness*, argues that "the historical relationship of liveness and mediatization must be seen as a relation of dependence and imbrication rather than opposition" (1999, 53). More specifically, "the history of live performance is bound up with the history of recording media; it extends over no more than the past 100 to 150 years" (52). According to this argument, it would be anachronistic to describe a performance from the early nineteenth century as live; in fact, as Auslander points out, the *OED* did not use the word *live* in relation to performance until the mid-1930s (52–53).

---

[6] For an extended discussion of "vibe," see Fikentscher (2000). See also Thornton, who connects vibe to authenticity through a reconfiguration of Benjamin's "aura": "What authenticates contemporary dance cultures is the buzz or energy which results from the interaction of records, DJ, and crowd" (Thornton 1996, 29).

But how, precisely, do the practices and technologies of sound recording mediate performances of electronic dance music? This is the central question of this chapter. I highlight two main axes of mediation: on the one hand, that between the performer and the sounds he or she creates; on the other, that between the performer and the audience that hears and responds to those sounds. In keeping with the orientation of the book as a whole, my discussion proceeds from the standpoint of the performer; audiences do play a quite significant role, but they are addressed from the perspective of the performers who were the basis of my ethnographic inquiry.[7] The chapter begins on the stage, with a survey of the technologies used in EDM performance. I describe a number of types of performance interfaces and the kinds of interaction they allow. I outline criteria for evaluating the potentialities that each interface offers, and I characterize this potentiality in terms of "affordance," a concept drawn from the fields of psychology and human-computer interaction. Framing interfaces in this way construes them as sites of possibility rather than highly determined spaces.

In the next section I broaden discussion to consider the general qualities that performers value in interfaces, and then move out into the audience in order to explore a variety of ways in which musicians communicate liveness and a sense of performance to them. It is this heightened sense of performance taking place that I reference in the title of this chapter, "Performing Performance." In speaking of this quality I will sometimes use the term *performative*, an adjective that will be familiar to scholars in linguistics and performance studies. Performative utterances, as first defined by J. L. Austin (1962), are those that accomplish an action, such as the "I do" of the wedding vow. The term has since been extended to the terrain of identity formation (particularly gender and sexuality) by poststructuralist scholars, most notably Judith Butler (1990). Butler framed gender and sexuality not as static categories but rather as sets of behaviors that we enact within the discursive systems available to us. In general, the sense of "performative" as cultivated by both Austin and Butler involves an expanded notion of what performance is, since it extends the concept into realms that are not conventionally thought of as such. Thus it might seem curious to speak of performances themselves being performative. As with the original meaning of the term, however, the actions I describe also *do* something; they perform a cultural meaning (of "performance-ness"). As meta-level performances

---

[7] A related question, and an important one, is *who* the audience in a club context is. The audience attending to a DJ or laptop performer in a club or similar environment is constantly in flux; this is particularly true for large clubs with multiple dance spaces. "Attending" thus becomes a key concept. In a context in which attending is explicitly optional, performers direct their performances to those who are choosing to attend at any given moment. They are trying to engage audience members who want to be engaged (and more generally, to maintain a critical mass of engaged audience members).

(performances of "performance"), they are therefore intrinsically performative.[8] Note also that my project shares an affinity with that of Judith Butler in that it seeks to deconstruct purportedly natural categories (e.g., the "live") and to reveal the mechanisms by which they are constituted.

The third and final section returns to the stage, addressing musicians' numerous epistemologically oriented descriptions of sound and explaining how their conceptualizations of performance highlight the pervasive incursion of recording practices and technologies into this realm. By focusing on the emergence of distinctive listening practices during performance, I reveal an increasing overlap between the seemingly disparate categories of performer and listener. I also describe how performers and audience members (who, as dancers in an ambient musical environment, can be understood as both performers and listeners) work together and interact to imbue mediated musical events with liveness.

Interface Design and Interactivity

When electronic dance musicians perform, they are always already working with recorded sound. Stored in the memory of laptop computers and twelve-inch vinyl, like seeds awaiting growth, is a wealth of musical raw material, the potential of which is unleashed through real-time, improvisational creativity. The actions of musicians in performance are mediated, however, not only through the omnipresence of recorded sound but also through the devices used to release sound from its dormant recorded state and transform it before an audience. As described in the introductory chapter, the technologies involved in EDM performances are diverse, encompassing devices such as analog turntables, DJ mixing boards, laptop computers, drum machines, synthesizers, and various kinds of MIDI controllers. As a category, I describe these technologies as "interfaces," a term that usefully emphasizes the mediation between the performer and (recorded, already mediated) sound. As a concept, however, "interface" denotes something more than simply the mediating technology; in particular, it refers to the actual site of mediation: the surface of the mixing board with its knobs and sliders, for example, or the graphical representations on the screen of a computer.[9]

---

[8] In the interest of clarity, I have restricted my use of the term *performative* to such actions. I have avoiding using it as a catchall term for "things that happen in performance," although uses along these lines do appear in scholarship on musical performance and are acknowledged in the *Oxford English Dictionary* (s.v. "performativity").

[9] The history of the word *interface* parallels that of recording technology in a strikingly close manner. The *Oxford American Dictionary*, for instance, notes that "the word **interface** is a relatively new word, having been in the language (as a noun) since the 1880s. However, in the 1960s it became widespread in computer use and, by analogy, began to enjoy a vogue as both a noun and a verb in many other spheres."

The potentialities that EDM interfaces offer performers can be characterized or evaluated according to a number of parameters. How specifically is their function defined?[10] To what extent, and how, are they customizable? At what rate do they change or evolve? For how long are they used before becoming obsolete? What is their response time or "latency"?[11] More generally, how direct or immediate is the relationship between a sound-producing action and its sonic effect? To what extent can one change an event after it has been initiated? How is the interface navigated— that is, how does the performer move through or around it in space and time? How tangible are the elements within or on it? Although it is not my goal to provide an exhaustive or comprehensive theoretical treatment of interfaces, these questions will arise as significant areas of focus throughout my discussion.

One can also consider the kinds of control elements featured on or in particular devices. A complete taxonomy of all possible devices would be huge; I am concerned principally with those that are used frequently in EDM performance. These include "continuous" controllers such as sliders and knobs, discrete or notched controllers (in which the controller must move along fixed points on a parametric scale), and binary (on/off) controllers such as switches or buttons.[12] Some interesting examples within individual categories are rotary controllers (such as knobs, dials, and turntables, all of which afford a particular kind of continuous control), table controllers (a category in which the interface is a flat horizontal surface on which objects are manipulated),[13] and cross-continuous controllers (in which the increase of one parameter occurs in inverse relation to the decrease of another parameter, the best known example being the cross-fader).

In lieu of a deterministic approach, in which the technical properties of an interface would be seen as inevitably driving the results it achieves, it is preferable to conceptualize interfaces in terms of *affordances* between users and objects. That is, what kinds of actions does an interface allow, suggest, or invite? The concept of affordance originated in psychologist J. J. Gibson's ecological theory of perception (1977 and

---

[10] Composer Tod Machover associates a certain generality of function with traditional acoustic instruments. Referring to recent academic electronic music, he describes the controllers and interfaces that musicians have designed as primarily "customized for particular compositions, performances, or performers, and...not standardized in a way that I associate with 'instrumentality'" (Machover 2002, 196).

[11] "Latency," which refers to the period between a directed action on the part of a musician (e.g., initiating a program, turning a knob) and the achievement of the intended result, has been a principal concern in computer music. Latency time can be substantial and obvious (as when one must wait several seconds for a program to complete a requested action) or slight but still perceptible (for instance, gaps of less than a second between controller actions and musical results can still be noticeable to performers). One of the significant improvements of recent software such as Live is the virtual elimination of latency time for key musical actions.

[12] Several kinds of controllers (particularly discrete vs. continuous) are theorized in Kvifte and Jensenius (2006). The authors propose the term *control organ*, which I will use subsequently, to refer to "the parts of the instrument that are sensitive to control" (221).

[13] For further discussion and examples, see Kaltenbrunner, Geiger, and Jordà (2004) and Kiser (2006).

1979). In an early definition Gibson states that "the affordance of anything is a specific combination of the properties of its substance and its surfaces taken with reference to an animal" (Gibson 1977, 67). By "animal" he means any living creature, including what he frequently calls "the human animal." The "anything" that has affordances is most easily conceptualized as an object or a surface, but Gibson also mentions mediums, substances, other persons/animals, and places. The properties of these things afford certain kinds of actions and preclude others. The closing phrase of Gibson's definition—"taken with reference to an animal"—means that affordance must always be understood in relation to the capabilities of the agent in question. For instance, a floor might afford dancing for a human, but not for a cat. In perception, Gibson argued, the relationship between agent and environment is complementary in an important way. An affordance is "equally a fact of the environment and a fact of behavior" (1979, 129); the two are co-constitutive.

Having developed in the field of psychology—and drawing key concepts from ecology—the concept of affordance was subsequently adapted within theories of design, especially in those areas of research that have come to be known as "human-machine interaction" (HMI) and "human-computer interaction" (HCI). Donald Norman's development of affordance in *The Design of Everyday Things* (2002 [1988]) has been particularly influential. Whereas Gibson framed affordance simply in terms of what an agent can do, Norman made the concept more context-dependent, suggesting we conceive of affordance more specifically in terms of what an agent *perceives* it can do. This has often been characterized in terms of what an object "suggests." Thus for instance, although a chair of reasonable weight affords sitting and being picked up equally well, it more strongly suggests sitting as a mode of interaction.

I use affordance as a theoretical lens for viewing interfaces and instrumental configurations as sites of possibilities, rather than as pieces of hardware that generate outcomes predetermined by their physical properties. In the rest of this section I discuss a range of interfaces used by electronic dance musicians, considering each in terms of the kinds of manipulation and interaction that it allows, suggests, or invites. I begin with the analog turntable, which has been the most widely used interface throughout the history of electronic dance music. Much has been written about DJ turntables, which differ in several respects from those intended for home listening. In particular, the literature on electronic dance music has emphasized adjustable speed, the direct-drive motor, and increased sturdiness as key technical improvements. The enduring significance of the turntable, however, has as much to do with its continuing legacy as a distinctive *interface* as with the ability to adjust a record's tempo or with the fetishization of vinyl. Specifically, the turntable is a special kind of

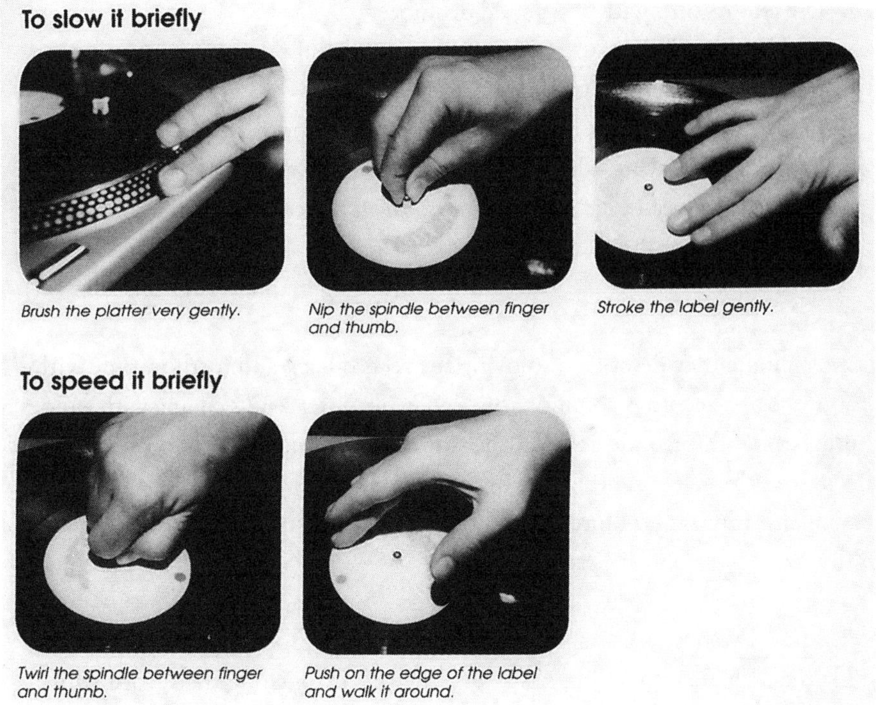

To slow it briefly

Brush the platter very gently.

Nip the spindle between finger and thumb.

Stroke the label gently.

To speed it briefly

Twirl the spindle between finger and thumb.

Push on the edge of the label and walk it around.

FIGURE 2.1 Some physical interactions with the turntable interface (from *How to DJ Properly: The Art and Science of Playing Records* by Bill Brewster and Frank Broughton, p. 55. Published by Bantam Press. Reprinted by permission of The Random House Group Limited.) ⬤

continuous, rotary controller.[14] It is different from other simple rotary controllers such as knobs, which affect a single parameter. Instead, it maps control directly from the spinning platter to the entire track. Form is represented physically and is manipulable through the interface; rotating the record forward or backward moves one in corresponding directions within the form. The turntable also has more dimensions affording control than other rotary control organs: one can touch any part of the flat surface, as well as the side and center of the record. These ways of interacting with records are important parts of DJ technique. One recent guide for would-be DJs, for instance, includes five depictions of "how to adjust a record's speed," as shown in Figure 2.1.

Touching the record is also an essential part of "cueing" it—that is, preparing it to enter the mix on the same beat as a currently playing record. Brewster and Broughton provide a concise pedagogical description of the process:

---

[14] See Andersen (2003) for a useful treatment of the turntable as interface. I derive the term *rotary controller* from this source.

1. Use two records with clear, solid drumbeats....
2. Set the mixer so record 1 is playing out loud and record 2 is in your headphones. You should have one record in each ear.
3. Find the first beat on record 2. Move it back and forth in time with the record that's playing—like you're tapping out the rhythm.
4. When you're ready, let go on the beat. The first beat of record 2 should play in time to record 1.

(Brewster and Broughton 2002, 51)

The technique they describe of moving the record back and forth in time with the beat of the first record is common; one can easily observe DJs cueing with a series of gentle back-and-forth motions on the side edge of a record. When I learned to do this myself, the tactile significance of the interface became clear to me in a way that was much stronger and more visceral than it had been before. Here is a description of this process from my research journal:

> Just now I've been learning to slip-cue. The whole process was even more tactile than I had expected. It wasn't just that I was touching the record while I was doing it; more specifically, I was controlling the very beat with my fingers. You can literally hear a single beat sliding backward and forward, and stretched out in time.

To be precise, the feedback that caught my attention was *haptic*; I was receiving information through my sense of touch. This quality, however, inheres in something more than simply the ability to control the interface with one's hands. Additionally, as one manipulates the record, as one pushes it back and forth, one feels the turntable's resistance—its give and take—in ways that are musically meaningful.[15] The beat, which is often treated in music-theoretical and cognitive accounts as an abstract element of "structure," becomes tangible and material.

Finally, the turntable is also interesting in that it is not *just* the platter that works as a controller. More precisely, it is the platter in combination with the record itself. The record's surface serves as part of the interface. As such, the categories or functions of sound source, controller, and recording cannot be strictly separated.

The other main interface associated with DJing is the mixing board. Its structure and design, though simple, have formed the prototype for many of the interfaces associated with the laptop set. Following the example of more elaborate studio

---

[15] Lippit (2006, 72) briefly mentions this property of the turntable, describing it as "force feedback."

FIGURE 2.2 Evolution UC-33 MIDI controller 🖥

mixers (and ultimately, the idea of multitrack recording), it divides musical space into "channels," which themselves divide into frequency ranges (typically three or four). Its principal controller types are continuous: they include vertical sliders for adjusting the volume of each turntable; knobs for adjusting the volume of individual frequency bands ("EQs"); and the cross-fader, a horizontal slider that works as what I have called a "cross-continuous" controller.

Many of the interfaces used in laptop sets fall into the broad category of "MIDI controllers." As MIDI, or Musical Instrument Digital Interface, is really just an agreed-upon design protocol for facilitating communication between instruments, a MIDI controller in theory could be almost any kind of device that meets these specifications. Reflecting practice, however, I use the term to describe a particular class of devices that have arisen since the turn of the twenty-first century in association with the laptop set. The majority of those in use are commercially produced; a typical example, from a widely used series by the company Evolution, appears in Figure 2.2.

The UC-33 is designed for variety and generality of function. Its interface contains a fairly even mix of sliders, knobs, and buttons, which allows musicians to interact with it according to their preferred method. Although it can be employed for production as well as performance, the manufacturers' descriptions of the product emphasize its functionality within performance-oriented programs such as

FIGURE 2.3 Faderfox Micromodul LV2 🎵

Live,[16] and its similarity to DJ mixing boards should be self-evident. EDM musicians have also treated these devices primarily as performance mechanisms. For instance, the Canadian performer Deadbeat (Scott Monteith) used the UC-33 in a set at Berlin's Maria club in August 2006, while Henrik Schwarz continues to employ an earlier and simpler version, the UC-16 (which features no sliders, only sixteen knobs and two sets of buttons).

The Micromodul series of controllers from the German company Faderfox is similar to the UC-33 in terms of its variety of control organs: it also presents knobs, sliders, and buttons, as well as a joystick and LEDs for visual feedback (Fig. 2.3). The Faderfox series differs in several significant respects, however. First, it is expressly oriented toward performance; beginning with its precursor, the LV1, the manufacturers have explicitly stated that it is "designed primarily for use with Live from Ableton."[17] In this regard, it demonstrates an increasing convergence between physical interfaces and software (particularly performance software). Second, it is noticeably simpler than other MIDI controllers; in fact, the number of elements on its interface was actually *reduced* when the second edition was produced.[18] This kind of technological devolution, which contrasts strongly with the general trend of devices becoming

---

[16] See, for instance, http://www.evolution-i.net/products/evo_uc33e.htm (cited April 9, 2008).

[17] Faderfox LV1 User Manual (2004), p. 6; available from http://faderfox.de/lv1-lx1-dj1.html (accessed February 7, 2014). The Faderfox devices also work with software such as Traktor, a program for DJing with mp3 files.

[18] The number of sliders was reduced from eight to six, and a cross-fader was removed.

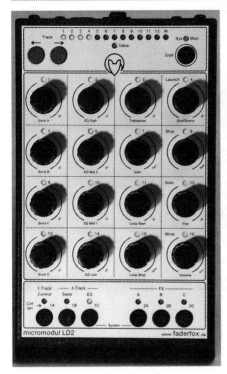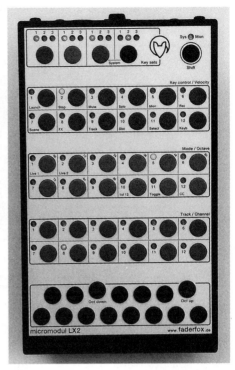

FIGURE 2.4 Faderfox LD2 (left 🖼️) and LX2 (right 🖼️)

more complicated as users demand more features, demonstrates a distinctive design orientation on the part of the manufacturer. In conjunction with this reduction of the number of elements is a noticeable emphasis on tactility: although the devices themselves are rather small (the advertising copy describes them as "pocket-size," a passable claim if one imagines a bigger-than-usual pocket), their knobs and sliders are large and made of soft, touch-inviting plastic. Third, as the name of the series indicates, the Faderfox controllers are markedly *modular*. In fact, the LV2 is the base unit for a network of up to three additional auxiliary units, such as the LX2 and LD2, pictured in Figure 2.4. As is visually evident, these supplementary devices are specialized according to the type of control organ involved: knobs in the case of the LD, and buttons in the case of the LX. The basic premise of the overall system is that musician can assemble a configuration of performance controllers using one or more LVs as the core unit(s) and other units according to their individual needs and preferences.

One of the most significant interfaces for contemporary laptop performance—more properly, a *set* of interfaces—is that found in the program Live. Musicians interact with Live through two main "views," which Figures 2.5 and 2.6 show as they appear in one of the "demo" tracks included with the program. The arrangement view (Fig. 2.5,) is basically a piano-roll notation: it proceeds through the piece from

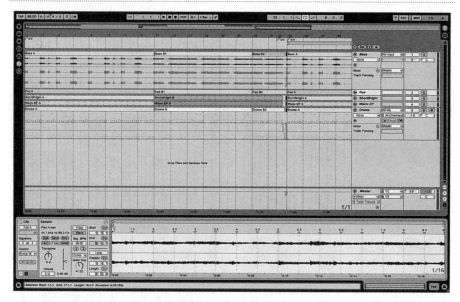

FIGURE 2.5 Arrangement view in Live

left to right, marking the music in measures and seconds.[19] As an interface, the arrangement view is intended primarily for studio functions such as composition, production, and recording; its design is similar to that of various sequencing programs. The other principal interface in Live, the "session" view, is the one used most often in performance. Its primary elements are short instrumental patterns called "clips," which are normally set to repeat in cyclical patterns (loops). Represented by small colored blocks, clips form a grid of vertical columns and horizontal rows. In Figure 2.6, twelve clips are arranged into five columns and three rows.

Rows contain formal sections or "scenes," which hold a mix of textural elements; in Figure 2.6, the scenes are labeled A, B, and B2 (see the "Master" column). The columns, meanwhile, consist of categories of related sounds, such as "bass," "pad," or "drums." For instance, the three bass patterns contained in the demo track are identical in timbre but differ in terms of loop length (the two "B" patterns are half as long as the A pattern). As Figure 2.7 reveals, their motivic construction shares various pitch and rhythm patterns, though each loop as a whole is distinct.

Both the arrangement and the session view use a "WIMP," or Windows/Icons/Mouse/Pointer interface (Andersen 2003: 30). Accordingly, one can drag representations of a waveform, cut and paste parts of a sound file, or type in values for param-

---

[19] In several respects, this representation of the music is comparable to the "textural graph" notation that I developed in *Unlocking the Groove*. See especially the small textural/formal summary that appears at the top of the screen; compare with the textural graphs that appear in Butler (2006), 268–323.

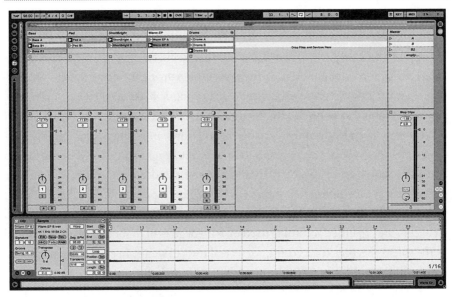

FIGURE 2.6 Session view in Live

FIGURE 2.7 Bass-line patterns in the demo track (transcription by the author)

eters such as tuning, transposition, or tempo. These ways of manipulating sound do not have counterparts in physical control devices, but rather originated within sequencing programs. At the same time, virtual analogs of physical controllers (such as knobs and sliders) do form certain parts of the Live interface; the basic design of the session view, for instance, has a readily apparent relationship to that of the mixing board. Other programs, the most widely used of which is currently Reaktor, develop this notion of "virtual instruments" much further, presenting software analogs of a wide range of synthesizers, drum machines, and other devices.[20]

---

[20] See http://www.native-instruments.com/index.php?id=reaktor5_us (accessed March 22, 2014).

It is possible to move through the session view in a prearranged, linear fashion, treating the scenes as formal sections and proceeding in order from top to bottom. However, the interface is deliberately designed in a way that facilitates nonsequential, extemporaneous navigation through the grid. The text accompanying the demo notes, "The Session View offers an improvisational approach to music-making, allowing you record, play and combine ideas **on the fly**" (original emphasis). Clips can be switched on and off at will, independently of their arrangement in rows; in Figure 2.6, for instance, patterns from three rows are playing, as indicated by the lit-up triangles on the clips of Bass B1, Pad A, ShortBright A, Warm EP B, and Drums B2. Indeed, performers who use Live vary greatly in their utilization of these technological capacities. When Pole performs with his band, for example, his use of Live is highly organized and relatively prearranged. First, clips are organized according to color, with degrees of timbral similarity indicated by the palette. Second, tracks consist of several rows of scenes. In combination with the use of one or more empty rows as spacers, this clearly delineates each track from the ones that surround it. In the course of performance, Pole mostly moves in descending order, activating rows as he proceeds through his set. These features are evident in Figure 2.8, a screen close-up from his performance in Montreal in June 2006; here, a band of orange and reddish clips (rows 3–8) represent the track currently in play.

Pacou's approach represents the opposite extreme. There is little organization by track in his set; instead, it is largely loop-based. In Live, this fact translates into a

FIGURE 2.8 Screen close-up from performance of Pole and band at the Mutek festival, Montreal, June 4, 2006

screen densely packed with clips, with many colors and no apparent systematization. He moves through this grid in various directions, turning loops on and off in a highly extemporized manner. In the passage shown in video example 2.1 🌑, for example, he brings two loops into the mix: first at about thirty seconds into the example, and then around 1:15 (in both cases, Pacou highlights a different row and then a new sound becomes audible).

Henrik Schwarz's approach is somewhere in between that of Pole and Pacou. Visual organization is readily apparent, as columns of the same color represent families of loops. Some of these are copies (duplication allows them to be placed into diverse textural configurations more rapidly), while others are variants (as described in the ontology chapter).[21] His source material comes from his tracks, but these larger entities are broken down into many short loops. These modular elements form the basis of improvisation, though which he significantly reconfigures his compositions (to the extent that their identities can be specified). In general, he uses drastically fewer loops than Pacou; in the passage shown in video example 2.2, for instance, note the amount of blank space on the screen. 🌑 At the same time, he works with individual sounds much more intensively. At the beginning of this passage, he manipulates parameters of a filter in ways that are both visible (see the bottom left corner of the screen) and audible. He then initiates an open hi-hat sound, the details of which are visible as a pink MIDI file.[22] After returning to the filter for a while, he uses his MIDI controller to distort the sound; this produces instantaneous cries of appreciation from the audience. Near the end of the clip, he scrolls down to a new configuration of sounds.

In these performers' approaches, interesting intersections emerge between the intent of the designers toward specific elements of the interface and the diverse ways in which musicians use them. Some musicians follow the leads suggested by particular program features: they use colors to indicate timbre, or they arrange tracks in series of textural "scenes." Others, however, disregard these elements entirely or even work against them (as when Schwarz arranges his set loosely into scenes and then moves freely between them in order to focus on individual loops). The way in which the interface suggests actions to performers should not be understood deterministically, as a case of feature x resulting in action y, but rather as series of affordances or

---

[21] In all of the examples I have presented, musicians assign colors to instruments arbitrarily; there is no fixed association between color and timbre in Live. This is evident even in the demo (Fig. 2.6), in which timbrally identical sounds within the same column are assigned different colors.

[22] As in other programs with sequencing functions, Live shows MIDI files as series of blocks representing digital information, in contrast to sounds that are played or sampled directly, which are shown as waveforms.

possibilities of varying specificity that musicians encounter and negotiate as they move about the performance environment.

Live facilitates variety among performers in part because it is customizable. Indeed, when musicians use the program to create clips and tracks, they are also producing the specific graphical interface they will use in performance. In this way, the "data" they record in preparation for performance can be understood as both text and context: these musical facts constitute the formative matter of performance (musical patterns) *and* the interface through which it is encountered (manipulable graphic representations of those patterns). Customizability was also seen as an advantage in the Faderfox controllers, although in that case the musician can generate variability only as a consumer (one can purchase and arrange configurations of controller units according to one's preference).

For some musicians, the customizability built into commercially available products has proven inadequate. In response, they have taken matters into their own hands, literally, by designing their own devices. Robert Henke (Monolake) provides one of the best examples. In 2003 he began performing with a unique controller, the "Monodeck," which he designed and built himself. On his website he explains the motivations behind his decision:

In 2003 I decided to build my first own [*sic*] MIDI controller, the Monodeck. A MIDI controller is a hardware unit made for controlling a computer in a musical way, turning a general problem solving machine into a true musical instrument. For my live performances I needed a very specific device. No commercial product matched, so I finally built my own one, a box with knobs, LEDs and buttons, with a layout optimised for my performance. It worked much better for me than expected, my concerts became more spontaneous and I became quite skilled playing it.

(http://www.monolake.de/technology/monodeck.html;
accessed February 7, 2014)

Especially notable in this description is the way in which Henke frames his device: he calls it a "true musical instrument," and mentions the skill he developed for "playing" it. In weighing the balance between generality and specificity of function, he clearly comes down on the side of the latter: not only does he want a controller that is specialized for music in a way that the computer is not, he also wants it to be oriented toward his particular approach.

The Monodeck, a photograph of which appears in Figure 2.9, features twenty-six binary controls (buttons), as well as continuous controllers in the form of knobs (there are no sliders). The buttons can provide visual feedback and stimulation by lighting up. The interface contains three main parts or regions. The central part

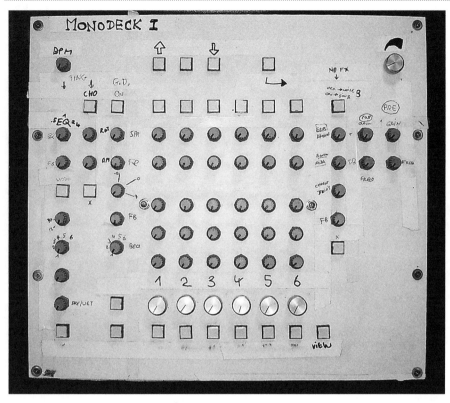

FIGURE 2.9 Monodeck (first version)

determines which sounds are present and their volume. Like a DJ mixer, it divides the texture into a number of channels (in this case, six), with volume controls and a three-band EQ for each. It also contains several features specific to Live, however, such as buttons for turning clips on or off and scrolling up or down through the grid. To the left and right of the central six channels are the other two regions of the Monodeck, which control effects.[23]

When I observed Henke using the Monodeck in performance, he alternated between periods focused on the controller and segments in which he scrolled and clicked on screen. Although this is a typical way of using a MIDI controller (as seen in performances by Henrik Schwarz and Apparat, for example), Henke clearly regarded it as a limitation: "the first Monodeck still only served as an additional interface and could not replace operating the computer with the mouse and staring at

---

[23] Apropos of customizability, it appears that the effects assigned to particular knobs or buttons in these areas are variable. Henke has written labels for them on masking tape, and there are considerable differences in labeling between the two photos of the Monodeck that he sent to me. Additionally, neither photo corresponds exactly to images of the Monodeck that I recorded in an August 2005 interview.

FIGURE 2.10 Monodeck II 🖳

the screen during my concerts" (ibid.). As a result, he developed a new Monodeck, which he calls "Monodeck II." With several assistants, he completed the Monodeck II in 2005–06 and began to perform with it in late 2006.

As is evident in Figure 2.10, the Monodeck II expands the features of its predecessor considerably. It is larger, and it contains many more control elements. The basic layout of the interface is the same, with a central section focused on the control and manipulation of texture and peripheral sections dedicated to effects; the number of channels, however, has increased to eight. The effects areas are more elaborate and hierarchized, containing small subsections for controlling individual parameters within the overall effect. Lighting is also noticeably more complex; the interface now includes ninety-two LED lights, each capable of seven colors. According to Henke, their purpose is to "provide constant optical feedback and facilitate navigation" through his set (http://www.monolake.de/technology/monodeck.html; accessed February 7, 2014).

Henke's work on the Monodecks complicates issues of determinism, intent, and agency in interesting ways. Scholarship on the design of interfaces and instruments has generally assumed a separation between makers and users, such that a device intended to function in a certain way might "determine" its resultant uses, or users might be seen to assert their creative agency in the face of apparent technical constraints or specific intended uses. These circuits of power begin to break down, however, when controllers are self-designed. Furthermore, whereas such self-designed interfaces are an ever-increasing trend in recent years, Henke represents a special case above and beyond this development, in that he is *also* the creator of the software that the controller is meant to manipulate. In particular, his work with the Monodecks and Live shows a striking convergence between software, controller, and music, in which all three elements are linked through specific design correlations.

These correspondences are most visible on the central part of the interface. In Figure 2.10, note how the eight channels are grouped into five rows (counting up from the bottom of the machine).[24] Each button in this grid controls a clip in the software, which in musical terms represents a loop. When a loop is playing, an LED beside the button is lit to display its status. Each loop is categorized in two ways. First, it is part of a textural configuration (a "scene" in Live), which corresponds to a row on the Monodeck; second, it is a member of a timbral category, which in turn relates to a column in Live and a channel on the Monodeck. The matrix on the controller always corresponds to a virtual matrix in the software, which as a whole represents one track in Henke's live set. In other words, Henke has developed an approach in which tracks consistently form structures of five scenes and eight columns, and the controller he has designed matches this organization exactly. Figure 2.11, which shows a screen in Live from an interview in which Henke explained this approach to me, reveals this patterning within the software: visible are two complete tracks, colored yellow and light orange, as well as three scenes from another, dark-orange track at the bottom part of the on-screen grid. The musical structure of a performed track thus has two visual analogs—the on-screen graphical interface and the grid of buttons and LEDs—one of which is physical in form as well. In Henke's words, "You cannot separate the instrument and the composition" (October 29, 2007; Berlin).

According to Henke, the constrained structure of his interface design facilitates freedom in performance. It does not force him, as one might assume, to follow an obvious or predetermined route through his set, proceeding in descending order from scene to scene and track to track. Rather, he moves through the highly controlled environment of five-by-eight tracks in a decidedly nonlinear fashion, combining clips

---

[24] The five-by-eight matrix at the bottom of the Monodeck II is separated from the other control organs by a row of double LEDs, above which is another row of buttons (labeled 1–8 to show the eight channels) that act as master on/off switches for each channel.

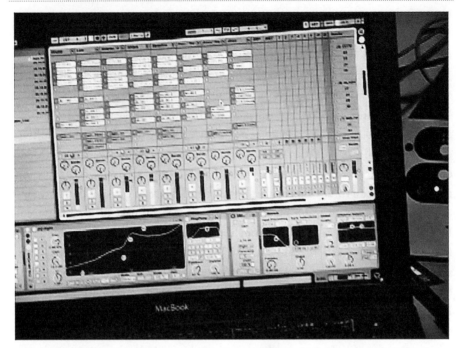

FIGURE 2.11 Screenshot of Live in relation to Monodeck II 🎧

from multiple scenes and even different tracks. Except in cases where he wishes to make a stark textural change quite suddenly, he rarely uses the prearranged scenes as wholes. Instead, the scenes function in a trifold manner: as strata of visual information, as documentation of how the track has been arranged up to the point of performance, and as starting points for musical reconfiguration.

In the course of our 2007 interview, Henke explained several ways in which loops from multiple scenes and tracks could be combined, presenting examples of how the procedure works on both computer and controller. The passage shown in video example 2.3 is part of a demonstration of the latter. 🎧 As the clip illustrates, another kind of freedom engendered by the Monodeck II is liberation from the computer—specifically, from the twin attachments of hand and eye to mouse and screen to which Henke objected in his previously quoted criticism of the original Monodeck. When I observed him performing with the Monodeck II at the 2007 Detroit Electronic Music Festival, for instance, I was stunned that he never once touched or looked at the computer after beginning his performance. Never before have I seen a musician refrain from at least periodically manipulating the computer. Henke relies instead solely on the physical interface; his laptop serves only as a source of data and of the program that the Monodeck controls.

It is remarkably ironic that a musician who has played a pivotal role in the popularization of the laptop set should himself design a controller that problematizes the very notion of what a "laptop set" is. Furthermore, it is equally ironic that someone who designed a program oriented specifically toward performance with laptops should be part of a trend *away from* laptop computers in favor of physical performance tools. As part of a performance environment that is self-designed to an unprecedented degree, "Live" remains in dynamic tension with the ideals of "liveness," provoking unexpected results in the context of performance. Paradoxically, it is through waves of technological mediation (electronic music, computer software, an intricate hardware controller) that Henke approaches an unmediated ideal, one in which he plays music only with his hands.

If Henke's work on the Monodecks represents the apogee of design customization—controllers that are specific not only to a particular software but also to one musician—the "Monome" interfaces produced by US-based Brian Crabtree and Kelli Cain constitute the flipside of this tendency. Their construction exemplifies Crabtree and Cain's mission statement: "We design adaptable, minimalist interfaces in Philadelphia" (www.monome.org; accessed April 20, 2008). Each of the three Monome models forms a grid of buttons, organized into rows based on powers of two: the 64 (eight by eight rows), the 128 (sixteen by eight; see Figure 2.12), and the 256 (sixteen by sixteen). These buttons are the only control element. As they are not pressure-sensitive, they are simple binary controllers; indeed, the complete absence of any kind of continuous controller on the Monome interfaces is unusual. Binary design also characterizes the only visual component, orange lights that are either on or off. Cain notes that "the binary on/off system is as minimal as you can get," while Crabtree feels that the utility of having many highly specific functions in certain contexts is overridden by the way in which such interfaces make it "harder to creatively cut right to the point."

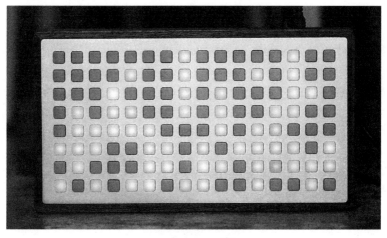

FIGURE 2.12 The Monome 128 (copyright by B. Crabtree)

The "adaptable" aspects of the Monome interfaces inhere first and foremost in their generality of function. The buttons have no set correspondence with particular musical parameters or functions; indeed, the interface need not control music at all. It can also be used for video, visual, or other functions; the Monome website mentions "live sample cutters, math simulations, drum machines, generative controllers, tonal maps, games, [and] visualizations" as potential applications (http://monome. org/series/; accessed April 20, 2008). The layout of the grid can be mapped to control elements using variable configurations such as rows and columns (most obviously), nested squares, diagonals, and so on, with regions of varying sizes. The lights and buttons are also separable, so that the former need not function as strict feedback responses for the latter. In the words of its creators, "there is no hard-wired functionality" (http://monome.org/series; accessed April 20, 2008).

Part of this generality involves the relationship between laptop and controller. Whereas the Monodecks are tied very specifically to the program Live, Monome interfaces have no set software association. This is not to say that particular programs have not affected the development of the interfaces: Crabtree devised the first Monome prototype after working for some time with Max/MSP; he valued the flexibility of this program, but sought a tool that would enable him and Cain to "perform and try to express ourselves with computers, which are traditionally very not [sic] expressive tools."[25] Today, both Crabtree and the majority of Monome users continue to favor Max/MSP; however, the interfaces are designed to function with a variety of other programs, including electronic-music applications such as Live and Reason and general programming languages such as C.

Crabtree and Cain have also framed the Monome project as reconfigurable in a way that is distinctly social: they have explicitly designated the software included with the interface as open-source, and the website serves as a starting point for a large community of users, most of whom freely share with each other "patches" they have written.[26] Their approach provides a distinct contrast to that associated with the Monodeck, which is tailored to a single musician's needs and is not publicly available. Nevertheless, customization remains a central tenet of both interfaces. The Monodeck can be seen as the *end result* of a substantial process of customization,

---

[25] http://cycling74.com/2008/02/11/a-video-and-text-interview-with-monome/ (accessed February 7, 2014). For various interesting video clips of Crabtree performing with Monome devices (using the performance name "tehn"), see http://www.vimeo.com/295006 (accessed April 23, 2008).

[26] In Max/MSP, a "patch" is a program; it carries out a series of actions in the form of algorithms or "objects." I describe Max/MSP in further detail below. For further information on the principles of open-source software distribution, see http://opensource.org/. Notably, Crabtree initiated the process of software sharing by posting a large number of his own patches to the original Monome website. See http://docs.monome.org/doku.php for a complete list of currently available documents.

beginning with a software program and moving through two versions of a hardware controller. With the Monome, by contrast, customizability inheres in and actually *persists in* the design of the interface, insofar as its quite indeterminate function is shaped and developed through the communally developed application of software.

There are also many clear similarities between the Monodeck and Monome interfaces.[27] For example, the initial motivation for each product was software—specifically, software that possessed strong performance capabilities but lacked clear methods of real-time, physical control. Furthermore, both Henke and Crabtree found commercially available controllers lacking, choosing instead to design their own products. In both cases, the central feature of their respective controllers was a grid of buttons that included lights for visual feedback. At the same time, the two devices are diametrically opposed in terms of the relationship to software that each has facilitated: as previously mentioned, the Monodeck virtually subsumes Live within performance, whereas the Monome project seems to have led to a proliferation of interest in programming. Kelli Cain highlighted a renewed emphasis on software within the Monome community; as they have learned to use the devices, many amateur musicians who have never programmed before have begun to write their own patches and share them with others. In this case, absence has fostered growth, for the emergence of this grassroots programming movement stems directly from the *lack* of software linked to the interface.

Henke, Crabtree, and Cain are among the most prominent of a number of musicians and interface designers whose work inhabits a zone of overlap between popular and academic electronic music. As described in the introduction, recent years have seen increased border crossing between these two realms, with artists such as Henke working from a popular-music base while also experimenting with sound installations and technical innovations drawn from computer-music research. Crabtree is an academically trained composer with a graduate degree from the University of California at San Diego (and to my knowledge, the only musician I have interviewed who uses staff notation as a significant part of the compositional process), yet his devices have become the center of a populist movement around electronic-music performance and software programming.

A related community, whose participants are mostly academic musicians or professionals working in the design industry, has developed around the topic of "New

---

[27] Furthermore, Crabtree and Cain are in communication with Henke, who recently used a Monome 256 as part of a 2007 sound installation called "Cyclone." (See http://www.monolake.de/installations/; accessed April 23, 2008.) In addition to his work as Monolake, Henke periodically develops various site-specific performances; in fact, I initially learned of the Monome devices through him, when he spontaneously decided to show me one during our 2007 interview. Moreover, although Henke's performance moniker derives from a lake in California and Crabtree and Cain's from monomial mathematics, the affective similarity of the names has obvious relevance for electronic musicians working in "minimal" idioms.

Interfaces for Musical Expression." This phrase (abbreviated NIME) is the name of a series of conferences, each resulting in an electronically published volume of proceedings, that began in 2002. More obviously, it denotes the chief point of interest for its members, who have been especially involved in designing distinctive interfaces for use in performance.[28] Whereas the interfaces developed for EDM contexts have generally been directed toward commercial markets (or, as with the Monodeck, in reaction to commercially available products), the trend within the interface movement has been toward single-use devices developed by and for a composer-performer.

The design of these interfaces often reflects a theoretical or conceptual orientation, such that the creation of the object becomes part of the artistic process. For instance, the category of "table controllers" includes examples such as Spencer Kiser's "spinCycle," an interface consisting of a large turntable with various brightly colored objects on its surface. Users move them around, generating visual patterns that are simultaneously translated into musical arrangements (Kiser 2006). A related device, the reacTable (Fig. 2.13), has been the subject of some media attention,

FIGURE 2.13 The reacTable (copyright by Xavier Sivecas)

---

[28] The NIME proceedings are available from www.nime.org (accessed May 9, 2011). Other important sources of academic work on interfaces include the *Leonardo Music Journal* (particularly since the editorship of Nicolas Collins beginning in 1998), *Organised Sound*, and the *Journal of New Music Research*. Although some work in this vein is broadly theoretical, much of it focuses on the design and implementation of a single interface. In general, this body of research engages with popular music only marginally if at all; some exceptions are Andersen (2003); Kiser (2006); Lippit (2004, 2006); Neill (2002); Ostertag (2002); Villar, Gellersen, Jervis, and Lang (2007).

perhaps because Björk played it in various concerts during her 2007 world tour.[29] Objects placed on its interface have specific shapes (such as squares, pentagons, cubes, and domes) that map directly onto particular functions (synthesis, tempo control, sampling). Circles around the objects afford touch-screen control of parameters such as frequency and amplitude, and connections between objects form chains of cause and effect. In essence, the design of the reacTable combines the approach used in the earliest synthesizers (in which users created modular "patches" by connecting cables between various sound generation and modification units) with the chains of linked objects found in software such as Max. The crucial innovation, however, is that changes to the interface take place *within* rather than prior to performance[30]; the designers note that "bringing these objects into proximity with each other constructs and plays the instrument at the same time" (Kaltenbrunner et al., 19).

Another category of controllers involves everyday functional objects, modified through the addition of sensors in ways that enable them to produce or manipulate sound. Burtner, who describes such controllers as "modulated objects," cites examples involving a mug, a hat, and a telephone (Burtner 2004, 193–94), while David Bernard mentions, among other devices, a "self-powered sound system in a dustbin pulled by 3 street sweepers activating rhythmical sound effects as they brush over different textures" (Bernard 2002, 189). At the 2006 Mutek Festival, one performance I attended featured three performers slowly manipulating Rubik's cubes in order to transform sounds on a nearby laptop.[31] Moving beyond desires for increased functionality and technological improvements in their controllers, the musicians who design these devices are also concerned with their theoretical content; Burtner, for instance, notes that the examples he describes are intended "to make the viewer reconsider common interactions we have with ubiquitous physical objects" (Burtner 2004, 193–94).

The Rubik's cube approach also combined elements of functional-object implementation and a strategy that Burtner labels "hand-based design"; "in HCI," he notes, "controllers that extend the human hands are possibly the most common of new musical interfaces" (195). He provides an example from one of his own performances: in this case, the object made into a controller (an oversized pair of wooden hands used by the shamans of an Alaskan ethnic group) is not mundane but rather drawn from ritual.

---

[29] See Kaltenbrunner et al. (2004) for a description of the prototype by its creators, and http://www.reactable. com/community/videos for videos of the device in performance (accessed February 7, 2014). In contrast to most NIME instruments, the reacTable has been released commercially.

[30] A second important feature is the visual feedback provided by the shapes and lighting.

[31] The Rubik's cube performance differed from those described in the preceding sentence in that the sound-controlling sensors were placed not in or on the objects themselves, but on the performers' arms and hands. Nevertheless, the visual focus of the audience was directed toward the objects in question.

Hand-based controllers also fall within a category that Michael Sharon describes as "gestural"; his own example is a sphere that the performer holds and turns (Sharon 2004). He also mentions a commercial product, the Alesis AirFX, which uses four infrared sensors to create left-right, front-back, and up-down axes that are manipulated through hand motions in the air.[32] Perhaps the most widely used nontraditional interface, however, is the Korg KAOSS Pad, a touchpad controller with which users can map various parameters onto a screen with an x-y axis (Fig. 2.14). In Berlin, both Phon.o and Apparat used the device frequently; see for instance video example 1.6.

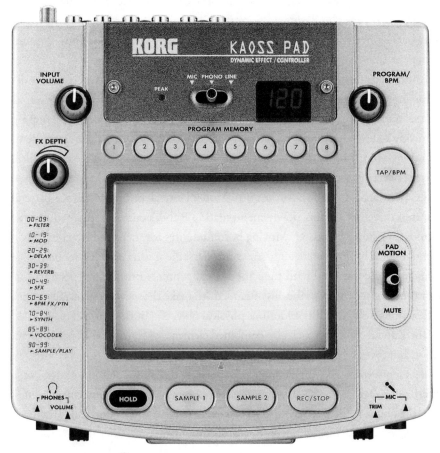

FIGURE 2.14 KAOSS Pad

[32] The AirFx is no longer commercially available, in contrast to the popular Roland MC-505, another device using an infrared beam (and also mentioned by Sharon). One musician who has used the latter is Neal Blue, whom I discuss in Butler (2006). Whereas the AirFx was a dedicated effects processor, the beam controller on the 505 is just one part of a multifunction sampler-sequencer. See http://www.rolandus.com/products/productdetails.aspx?ObjectId=173 (accessed May 10, 2008).

Academic musicians interested in "interactivity" have also created many interfaces that extend, modify, or imitate the design or playing techniques of traditional acoustic instruments. Composer Tod Machover, for instance, has designed a series of "hyperinstruments" (hyperviolin, viola, cello, bow, and keyboard); these are performed in the manner of an acoustic instrument, but augmented in real time by a computer program that responds to and modifies the sound. Ultimately, the range of devices already created under the rubrics of interface design and interactive performance is huge; I have cited a number of representative examples here, but an exhaustive treatment would take us well beyond the boundaries of this study.

In performance, individual technologies usually serve as parts of a larger assembly of devices. Although some musicians (such as Henrik Schwarz) employ a minimal setup of laptop and MIDI controller, most use larger amounts of gear, arranged in complex configurations on a performance table. Bowers theorizes these sets of materials as "ecologies," writing that "In most of my performance work, I have adopted the strategy of *having a varied set of musical resources* before me which I have structured as an arena for activity, *a performance ecology*" (Bowers 2002, 57; original emphases). This way of conceiving performance conveys an inherent contextuality; it posits the musician as an agent inhabiting and navigating an environment. In this respect it is also it is intrinsically Gibsonian—not only in its deployment of "ecology" to broader ends, but also in its emphasis on the environment as a *set* of resources.[33] In broader terms, Bower's conceptualization also counteracts potential overemphases on technology and physical devices at the expense of human agency.

Bowers further theorizes the variety of ways in which musicians may interact with the tools at their disposal—he points out delegation, supervision, direct manipulation, and inhabitation as distinctive modes of engagement (ibid., 57)—and the contingence of technological configurations themselves, which often change in response to particular performance contexts. In fact, in comparing performances by the same musician on different occasions, I have often seen a surprising variety of materials used. For instance, when Pacou played at Berlin's SO36 club on July 15, 2006, he used two drum machines (a Korg Electribe mkII and a Roland TR-727), two analog synthesizers (a Future Retro 777 and a Roland SH-101), an effects processor (a Pioneer EFX-500), and a laptop with Live. At the Tresor club on November 2, 2007, he preserved the laptop with Live and the effects unit, but used three different drum machines (the TR-606, 707, and 909, all by Roland), a MIDI controller, and no synthesizers. His general approach remains the same—an emphasis on hardware over software, with a preference for vintage and analog devices—but he substitutes

---

[33] Most tellingly, Gibson's discussion of environments (in his case, perceptual environments) draws on the ecological concept of *niche*, which he defines as "a set of affordances" (Gibson 1979, 128).

similar devices freely within his basic setup. Indeed, his selection of instruments is often somewhat spontaneous. He told me, for instance, that he was unsure exactly which devices he would take until shortly before leaving for the 2006 performance; for a while, he had considered another synthesizer in place of the 101.

The notion of a performance ecology also has ontological implications. What are the "things" within the performance environment? What are the objects of manipulation and interaction? In Live, these are clips and scenes; in a DJ set, they are records; in almost all of the interfaces I have described, musical space is divided into "channels." Perhaps most obviously, the program Max employs shapes—called "objects"—to generate actions within the software. Objects are connected graphically with lines denoting series of cause and effect. A complete arrangement of objects, called a "patch," is an algorithm for carrying out some sequence of actions. In this way, the "object-oriented" interface of Max reveals itself to be actually structured around *processes*. Indeed, the physical appearance of patches is strongly evocative of the lateral, processual assemblages and "distributed objects" described by Born (2005, 27), as shown in Figure 2.15, a patch for use in MIDI sequencing.

The ontology of Max is also socially implicated. Users can customize objects as well as write them from scratch; through these techniques, they not only inhabit but also construct their own musical environments. Furthermore, the program is written so as to expressly facilitate the sharing of patches (they can easily be emailed or otherwise transmitted from the program as digital information). The implications of this orientation are realized most clearly in the community of Monome users, with their exten-

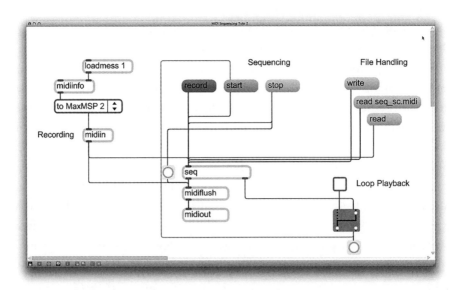

FIGURE 2.15 Sample Max patch

sive sharing of open-source materials written for performance with the device. Crab-tree, like a number of other interface designers, reveals recognition of his device as not just a purportedly neutral "tool" but also as a nexus through which power can be transmitted and expressed. The Monome's generality of function, like the reconfigu-rability of Max (which can serve a variety of functions other than musical ones), is a specific response to this awareness. Crabtree explained that he wanted to avoid creat-ing a controller that would lead others to reproduce his own working methods; "for me to make a device that lets everybody be exactly like me," he noted, "that's actually horrible." In a related vein, Bowers asserts that "it does not seem idiomatic for my design work to fix the sociality of performers" (Bowers 2002, 58).

The programs and devices I have described—Live, Max, turntables, mixing boards, mass-produced MIDI controllers, the self-designed Monodecks I and II, the "mini-malist" Monome devices, and various NIME controllers—function as sites of possi-bility for electronic musicians; their physical properties invite particular modes of use and interaction, the ramifications of which are both musical and social. In the next section I move from a focus on the characteristics of individual interfaces to consider the technologically mediated relations that arise between performers, devices, and audi-ences in broader terms. Two questions in particular guide my exploration: first, which general properties do musicians seek and value in their interactions with technology? And second, how do they communicate qualities of liveness to their audiences?

Conveying Liveness in Performance (Or, "I Don't Want to Look Like I'm Checking My Email")

Playing an instrument involves physical interaction with an interface, which I have described in terms of affordance. When this interaction enters the realm of musical performance it becomes an observable, communicative act. Of the various interfaces used in electronic dance music, none reveals the communicative issues at stake in technologically mediated performance more strikingly than the laptop computer. The laptop is the most general-purpose of the devices involved in EDM perfor-mance, and the one element common to virtually every mode of performance other than the DJ set. As such, one might expect it to occupy a neutral position within the discursive frameworks of performance, yet this is not the case. Instead, it provokes more intense manifestations of anxiety than any other technology, for both per-formers and audiences alike.

The following description from an interview with Pacou illustrates a very common way in which musicians characterized the problems associated with performing with laptops:

I know a lot of people that are also using Ableton, but in a very boring way. They are just clicking the parts on, in a sequential order, and from an audience point of view it looks like they are checking emails or playing Tetris or things like that. Very boring presentation. And these guys are charging money for this?

(July 26, 2005; Berlin)

In conversations with performers, negative comparisons to "checking email" came up time and time again. This image evokes several key dimensions around which musicians' concerns coalesce. The first concerns the perceived purpose of the laptop: whereas devices such as turntables, drum machines, synthesizers, and sequencers are clearly designed for music making, if not of a traditional sort, the computer is associated primarily with nonmusical pursuits and is certainly not thought of first as a performance instrument. The second focal point of anxiety involves the visual appearance of the performer to the audience (in Pacou's description, this appearance is expressed as imagined by the performer). The latter point is broad, involving several distinct subpoints.

First, the interface elements of a laptop, which include virtual elements on the screen as well as the keyboard, physical display, and mouse or touchpad, are for the most part invisible to the audience. This is partly due to size—they are too small to be seen clearly from a distance—but more significantly due to the orientation of the computer, which faces the musician. Second, the only visible controller, the mouse (if used), is itself employed to manipulate onscreen elements; as a result, there is a lack of perceptible connections between the musician's physical gestures (specifically, hand and arm movements) and the sounds that arise. Third, whenever the mouse comes into play, the musician must devote full attention to the screen; this precludes the performer from making contact with the audience, particularly eye contact, suggesting instead the self-involvement intrinsic to the "personal" computer. Several of these elements are evident in video example 2.4. 🔊 In this excerpt from our 2005 interview, Robert Henke performs an amusing imitation of a problematic laptop performance. Speaking as both audience member and performer, he evokes a lack (and perhaps avoidance) of eye contact on the part of the performer, as well as a disturbing gap between the intensity of the music (in particular, its volume) and the performer's unexpressive demeanor.

One significant consequence of these issues is that rarely if ever is a "laptop set" *only* a laptop set. Instead, the internal, digital elements of the laptop environment are externalized—made physical in the form of MIDI controllers and other hardware devices. The manual for the Faderfox Micromodul LV1 provides an interesting gloss on the attitudes behind this development:

It is 2004. Music is being made with electronic instruments that were originally intended to replace the typewriter. PC's and Mac's are replacing more and more synthesizers, pianos, CD players and LP turntables in the inventory of today's musician.... Since computer music should also thrive from improvisation, we...designed a controller to support the playful use of loops....Let's face it, who wants to drive a car with a computer keyboard or a mouse? Fact is, slide controls, knobs, joysticks, buttons, and LEDs are as much a part of electronic music as a steering wheel is to a car.[34]

Providing an unusually explicit explanation of their intent, the designers of the Micromodul contrast the mouse and keyboard of the computer (which they relate to the typewriter) with slide controls, joysticks, buttons, and LEDs. How ironic that so much technical geekery should come to seem warm, live, and human! Devices and interfaces that would be the *ne plus ultra* of *in*authenticity in a traditional rock performance—if they were associated with performance at all—come to serve as ways of grounding performance, of locating something physical that one can manipulate in a visible, visceral manner. The knobs and levers of MIDI controllers, drum machines, and mixing boards—all of which originated as recording or playback equipment—become conveyors of liveness. In so doing, these machines reveal that they are not mere technical auxiliaries to the laptop's digital environment, but rather physical manifestations of the principles of interactivity and visible performance. Ironically, an increase in the amount, variety, and presence of technology addresses a problem that originated in technological mediation.

Although the rhetoric of technology, suffused as it is with images of advancement, might lead one to expect that musicians would seek hardware with as many improvements and options as possible, the opposite is often the case: to facilitate spontaneous changes and directness of control, most performers favor simplicity of design. As a general rule, they seek to avoid technological clutter. Apparat, for instance—whose name after all means "device" in German—told me that the twenty-four knobs of the Evolution UC-33, at the time the most widely used MIDI controller, were "too many" for him. The makers of the Faderfox controllers seem to be aware of such viewpoints, for their competing product features only four knobs and six sliders (with the latter number reduced from eight in the original version). The most pronounced manifestation of simplicity, however, is clearly found in the Monome devices, which boil the idea of "controller" down to a grid consisting solely of on/off buttons. At the same time, when I asked Crabtree and Cain what they meant by "minimalist," they were quick to clarify and nuance the term. Crabtree explained that "it's not just about it being simple and having a reduced functionality." Rather, they highlighted "openness" in design as a particular kind of simplicity that

---

[34] No author cited: 3. Available from http://faderfox.de/lvɪ-lxɪ-djɪ.html (accessed February 7, 2014).

facilitates diverse uses: it is for this reason that the buttons on their controllers have no specified function.

Simplicity or complexity may also inhere in the number of decisions that an interface might require or engender. For instance, in explaining the limited number of devices he employs, Apparat described a scenario in which multiple options become excessive: "At some point I figured out it's better to have just a little bit of equipment, which you use very intensively, rather than having loads of equipment, because I found myself behind it sometimes, thinking about 'hmm, what can I do next?'" Explaining the design of the Monodeck in 2005, Robert Henke noted that he kept it basic because he was afraid of having "too many choices." When we spoke again two years later, he reiterated the same point, but in the past tense: this first controller had not been "basic" enough, for its use continued to require more decisions than were desirable.

Henke developed the Monodeck II in response to these issues. The grid on the new controller, in combination with its direct linkage to a five-by-eight compositional structure, placed much tighter restrictions on his performance activities. Henke consistently emphasized the importance of these limitations, which he described as "constraints": "Nowadays I try to make music which fits within the constraints of the Monodeck. And those constraints are massive." The direct connections between controller, program interface, and musical design therefore balance the indeterminate aspects of his performances with a "very, very fixed structure." Commenting on the Monome interfaces, its designers used similar language. Cain, after pointing out the absence of velocity-sensitive buttons or multicolored LEDs, noted, "There is a certain amount of constraint that's also liberating." Crabtree concurred, saying that "by reducing that set of parameters, it kind of requires more flexible thinking" and "there's a point where having constraints is actually really helpful."

Notably, all of these constraints are self-imposed. In other words, they arise when musicians choose, arrange, use, or design technology in ways that deliberately produce restrictions; it is not as if there is only one available technology to which performers must learn to adapt.[35] A further way in which musicians limit themselves, specific to laptop performances, involves the preparation of incoming sounds. In a DJ set, the cueing of the next track is usually inaudible to the audience; the DJ prepares the next record using headphones, comparing this internal sound to that being projected through the club's stereo system. By contrast, laptop performers usually forgo prelistening when bringing a new loop or track into the mix. To perform without evaluat-

---

[35] See also Bowers' discussion of interfaces, which includes a section on "restricted technique" that mentions examples such as slackening the strings of an electric guitar so that it can be played with one hand (ibid.). At one point while demonstrating the Monodeck II, Henke jokingly suggested that perhaps he should regularly perform while holding something in one hand, or with an interviewer asking him questions, in order to limit his interaction with the interface to the most essential uses.

ing possible sonic combinations beforehand requires both significant foreknowledge of the sounds involved *and* a significant level of spontaneity and flexibility—in other words, improvisational skill. Through this restriction musicians find another way to reduce the number of decisions that must be made during performance.[36]

Performers further evaluate technology in terms of the ease with which it can be manipulated. Musicians seek devices that facilitate *directness* of control, that enable them to touch one part of the machine and receive an instantaneous, audible response. This is one reason Pacou, for instance, prefers analog over digital synths: although the latter contain many preset timbres of a quite specific nature, which might seem to simplify matters in certain respects, they also require one to hunt for these sounds through a variety of elaborate submenus. By contrast, when Pacou uses analog synths such as the Roland SH-101 he has *no* presets, *no* memory, and just one basic sound source—yet every knob on the machine affects the waveform directly. He described the flexibility this affords as "hands-on," noting also that "I'm trying to get as close as possible to actually playing things." Apparat used similar language, at one point describing the Max patch he uses within performance as "basic," and saying that he knows the program so well that he can "play it like a guitar."

When technologies afford direct control, they establish clear links between performance actions and sonic results, thereby providing the quick and unambiguous feedback that is essential for musicians. To the extent that they are expected to convey liveness in performance, musicians must also communicate connections between physical gestures and resultant sounds to their audiences. This is especially important in an electronic dance music context, in which many of the musician's interactions with interfaces may be invisible, and the unfamiliarity of the instruments renders their performance techniques gesturally opaque to most audience members.[37] Indeed, a common theme among performers of electronic music (both popular and academic) is "legibility." Bowers, for instance, remarks on the "loss of legibility that gestures can have in technologically mediated performance environments" (Bowers 2002, 47); he is also concerned about the disappearance of "intelligibility."[38] Later he describes how certain performances can "make interaction into a puzzle for the audience to solve: do you see how it is working (this time)?" (57). For him, (il)legibility is crucially linked to interactivity between the performer and audience; he writes, "Clearly

---

[36] Apparat, who does not use Live, noted that he could set up pre-listening within his current performance environment, but it would not be "direct" or "rock and roll" enough. In this way he makes a clear connection between a self-imposed restriction and liveness.

[37] See Sharon (2004), Zadel and Scavone (2006), and especially Kvifte and Jensenius (2006) for further commentary on gesture-sound mappings.

[38] Ibid. These two orthographically similar words have different Latin roots: *legere* (to read) and *intelligere* (to understand).

legible interactive works—once the audience solves the puzzle, or the performer is well enough rehearsed—phenomenologically cease being 'about' interactivity."[39]

Echoing this connection between legibility and interactivity, Kelli Cain described how certain Monome performances might engage the audience in figuring out what is going on: "[When] someone has made their own program that doesn't have a level of transparency, then there's this new facet of the whole performance, that...you're not just watching someone be amazing, but you're also actually wondering what they're doing." Many EDM performances have captured my interest in this way; the live sets of Sender Berlin—one of the few non-solo acts whom I observed—are a particularly good example (see video example 2.5 ⬤). The collaborative aspect of their approach, which is unusual in its own right, imparts an additional degree of liveness to the events on stage as they communicate in real time and engage in complex coordinated actions that move beyond the simple operation of equipment. Particularly noteworthy are the intricacy and spontaneity of their movements: their arms intertwine elaborately, and they execute numerous seemingly sudden gestures in perfect synchronization.[40]

Crabtree and Cain clearly regard the "reading" of a performance as a positive attribute connected to their "minimalist" aesthetic. For example, Cain pointed out that "minimalism is about transparency too, how much of everything is visible.... What you see is what you get." Crabtree continued this thought, mentioning that "there's nothing secret" about the Monome. These remarks articulate an important connection between legibility and visibility. When audience members read a performance in order to determine how a musician is using an interface to create sound, they draw on feedback that is significantly visual as well as aural; in effect, they are listening with their eyes.

Robert Henke describes this feedback process quite explicitly in his comments on what is valuable about the Monodeck's function: "The way the audience reacts to this box is really good. Because the audience is happy that they can see something. It's more explanatory than if someone is just using a mouse and a laptop. Because I press a button; something goes on; and they hear a change." His remarks place particular emphasis on hardware, on the way in which physical controllers make sound

---

[39] Ibid. Bower's claim would not be applicable in an electronic dance music context (nor he does he intend it to be), in which interactivity inheres in many domains (e.g., between audience members as well as between them and the performer). Rather, he is critiquing certain modes of academically oriented electronic music that are avowedly "interactive," in a context in which music is assumed to be "about" something (note the quote marks Bowers places around this preposition).

[40] Naturally I asked Sender Berlin in interviews how they were able to coordinate their movements so precisely. They did not identify particular tricks or techniques, but rather emphasized the intuitive understanding that comes from having played together for more than nine years and knowing their tracks very well. I discuss coordination and collaboration within their performances in much greater detail in Chapter 3. The timing captions that appear in video example 2.5 will also be explained in that chapter.

manipulation external and visible. Similarly, Bowers asserts that "knobs, sliders, keys (both qwerty, and ebony and ivory), mice, joysticks, touchpads and so forth should be exhibited and not hidden" (2002, 58). "My devices are on a table and on show" (ibid.).

Another very important site through which liveness is communicated is the musician's body. Note, for instance, how Pole interacts with the mixing board during the passage shown in video example 2.6. ◉ Near the end of the clip in particular, he seems to put his whole body into the extended turning of a knob.[41] I have seen many such instances in performance; in my field journal I began to call them "passion of the knob" moments. This term evokes the strange incongruity that arises when a musician directs exceptionally intense expressivity toward a small, technical component associated with sound engineering. Passion-of-the-knob moments communicate through intensely exaggerated gestures; they are performative enactments of "performance" as a culturally situated behavior. Note also how Apparat moves in video example 2.7, from his 2005 performance at Maria in Berlin. ◉ His gestures are large; they sweep through space extravagantly, marking certain moments as especially expressive or significant. Indeed, his movements are so wide-ranging that at one point he knocks a piece of equipment (a guitar distortion pedal) off his performance table! In terms of directed expressivity, his interactions with the KAOSS Pad are particularly notable.[42]

Facial expressions are another way in which intensity and involvement may be conveyed.[43] Furthermore, performers sometimes move demonstratively to an already unfolding sound, almost as if they are conducting the music that they themselves produced, or "playing" it in the manner of an air guitar. All of these features are evident in Henrik Schwarz's performance video example 2.8. ◉ During most of the passage, Schwarz is manipulating sounds with his left hand via his UC-16 MIDI controller, all the while keeping the appropriate clips in play on the computer using his right hand and the mouse. The process of sound manipulation intensifies as the passage unfolds: the loops become shorter, thereby increasing the frequency of repetition, and Schwarz applies distortion to them. Near the end of the passage,

---

[41] Also striking in this performance is the discrepancy between the intensity that Pole, the electronic musician, displays on stage, and the two musicians playing "traditional" instruments, who seem quite mechanical in affect.

[42] Passion-of-the-knob moments can, of course, involve the manipulation of components other than knobs. Another account of this type of performative gesture, written by a performer-composer in an interesting reflexive style, appears in Bowers (2002, 32): "To run up the final hill, I need to load sound Q.... This requires my left hand to reach over to the Q on the laptop, itself placed to my left, while I disengage my right hand from the touchpad to grasp a knob on the front panel of the synthesiser, placed to my right. My body takes up a noticeable sprawl over the equipment before me.... I bring down my finger onto the Q and turn the knob down with a whole arm twist which I continue into a whole body turn as I disengage from both knob and key."

[43] This tendency is less widespread than expressive movement, however. Some musicians, such as Pacou and Jeff Mills, perform with relatively little facial affect.

the process climaxes and then arrives at a plateau, which is characterized by the entry of a sampled, brass-heavy sound.[44] Schwarz and the audience ride this moment out together: he lets go of the performance equipment to raise his hands in the air, and they cry out and dance more intensely. Indeed, in the passage as a whole, increases in musical intensity are closely matched by Schwarz's movements and the audience's responses. This reveals that passion-of-the-knob moments and other actions are not interior to the musician's world, but rather are intensely meaningful communications: they reverberate outward to the audience and then are reflected back to the stage as formative elements of a milieu whose participants seek to actively cultivate and sustain liveness.

One specific type of motion noticeable in all these performances is dancing. In most cases the musicians manage to dance quite energetically even though their hands are almost constantly involved with their interfaces. Occasionally (usually at climactic moments such as the one described in the preceding paragraph) a performer will momentarily disengage from the interfaces and involve hands and arms in the dance as well. Each performer's dancing reveals a general level of engagement, of course, but it also highlights the recorded nature of the medium at hand: one is dancing, after all, to one's own tunes. As a classical pianist, I was always discouraged from moving to music during performance. "Sit still!" my teachers said. "You're dancing the music, not playing it!" I was supposed to be a vessel for a composer's ideas; I was not to distract by calling attention to my own expression. Here, however, the moving body invites an identification that is welcome. As a dancer responding to the sounds that have been created, the performer enacts the role of the audience on the stage.

Performers' movements fill in the visual gaps opened by the acousmatic nature of recorded materials, locating performance within the moment through actions that can be followed with the eyes and providing general stimulation for a sense that is otherwise underengaged in this context. For audiences, establishing connections between physical gestures and their musical effects is a key strategy for understanding the performance. Musicians accordingly seek to maximize the legibility of their actions through the ways in which they interact with interfaces as well as through the interfaces they choose to use; hence Henke's description of the Monodeck as "explanatory," for example.

Many of the actions I have described, however, exceed the boundaries of explanatory functions. Using one's entire body to turn a knob, contorting one's face intently,

---

[44] This new sound is a clear example of the "reflective" sampling practices described in Chapter 1; it contrasts noticeably with the more abstract electronica surrounding it and is thus clearly comprehensible as "music" in an intensely ontic way.

dancing intensely to the sounds one has set in motion—all of these behaviors do more than what is necessary to make a sound; they go beyond the basic requirements of legibility. What is conveyed through these performative excesses?

First, such behaviors may communicate a broad sense of "expressivity." On the part of the performer this communication may be intentional, although it is entirely possible for an action to be perceived as expressive without it having been intended as such. As a whole, performers' movements run a gamut from the fully deliberate to the unconscious. Although audiences generally regard the gestures they see as meaningful, their interpretations may or may not align with the performer's intent. The strongest possible case occurs when a performer moves in a way that expresses something felt in or through the music, intends for it to be understood as such, and succeeds in conveying this perception to the audience. In addition to expressivity, the musician's combined actions convey a more elusive sense of "personality": Pole the serious musician who enjoys dub, for example, or Apparat the rock 'n' roll badass.

Second, musicians' performative actions serve additional purposes that might be described as demonstrative or rhetorical. A chief function is *proof*: the performer's movements on stage, and all of the hardware that is manipulated, shows that she is really doing something, that she is actively engaged in music making rather than email checking. At the same time the performer demonstrates *agency*: *he* is the author of these sounds, recorded though they may be. A further quality is *exertion*. This should be familiar enough as a conveyor of authenticity in other contexts, and it works in the same way here: signs of physical exertion tell us that these sounds are produced through the musician's own labor; they are not easy to come by, but rather require both work and exceptional skill. The musician's efforts on stage validate the audience's exertions on the dance floor.

My discussion of technology and liveness has emphasized a series of communicative flows along axes of mediation. Feedback, both aural and visual, travels between performers and instruments and from the performer to the audience. It also moves in meaningful ways from the dancers back to the stage. Musicians are clearly aware of and concerned about audience responses; they understand, as Nicholas Cook has written (1995a, 33), that audiences are interested in performances and not only in compositions. Indeed, every performer I interviewed, irrespective of how "mainstream" or experimental their style might be, commented on the importance of audience feedback to their playing. How is this feedback received? Is it primarily visual, aural, both, or otherwise? Robert Henke responded to these questions as follows:

> I found it actually quite difficult to maintain communication with the audience while performing, because it's something which actually needs all my concentration. So I force myself to look at the audience from time to time. Not so

much because I want the feedback; I feel the feedback even if I'm staring at my screen. But just to be present for the audience. I try to react to their reactions.

These remarks are representative; many performers asserted that they "feel" the reaction of the audience. I take this to mean that they absorb some combination of visual and aural responses without always attending to them directly. Performers cannot look directly at the audience all the time, of course, but in most performance spaces they are facing them with varying degrees of closeness. They also see them peripherally, and hear their sounds, which excited audiences make with fervor. Several musicians indicated a further specific preference for being at the same level as the audience rather than on a stage above them. Apparat explained that such a placement facilitated "feeling" the feedback without always having to look, while Henke spoke in terms of a desire for intimacy and closeness to the audience.[45]

Musicians frequently also direct their music toward the "kind" of audience present at an event. The criteria through which they assess the audience are qualitative rather than systematic, but they involve factors such as the time frame in which their set occurs, the time of year (including possible associations with particular events, such as the Love Parade), and the kind of patrons the club draws (with "kind" encompassing all manner of variables: age, gender, nationality, sexual orientation, musical preferences, level of drug intake and preferences, insider vs. "mainstream" status, and so on). In many cases, musicians framed the opening tracks of their set as "testers"; by playing records they had used in several contexts already, they could compare the current response to past experiences and respond accordingly.

Most of the musicians with whom I spoke expressed a distinct preference for smaller, less "party-oriented" venues, and for audiences with a degree of insider musical knowledge. They perceive the audiences at such events to be more open-minded and responsive, and hence more likely to respond favorably to experimental and extended approaches. In such contexts, they tend to play tracks in new ways and for longer periods of time and are more likely to improvise extensively. They do not usually resent playing for rave or "party" crowds, but they describe such performances in terms more associated with work, with simply "doing their job." Furthermore, they may refuse to meet the demands of such audiences if they find them to be excessive. As an example, Dan Bell told me after his July 2006 performance at Watergate in

---

[45] In general, Henke also prefers to be surrounded by the audience instead of in front of it, as he explained to me in a critique of his performance at the 2007 Detroit Electronic Music Festival (which he found frustrating because he was on a huge stage, high above the crowd and facing them). His comments on liveness and performative performance also appear in print; see Henke (2007, esp. chap. 4).

Berlin that the crowd had wanted him to "bang it," but he could not, as that would have transgressed the boundaries of his personal style (which is generally associated with "minimal" techno).

The phenomena I have described also raise questions concerning the overall visuality of performance. When did DJ and laptop sets become so visually oriented? It is now commonplace to see audiences facing the performer while dancing. Was this always the case, or were earlier crowds more internally oriented? If there has been a significant change, what has caused it? One possible explanation would be some sort of influence from rock; however, I do not find this compelling. Why would a genre that has often defined itself in opposition to rock suddenly begin to adopt its performance conventions? Rather, I contend that it is precisely the direct relationship between technological mediation and liveness that necessitates this giving and receiving of visual proof. In short, the greater the incursion of recording techniques and technologies into performance, the stronger the need for performative displays of involvement.

Playing with "Something That Runs": Listener Orientation Among EDM Musicians

> I think the main difference is, in electronic music, there's a lot of ways to create something that runs—that is static, but nevertheless, it's creating something. Take a drum computer: you turn it on and it plays a pattern. And you cannot turn on a drummer. A drummer always has to do something in order to work. And the drum computer, you turn it on and the pattern is there, but the action of the person who is playing the drum computer is changing the pattern.
> —ROBERT HENKE (MONOLAKE), interview with the author, Berlin, Germany, July 22, 2005

In this statement Robert Henke contrasts electronic music with styles played on traditional instruments. He makes a distinction between continuously "doing something" in order to produce a sound, as an acoustic drummer would, and initiating a process that runs on its own once set in motion. He also articulates a tension between a process moving inexorably forward through time and the "static," almost physical sense of presence that a pattern evokes when it is just "there." In speaking about his musical creations, he describes independently functioning sounds from an external perspective—almost as if he were listening to someone else's music—rather than as finished compositional products to which authorship might be ascribed.

The sites of contrast in Henke's remarks consistently express a divided perspective: on the one hand, he speaks as an agent of sonic genesis; on the other, as someone who stands outside the event he has initiated, hears it, and evaluates it. In the latter role he acts particularly as a *listener*. I describe this kind of perspective on sound as "listener orientation." This term captures a widespread set of attitudes within electronic dance music. A DJ or laptop set characterized by listener orientation is simultaneously performance-based and interpretive; it encompasses both the production and consumption of sound. The musician's attitude is reflective, and characterized by a dual consciousness. I elaborate these qualities next; although I will be speaking primarily of performance, listener orientation is equally characteristic of EDM's compositional processes and can best be understood as a way of perceiving an unfolding sonic event.

I begin my account with a personal anecdote. Although I had begun to notice some of the attitudes I describe here after interviews with musicians, I first became keenly aware of listener orientation as I was learning to DJ, especially during a period in which I frequently practiced classical piano and DJing in immediate succession. The former was a discipline I had been practicing for most of my life, while the latter was completely new to me. The resulting gaps in my experience and knowledge drew the discrepancies and points of contact between the two activities into sharp relief. After practicing, I often recorded my thoughts immediately in journal entries.

While DJing, I was struck by the way in which I could step outside a sound as I was making it happen. In fact, this oscillation between listening and doing is an essential part of this kind of musical performance: DJs are continuously evaluating the current configuration of sounds; determining if, when, and how it should change; and thinking about what sort of sound or record should follow next. While this is happening, the record continues to turn, and loops and sequences continue to repeat, until the next sonic action is undertaken. Referring back to Henke's description, the sound is always "there"; it is always running. This sonic presence arises through the combined effects of repetition and an endless flow of sound, two of the most distinctive features of this musical style.

By contrast, classical pieces offered me rests, chances to breathe, breaks between movements. Yet they also required me to be continuously involved in the production of the sound; if I became too enraptured by what I was playing—if I became too much of a listener—the piece fell apart. At the same time, I noticed I have often been drawn to pieces featuring constant rhythmic motion, such as Chopin's etudes or Schubert's Impromptu in E-flat major, D. 899. These works also offer an uninterrupted flow of sound and cyclical temporal organization. Structuring time in recurring cycles fosters a certain reflectivity; one can begin to stand outside a temporal unit and perceive it even as it unfolds.

As a classical performer, I sought to bolster my abilities as a listening performer by practicing listening outside of a performance context. While pursuing a graduate degree in piano, I began the discipline of "silent practice." Often advocated by piano teachers, but rarely (I suspect) carried out, this mode of exercise involves running a composition silently through one's head, away from one's instrument. I turned to the technique in desperation, during a period in which my teacher was pushing me to learn large amounts of repertoire in a very short time. I was having particular problems memorizing the finale of a late Schubert sonata, a rondo-movement in which the A theme appears in a seemingly endless series of keys and textures. I could imagine the piece in my head in a loose, fuzzy way, but when I tried to really make myself hear *every note*, I was startled to discover how vague my knowledge was. Even more surprising, I made the same mistakes *mentally* that I did physically! Practicing silently became a helpful discipline for me, something that freed me from the rut of pointless physical routines and allowed me to refine my inner hearing in new ways.

At the same time, there is a strangeness to the idea of silent practice, a curious separation of music from the body. It reveals the extent to which an understanding of sound as recorded object has permeated our consciousness, even with regard to styles whose origins predate recording. By silently practicing, I slowly and surely produced a full recording in my memory, which in turned enabled me to play it back for others. And—to invert the sequence of cause and effect—one might also ask whether I needed to know a piece this well *because* I was so accustomed to experiencing music through recordings. For me (and presumably for many other classical performers) there was often a huge disjuncture between my primary activity as a musician—practicing—and the performances for which I was supposed to prepare. One required many hours of daily maintenance, centered in particular around *repetition*, while the other proceeded irrevocably forward through time and was over in an instant. A bad performance was like a recording that one could not stop; a good one, like the playback I had inscribed in my mind.

These reflections highlight some of the effects of recording practices on musical epistemologies in contemporary classical performance, a context in which the pervasiveness of these practices is rarely admitted or discussed. In electronic dance music, conceptions of sound as recorded object are more immediately apparent. What is perhaps surprising, however, is their incursion into the domain of performance. In characterizing their performances, for instance, laptop musicians frequently use the language of discovery: they "find" a perfect combination between two loops; they "realize" a new way in which a track might be arranged; they "hit upon" previously unknown sonic possibilities. What almost escapes notice is the serendipitous, externally oriented attitude they display—projected, after all, onto music *they themselves* wrote. Similar emphases appear often in descriptions of DJing, as in this characterization by DJ Shiva:

What's really fun is when it's completely off the cuff, just accidental. You were playing this song, and you're flipping through your crate, thinking, thinking,

thinking, "What's gonna go? Ok, that!" And you put it down on there, and you cue it in, and you're like, "Holy shit! I didn't know that!" Because it has a sound that's exactly the same as the sound in that record, only it's on another beat.

In the context of a DJ set, this attitude of discovery is less surprising, since DJing is in fact about finding novel combinations of other musicians' records. The more significant quality evident in both descriptions is the aforementioned view of musical sound as recorded object. Notably, this perspective holds even when the sounds in question are self-generated. And it continues to interact with more traditional concerns about music's technical qualities: DJ Shiva, for instance, pinpoints timbral and rhythmic qualities (two sounds that are "exactly the same," but one is "on another beat") as the key to the discovery she describes. The constituents of this musical play, however, are entire recordings.

The attitudes that I describe as "listener orientation" are thus inextricably intertwined with the penetration of modern media practices into all forms of music. In electronic dance music this interpenetration reveals itself in a particularly striking fashion, as performances themselves are crafted from the alteration and reconfiguration of recorded elements. The physical technologies of its production and performance also promote listener orientation. By shifting some of the responsibility for sound production from the performer to the machine, EDM technologies cultivate the emergence of a distinctively interpretive role *during performance*. Whereas a conventional musician "always has to do something in order to work," the DJ or laptop performer can turn on a device such as a drum computer, and "the pattern is there." The performer's agency does not disappear, of course, for the ever-present pattern is only raw material for a musical improvisation. Freedom from continuous concentration on producing "the notes," however, enables the performer to be a better listener, for he or she can step outside the performance and evaluate it while it is ongoing. It is in this way that the technologies of electronically mediated performance support the quality of listener orientation that I have described as "reflective"; they make it possible for the performer to create and experience a musical event at the same time.[46]

Scholarly and journalistic writing on technology in EDM, however, has not addressed such effects; instead, it has generally emphasized one or both of two main

---

[46] One modality through which musicians may further perform a response to recorded sounded is dance. When musicians embody their responses through dance, they perform listener orientation in a visible manner. This is most evident when they let go of their interfaces and dance with the whole body, as described in the preceding section. This would not be feasible without technological support, of course.

themes. The first is the low cost of the technology involved in EDM production, which in the mid-1980s allowed house and techno musicians to make records with cheap analog devices such as the 808 and the 303, and more recently has enabled the production of internationally distributed recordings from relatively simple home studios. The second recurring theme is the low degree of technical training required for EDM composition. In time, the technologies involved can be mastered on one's own, and most EDM musicians are self-taught.[47]

These emphases, though not irrelevant, do not tell the whole story, for they fail to address the experiential possibilities fostered by EDM technologies.[48] Indeed, very little critical attention has been devoted to the actual experience of performing, despite the rise of "performance studies," music-theoretical literature on "performance and analysis," and other areas of inquiry. The same gap exists in fields in which performance is a primary activity. Earlier in this chapter, I provided several accounts of my experiences as a classical performer. After writing these narratives, I was struck (and refreshed) by their unfamiliarity; in my twenty years of formal instruction, I can recall no extended discussion of what a performance should feel like for the musician(s), or how it *does feel*. Instead, discourse around performance focused almost exclusively on issues of mastery and interpretation.

For contemporary audiences and musicians, the dual perspective afforded by listener orientation likely derives from the rise of the recording as the primary format through which we encounter music. Prior to these infinitely repeatable, rewindable, pause-able objects, performance was more strongly characterized by evanescence. Now, while musical events continue to move forward through time as always, there is also a novel sense in which we can "hear," or understand in an auditory manner, the disruptive effects of recording on the linear flow of time.[49] And perhaps we also desire this kind of experience, this enhanced ability to reflect on musical sound as it unfolds, precisely because the epistemology of recording practices has so thoroughly pervaded our consciousness.

---

[47] I deliberately use the word *training* rather than *skill*. Although the latter does appear frequently in arguments of this sort, it is problematic. EDM requires substantial skill in both composition and performance, and respected musicians spend years developing their abilities.

[48] The only exception to this lacuna of which I am aware appears in Bowers, who briefly describes machine-facilitated listener orientation (without using this term) in a section on "variable engagement." "Different forms of engagement have different *phenomenologies* associated with them," he writes (original emphasis). "Listening can take different forms depending on whether one is listening as one is bodily engaged or listening to an independent machine production.... Algorithmic material or the playback of recordings may 'buy time' for the set-up and initiation of other materials" (Bowers 2002, 46–47). As an ethnographically informed and self-reflexive account of interactive electronic performance, Bowers' thesis is unique.

[49] The way in which recording "stops time" is a recurring theme in the literature on sound technologies; see especially Katz (2004).

Music's status as recorded object is also inextricably linked to processes of proliferation. An inescapable immersion in and bombardment by media objects has become a commonplace of postmodern life. In sonic terms, the whole world of music is available to us, and we experience it constantly—not only through radio, television, and the recordings we purchase, but also through recent technologies such as podcasts and file sharing as well as in many public spaces. Musicologist Robert Fink (2005, 2) has described this "torrential flow of information"—and the water image is a recurring one—as the "media sublime." He applies this idea to various kinds of minimalist music, suggesting that it functions as a way for musical consumers to regain control:

> Music can drown out the omnipresent barrage of commodity culture with a barrage of its own. Music can even place that barrage under the control of the listener, and encourage her to toy with it, dominate it, experience it as an alternate, equally "full" space where she is free to pay attention or not, a space within which the mind can "wander" without anxiety.
>
> (Fink 2005, 205)

In turntable-based styles, the DJ can be understood in similar terms as a kind of *über*-listener. DJs mediate this sea of media for their audiences, providing an ordered response to the excess of information the world presents to us. From a vast array of available music, the DJ carefully chooses a set of interesting and stylistically related material and arranges it coherently. This view of the DJ set emphasizes the performer's identity as a consumer. Playing a DJ set is a way of performing consumption.

Conversely, DJs also "perform" when they act as consumers in a more conventional sense. In the record store, the roles of DJ-as-listener and DJ-as-consumer come together. The first stage of "selection," one of the key components of DJing, begins in this location, where the process of choosing records becomes more challenging than the leisurely connotations usually carried by "shopping." The specialist stores in which EDM is sold typically carry thousands of records. Although they are organized by genre and label, the sheer amount of product available is overwhelming. Many records are minimally labeled, and the day's best purchase might come from a previously unheard-of artist or be found on the B-side of a more popular track. DJs choose tracks in several stages: they pull records that interest them from the bins, listen to them at turntables set up in the store specifically for this purpose, and then discard the majority of their selections.

I learned about DJ shopping through my own experiences purchasing records (an activity that, for my own purposes as a "bedroom DJ," carried considerably lower stakes than it does for those playing to thousands in high-profile clubs) and through interviews in which I asked DJs questions such as, "How did the records in your crate end up there? How or why did you choose them?" Most DJs emphasized the continuing importance of the record-shopping process, an activity that stands out in an era in which music as a commodity is increasingly digital. For instance, Daniel Bell, a DJ who is extremely successful on a global scale, described the significant amounts of time that he still spends in record stores, as well as listening online. Before choosing a record, he often puts it aside after a first listen and then returns to consider it again later. He noted that a record must fully hold his attention in its entirety, not just in parts of the track. DJane Aroma also emphasized the evaluation of records in her account of this process, though she prefers to zero in quickly on essential parts of a track[50]:

> AROMA: When I go to record shops, for example, I don't look first for labels; I just look for the music, and then I listen to eighty or one hundred records and buy two. But that's the quota, you know? Two from a hundred. So this is how I deal with finding good stuff.
>
> MARK BUTLER: So, that's pretty selective. I'm not sure even how to ask this, or how to put it, but what do you think about, what things sort of grab you and end up making you choose something?
>
> AROMA: I know it in four bars. I cannot tell you why, but I can tell you it's four bars of listening. I mean, in four bars you know: Is the production good? What sort of beats does this person use? That's like the first criteria. And then, does this person use vocals?... [Vocals] can really mess up a track. They can elaborate a track perfectly or they can mess up a track completely, so I would not play them. So that's like the basic three terms. And then it's "Do I like it or do I not like it?"
>
> MB: And do you usually listen to the middle of the track?
>
> AROMA: No, I go [to the] first one-third, and then you can see it on the vinyl, like: "Where's the break? How does the break end up?"...
>
> MB: So partly you like to look at the record and sort of scan the form...
>
> AROMA: Mm-hmm.
>
> MB: and you can tell if it's going to be a really predictable kind of form.
>
> AROMA: Yes, sure.

In sifting through large numbers of records and choosing only a few, DJane Aroma enacts a process that has an obvious parallel within the DJ booth. Although "diggin'

---

[50] In Berlin, female DJs such as Aroma sometimes use the title "DJane" to highlight their gender, as well as to problematize the fact that the "DJ" is normatively defined as a masculine figure. This practice also reflects the grammatical structure of German, in which feminine gender in professions is denoted through the addition of the suffix –in.

in the crates" has mainly been written about as something that occurs in preparation for DJing,[51] it occurs within DJing as well. When preparing to lay down a new track, musicians such as Bell sift through the hundred or so records they have brought with them in order to find the one that will work best. Both kinds of "digging" involve improvisation, in the sense of spontaneous, real-time decision making, and both behaviors involve musically constitutive actions. In the latter sense, therefore, the "performance" that is a DJ set begins well before the actual evening on which it takes place.

If DJing performs consumption, and DJs perform when they consume, the same is true for the audience. By collectively responding to recorded music, they perform the act of consuming, and what they consume is not only music but also "performance."[52] More broadly, they may also be said to *listen* performatively. In an earlier work, I proposed the term *performing audience* in order to emphasize the active role the audience plays in shaping the musical outcome of an event (Butler 2006, 47 and 72–74). Here, as I conclude, I would like to extend this term to include the performance of *liveness*. Without the audience's cooperation and participation, this crucial quality will not emerge; a performance becomes an event through a *collaboration* between the musician and the dancers.[53] Communication travels along multiple paths, circulating constantly from the musician to the audience, between dancers within the crowd, and from the dancers back to the stage. Not only in spite of but also through the myriad technological mediations I have described, the participants within this performance work together to produce liveness.

---

[51] See Schloss (2004) for the most thorough discussion of "diggin'."

[52] See Malbon (1999, esp. 29–31) and Fikentscher (2000, esp. 60–61) for related but more general points about consumption and performance on the dance floor.

[53] This fact will be clear to anyone who has ever heard an excellent performer playing in a club in which the crowd has not reached critical mass. It was also revealed to me in an even starker fashion while studying Henrik Schwarz's 2006 Mutek performance. After analyzing the video of the performance closely and interviewing Schwarz about it, I listened to an audio recording of the set that Schwarz had given me. Although the sound quality was excellent, I could scarcely believe it was the same performance. The intensity and fervor with which he performs was somehow missing. Reduced to audio, his set seemed remarkably mellow, almost low energy: it was, in effect, a de-vibed performance.

3 Making It Up and Breaking It Down
IMPROVISATION IN PERFORMANCE

THE PREVIOUS TWO chapters have shown a number of ways in which the creative practices of electronic dance music break down oppositions between seemingly entrenched conceptual binaries such as work/performance, prerecorded/live, technological/human, fixed/fluid, and product/process. Chapter 1 revealed the work of electronic dance music as multiple, contingent, and in flux. Understood as a web of interrelated creative events, EDM's ontology draws together manifold forms of musical identity that arise both prior to and within performance. Chapter 2, meanwhile, explored the ways in which performance built around recordings and recording technologies can become live and immediate. This immediacy is negotiated between a performer and the sounds he or she creates as well as with the audience members who hear and respond to those sounds. Both performer and audience are active co-producers of "liveness" and hence of "performance" experienced consciously as an event.

This chapter addresses the ways in which performance in EDM is *improvised*. The conceptual axes with which it is most concerned are product/process, fixed/fluid, and especially composed/improvised. These frameworks have been essential to scholarship on improvisation, and the first section of the chapter will provide an overview of the principal ways they have been articulated. Teasing out the components of the composed/improvised binary in particular, I will argue for a clearer understanding of the relationship between musical events specified prior to performance and those determined within the event itself. Because of the special way in which EDM brings together prerecorded elements and live performance, it offers a very revealing lens through which to consider the interaction between these two modalities.

After exploring the insights and limitations of current research on improvisation, the chapter turns to two in-depth analyses of specific performances. Each analysis addresses a set of interrelated examples, thereby bringing out the work/text/performance relationships described in Chapter 1 through detailed engagement with the material in play. This engagement is deliberately multifaceted: it involves explanation of the artists' approaches to composition and performance, description of the context of each performance under consideration, identification of the constituent elements (tracks) heard in each performance, and close analysis of one or more tracks played within that performance. Each track addressed in this way is considered both in its recorded, pre-performance form and as realized within the specific event.

The examples chosen represent the two primary forms of EDM performance, DJ and laptop sets. The first group of examples revolves around three laptop performances from 2006 and 2007 by Hendrik Vaak and Torsten Litschko of Sender Berlin. I zero in on a segment of three tracks that appears in each performance, describing how these preexistent elements are transformed through improvisation. This analysis also speaks to collaboration, another recurring theme in improvisation studies. The second set of examples centers on the track "The Bells" by DJ and producer Jeff Mills. I consider the design of "The Bells" not only as encoded on twelve-inch vinyl—in short, as a product that would seem to be fixed in the most literal sense—but also as manifested in a DJ set by Mills himself. In both cases, exploration of the rich work/text/performance relationships involved illuminates a network of creative events as described in Chapter 1. The analyses also demonstrate the ways in which liveness is connected to improvisation for these musicians.

Studying Improvisation(s): Conceptual and Scholarly Bases

Although known for generating novel musical outcomes during the time frame of musical performance, improvisation is not a process of "making it up as you go along" or creating something out of nothing. Rather, it always brings real-time musical processes into dialogue with certain preexistent constraints, be they a repeating chord progression, the form and melodic structure of a Tin Pan Alley song, a raga, or a particular kind of rhythmic cycle. Thus, as Stephen Slawek writes, the "activity of improvisation" can be viewed as a "dialectical process" between elements that are fixed or flexible to varying degrees, that are simultaneously distinct but overlapping.[1] Although apparent to some degree in most improvised traditions, tensions between fixed and variable components are revealed in an especially striking fashion within the technologically mediated improvisations that characterize EDM.

Unfortunately, emphases on *synthesis* between these two dimensions of improvisation are uncommon within musical scholarship, which has tended instead to situate various improvised styles on either side of an ideological divide: on the one hand, composed, permanent, and recorded *products*; and on the other, improvised, ephemeral, and "live" *processes*. For instance, many early studies of improvised traditions, seeking to impart academic legitimacy to jazz and other styles, sought to emphasize their compositional dimensions. Authors advocated the analysis of transcribed improvisations, finding within them the pervasive, hierarchically structured coherence associated with canonical art music. Lewis Porter, for instance, finds within the music of John Coltrane "long-range structural connections" (Porter 1985, 584) and an "extremely rigorous, improvised compositional structure" that involves (among other features) a symmetrical tonal plan presenting the successive key scheme F, E♭, B♭, and C, representing a large-scale motion from I to V, while also drawing on pitches found in the initial F pentatonic scale (598 and 605). While noting that "process and product tend to fuse in improvisation," Frank Tirro writes that "the best jazz solos are indeed constructive in nature and may be evaluated syntactically as are other teleological compositions of the notating Western composer" (Tirro 1974, 285–86).

Teleology also emerges as a major concern in the small but well-defined area of jazz research by music theorists (see Folio 1995; Larson 1987, 1998, 1999, and 2006; Martin 1996 and 2006; Strunk 1979; and Waters 1996). Most of these authors employ methods that are Schenkerian to varying degrees.[2] Accordingly, their analyses exhibit strong emphases on coherence (especially long-range coherence), on connections between small details and high-level design, and on hierarchical, recursively structured pitch organization. Some treat these qualities as markers of aesthetic value: Larson, for instance, remarks that lesser jazz musicians (in contrast to Bill Evans) may not possess "real artistic long-range hearing" (1998, 241). Martin adopts a more relativistic stance, noting the "intrinsic weakness of applying the European model of large-scale structure, with its sense of single harmonic closure, to a body of work whose form, by nature strongly sectional, cadences repeatedly and nonhierarchically" (1996, 31).

---

[1] In Nettl and Russell (1998), 336. Within the context of his essay, Slawek's remark refers to Indian music, though I wish to extend it to improvised music more generally. Slawek also cites Paul Berliner as sharing a similar view: "the spontaneous and arranged elements of jazz presentations continually cross-fertilize and revitalize one another" (Berliner 1994, 383; cited in Slawek 1998, 365 n. 6).

[2] The analyses of Folio and Waters, who address rhythmic phenomena, are the only two exceptions in the list.

This area of scholarship provides powerfully detailed accounts of the music of a number of well-known jazz artists, as well as useful theoretical overviews of rhythmic, harmonic, and voice-leading procedures in particular repertories (especially bebop). Yet even though the authors analyze a great many improvisations, they very rarely discuss improvisation as a topic per se. As such, their work does not attempt to address the distinctive qualities of improvisations or the ways in which they are produced. Instead, improvisations are treated as compositions. "The listener"—that is, the abstract listener of analysis—is the focus of discussion more than musicians or their methods.

In these ways, music-theoretical work on jazz presents clear examples of the approaches for which Porter and Tirro argue. At the same time, these music theorists remain surprisingly silent with regard to metatheoretical and methodological considerations, an area that has been explored almost obsessively within other jazz scholarship.[3] In most cases their analyses succinctly establish a focus on the musical parameters under consideration and then move into detailed discussion of specific examples. Transcriptions are treated with the same level of permanence and authority as scores, and ambiguities in notation are only rarely acknowledged or discussed. The way in which these authors notate and ascribe "structure" results in particular accretions of ontological significance. The analytical method both generates and nurtures musical objects.

In recent years, with improvised repertoires being taken more seriously within at least some circles of academia, trends outside of music theory have shifted toward greater scholarly emphasis on the fluid, processive qualities of improvisation. Approaches have tended to be event-oriented, as well as decidedly opposed to scores and notation (as scholarly tools, but often more generally as well). These emphases are clearly evident in a recent work by David Borgo, who lays out the following claims as axioms:

—Music is an event centered on the real-time production of sound; music is not an abstraction, such as a score, transcription, or recording.

---

[3] By contrast, music theorists studying popular music have been just as vocal as their peers in other disciplines with respect to metatheory and method. The most significant exception to the generally nonreflexive tendencies of jazz theory is Larson's article "Schenkerian Analysis of Modern Jazz: Questions About Method" (1998). Here the author addresses certain recurring concerns explicitly, making an important argument against critiques of analysis based on the assumption that "improvised music differs fundamentally from composed music" (211). Martin's 1996 book also includes a brief but substantive discussion of issues around transcription, noting that "transcription is an analytical statement" (5). In general, however, it is striking to observe that the tendency toward silence around methodology in this literature is not all encompassing, but rather quite specific to the *improvised* dimensions of jazz. By contrast, these works address the particulars of *Schenkerian* methodologies in considerable detail.

—Music lives when it is heard and understood; the active, human process of listening is the essence of music. Therefore, the physical and cognitive capabilities and limitations of human listeners are crucial for analysis. What cannot be heard and understood is not (human) music.[4]

Notable in particular are the essentializing tendencies of these claims, the directness with which they define what music is (and what it is not). Similar drives toward definition appear in many sources that advocate a process-oriented approach. Most frequently, authors seek to specify the essential qualities of improvisation, distinguishing it from composition. Consider, for instance, this excerpt by John Brownell, from an essay that reviews several decades of jazz scholarship from a metatheoretical perspective:

It is the essential nature of jazz as a performing art, as something that takes place in real time, that has made the analysis of improvisation a slippery proposition. What are we talking about when we talk about an "improvisation"? Are we talking about the electromagnetic record left on a piece of audio tape after "the improvisation" itself has long been completed? What about a graphic representation of such a recording in the form of a transcription? If we accept these artifacts as somehow representing "the improvisation," is it then valid to apply analytical methods developed in the context of music of a different sort (composed European art music) to these bits of tape and marks on paper?

(Brownell 1994, 9)

In its immediate context, this last question is rhetorical, for its answer is a foregone conclusion—a resounding "no," argued explicitly and forcefully throughout Brownell's paper. For Brownell, improvisation is fundamentally different from composition: the former is essentially process-oriented, while the latter centers around products. In his view one such object, the score, is the total object of music-theoretical and musicological inquiry—"the traditional approach of Western music theory," he writes, "has been to treat music as being capable of being completely represented by a graphic record" (23)—and any analytical method developed in association with scores is therefore inherently object- and product-oriented. The article concludes with a chart that conveniently places the work of ten authors into columns representing either "improvisation as product" or "improvisation as process" (ibid.).

Another author advocating a process-oriented approach, Keith Sawyer, articulates a more nuanced argument. In particular, he highlights the *contingent* qualities of

---

[4] Borgo (2005, 5). These quotations appear as the first and second of four bullet points. I have used dashes instead of bullets in order to avoid confusion with my own textual marks.

improvisation, that is, the way in which the structure of an improvisation emerges within performance. In other words, events within the performance are not necessarily implied at the outset, but rather emerge as the result of other events originating within its unique context. Musicians are certainly aware of these conditions; in an interview with Paul Berliner, for example, the jazz musician Max Roach makes a powerful evocation of contingence from a performer's perspective:

> After you initiate the solo, one phrase determines what the next is going to be. From the first note that you hear, you are responding to what you've just played: you just said this on your instrument, and now that's a constant. What follows from that? And then the next phrase is a constant. What follows from that? And so on and so forth.
>
> (Berliner 1994, 192)

Sawyer makes an important point about how the form of an improvisation develops. At the same time, his model evinces similar biases to those of Borgo and Brownell: a desire to define improvisation (through characteristic processes of differentiation) and to contrast real-time sonic events and objects such as scores:

> The unanswered questions in studies of improvisation are: how does an improvised performance, a socially constituted *text*, differ from a creative product such as a musical score, a *text artifact*? How can the analyst represent the contingent and collective aspects of improvisational performance? Tools appropriate for the compositional analysis of text artifacts seem to lead the researcher away from these defining, unique elements of improvisational performance.
>
> (Sawyer 1996, 271; original emphases)

Certainly it would be simplistic and reductive to draw one-to-one equivalencies between notated compositions from the art-music tradition and improvisations such as those that occur in jazz or electronic dance music. Nevertheless, it is also problematic to exscribe the products involved in improvisations, or to always characterize them, *contra* "dynamic" improvisation, as static, dull, and lifeless "artifacts." Texts, and the abstractions that underlie them, are central parts of many improvised styles. In opposition to Borgo's claim, music *is* experienced through objects, through records and scores and posters and t-shirts. The materiality of these products, as well as their specific properties, is not irrelevant to discussions of how music is heard. Music is also made with and through various objects; increasingly, as occurs in DJ sets and sample-based hip-hop styles, the constituents of musical performances are themselves media objects. Ultimately, drawing lines between musical "processes" and "products" and placing improvisation on one side or the other compromises its messy complexity. Instead, in a world in which music circulates as a mass medium, it becomes more productive to ask how the coexistent possibilities of music as activity and music as product might interrelate and inform each other.

The relationship between improvisation and composition in particular constitutes another major problematic for the development of conceptual models. All of the previously cited processual approaches, for instance, oppose composition and improvisation in order to specify what is unique about the latter. As an intellectual strategy, this tactic seems straightforward at first: one defines the object of inquiry, and then formulates appropriate methodological tools. When both sides of the dichotomy are contemplated fully, however, their polarity begins to weaken. A number of authors, particularly within ethnomusicology, have challenged the dynamics of this binarism. Stephen Blum, for instance, has noted that in the West "improvisation" is a marked term (Blum 1998, 36). It is often defined negatively, as against norms (e.g., "performed without preparation"). Moreover, as "one of the most heavily mythologized of all cultural practices" (Cook 2004, 10), improvisation evokes particular aesthetic connotations within contemporary Western culture, such as freedom, spontaneity, unpredictability, directness, and intuitivism. In some contexts, it may also be associated with a lack of discipline or precision (Nettl 1998, 7).

In many performance traditions, however, the concept of "improvisation" is not operative; rather, what seems improvisational in contrast to the faithful performance of precomposed works may simply be how music is made. Indeed, as Stephen Blum points out, "improvisation" and "improvise" emerged as general terms in Western European languages only during the nineteenth and twentieth century (Blum 1998, 36–38). Nor is this timing coincidental. As Cook has written, "the concept of improvisation in the modern sense tends not to exist in traditional cultures, but arises in tandem with musicology and the associated idea of the reified (or commodified) musical work" (Cook 2003, 159)—which, as Goehr notes (1992), became dominant in European art music during the nineteenth century. In this context, therefore, improvisation emerges as composition's Other.

In light of these historical and cultural challenges, a number of voices have questioned the improvisation/composition dichotomy. An important early challenge, still widely cited today, came from Bruno Nettl, who asked, "Should we not then speak perhaps of rapid and slow composition rather than of composition juxtaposed to improvisation?" (Nettl 1974, 6). Nettl claimed that improvisation is also fundamentally creative, and that the "suddenness" of the creative impulse distinguishes the kinds of activities that we generally call "improvisation" (3). In response to these insights, a number of authors have suggested alternative ways of situating improvisation. Free-jazz musician Evan Parker, discussed by Borgo, suggests that we might more accurately think of improvisation as opposed to notated music (Borgo 2005, 57). Sawyer makes a similar point; in a critique of Nettl's argument, he asserts that it "overlooks a qualitative distinction between composition and performance: the presence or absence of an ostensible text artifact."[5]

Parker and Sawyer's comments call attention to the role that *texts* may play in construing improvisation. At the same time, however, it is striking to observe the new polarities that seep into the gap left by "improvisation" versus "composition." Within scholarly conceptual systems, improvisation need not be opposed to other musical activities in these ways (that is, on the basis of presumed essential differences). By contrast, echoing Cook and Blum, I assert that "the attempt to categorize between different types of activity (improvisation, composition, performance) may be less productive than 'discriminations between *more or less* improvised aspects of performance'."[6]

In the analyses that follow, I conceptualize musical creation vis-à-vis performance as situated along a continuum measuring the relationship of musical specificity to time. Sonic outcomes that are specified only *in time* form one end of the continuum, while those that are maximally specified *ahead of time* form the other. This suggests a series of framing questions for any potentially improvised performance: *What* is specified? How is it specified? Who specifies it? How specifically is it delimited? And, with particular regard to relationships among texts, works, and performances: To what extent does the inscribed form specify the sonic result? To what extent does prior planning specify the sonic result? To what extent are precomposed entities involved? These questions function as starting points for the analyses in section two of this chapter.

First, however, it will be helpful to consider the matter of prior specification from a theoretical point of view. Almost all improvisations involve an interplay between

---

[5] Sawyer (1996, 273). It should be noted that Nettl and Sawyer use "composition" in different ways: Nettl employs it to denote musical creation in general, whereas Sawyer uses it to describe practices specific to art music. In his 1998 essay, Nettl suggests "precomposition" as a term for the creation of relatively permanent works prior to performance (5). As quoted above, Sawyer's assertion is not supportable in point of fact, for Nettl does explicitly suggest that we might cease "making the presence or absence of notation the major criterion for improvisation and composition" (Nettl 1974, 11). Nevertheless, it is possible that Nettl elides or deemphasizes certain functional or discursive distinctions between improvisation and composition in his eagerness to break down this dichotomy. Nicholas Cook also perhaps goes too far in this regard when he suggests that almost "everything *other* than the notes is improvised" in a Western classical performance (Cook 2003, 159; original emphasis). In my own experience with classical training, which I believe to be relatively typical, one of the chief purposes of practice was to get as much as possible (including negotiable parameters such as "interpretation") settled prior to performance.

[6] Cook (2003, 155, quoting Blum 1998, 28). Original emphasis.

real-time creativity and preexistent musical elements.[7] This tendency applies cross-culturally, even as it manifests in a diverse range of approaches. Entities that might be used as the basis for an improvised performance include the ragas of Indian classical music (modes with characteristic melodic gestures and patterns of development), a loosely defined composition associated with the Persian *dastgahs*,[8] or a bell pattern used as a "timeline" within West African drumming (where it serves as a backdrop for virtuosic patterns extemporized by the master drummer). In jazz the most important elements structuring performance are the melodies and harmonic progressions of Tin Pan Alley song choruses, whereas an organ improvisation might be based on a given fugue subject or bass ostinato. In electronic dance music, preexistent elements include twelve-inch records, preset patterns stored in the memory of synthesizers and drum machines, samples from other recordings, and loops and tracks composed ahead of time by the musician.

A related multiplicity appears in scholarly descriptions of these preexistent elements. Some of the terms that have been used to refer to them are "referent" (Pressing 1998), "model" (Nettl 1974), "preform" (Titon 1978), "template" (Slawek 1998), "ready-made" (Sawyer 1996), "building block" (Nettl 1974, Butler 2006), and "module" (Butler 2006). "Referent" is perhaps the most semantically neutral of these words; as an independent term it seems simply to suggest something to which a performance refers.[9] Pressing, however, defines the referent in terms associated with music cognition, as "a set of cognitive, perceptual, or emotional structures (constraints) that guide and aid in the production of musical materials" (Pressing 1998, 52). "Template" seems to have more synoptic implications, its associations with printing and design connoting a pattern underlying an entire performance. Slawek, writing about Hindustani instrumental music, employs it to refer to the overall shape and components of a good performance.[10] "Model," meanwhile, seems to imply a heuristic function: when used as a basis for performance, a model suggests how an improvisation should proceed. Nettl recognizes this purpose when he notes that highly regarded compositions often function as models (1974, 12). However, he also points out that models may be theoretical entities such as a raga or a dastgah (11). The key factor linking these rather disparate kinds of models is time: they each serve in some way as a guide for the temporal unfolding of a performance (12).

---

[7] One apparent exception would be "free jazz." Even in this style, however, patterns and formulae known by the musician surely inform the result (although subverting this tendency is presumably a goal of most free-jazz performances).

[8] *Grove Music* ("Iran") notes that "Persian classical music is represented by a corpus of amorphous pieces that are subject to extemporized renditions." See also Nettl (1992).

[9] Noting its origin in linguistics, the *Oxford English Dictionary* defines *referent* as "the thing that a word or phrase denotes or stands for."

[10] Slawek (1998). Such a usage does not particularly emphasize the preexistent per se.

Used as a musical term, "building blocks" refers simply to constructive elements. It does not necessarily imply that these elements precede the performance or that they have independent musical identities; a building block could be something as neutral as a short scalar pattern, for instance. "Module" or "modular elements," as they appear in Butler (2006), have very similar senses, although they place greater emphasis on interchangeability. "Readymade," by contrast, clearly denotes something preexisting; its history within the visual arts evokes the found objects that appear in styles such as collage. By analogy, musical readymades can be understood as "objects" subject to appropriation within performance. At the same time, the past participle ("made") suggests that the object itself is closed; there is less emphasis on its transformative potential. Sawyer, in accordance with these implications, uses the term to describe chunks of material that cannot be changed. He cites Javanese *gamelan*, Rotinese parallel oratory, and Slavic epic poetry as contexts in which such entities might appear.[11]

One particular aspect in which these terms vary significantly is the extent to which they denote a specific musical entity. A readymade, though not necessarily complete in itself, is certainly clearly defined. A model could be a particular composition or a relatively abstract theoretical entity. Templates and building blocks seem to suggest formal elements and guidelines, while referent as Pressing uses it describes both a mental construct ("a set of cognitive, perceptual, or emotional structures") and a musical thing ("in jazz," he writes, "the referent is the song form, including melody and chords" [Pressing 1998, 52]). Within recent scholarship on improvisation, two streams of emphasis begin to emerge: one stressing referents and the like as external musical entities that precede a performance, the other framing them more as internal guiding conceptualizations of musical structure and form.

I will describe the musical constructs on which improvisational performances are based as *preexistent elements* (PEs). This term is broad enough to be applied flexibly and to address a wide variety of phenomena, although it emphasizes the first of the two streams described above. In part this strategy reflects the greater prominence and recurrence of preexistent elements as a theme within scholarly accounts of improvisation as a whole; however, it is also a response to the particular tendencies of

---

[11] Sawyer (1996, 285). He opposes these genres to jazz and Indian classical music, which he describes as being "without ready-mades" at the level of genre, allowing the performer to "make an innovative decision at virtually every note" (ibid.). Although problematic in its modernist valorization of "innovation" and change over repetition, this opposition can be understood in the context of a distinct stream of scholarly discourse that downplays the creative significance of "formula"-based improvisation. Music-theoretical literature on jazz, for instance, configures this distinction in a particular way, arguing that performers improvise on the underlying structure of compositions rather than stringing together formulae on the musical "surface." See especially Martin's notion of "thematic improvisation" in the music of Charlie Parker (Martin 1996).

EDM performance, in which tensions between musical "things" and improvisational indeterminacy are particularly stark. At the same time, the term does not preclude the validity of the other stream of emphasis.

It is important to note that the presence of these two senses does not only constitute evidence of differences in scholarly opinions or across various music cultures. Above and beyond those factors, the divergence is a sign of fundamental tensions in how preexistent elements operate. On the one hand, it is clear that PEs do not become objects of improvisation without internalization by musicians, a process that opens them up to transformation. For instance, jazz musicians are often said to improvise on the "melody and chords" of a standard tune, but it is clearly their *structural understanding* of that tune and its harmonies, distributed in time in a particular way, that forms the basis of what they play.[12] At the same time, there is a clear drive to ontologize within accounts of improvisational practice. This tendency is most obvious in descriptions of the musical entities that inform improvisations; model compositions, ragas, fugue subjects, and dastgahs all have musical identity. The presence of "exist" within the term *preexistent elements* also highlights the role of ontology in conceptualizing these constructs. But ontic qualities also manifest themselves in structurally and cognitively oriented accounts. The formation of a structural understanding is an ontological act of cognition. To determine "structure" is to locate essence; what is structural is also essential.[13]

Any ontological weight that a preexistent element has, however, is conferred rather than immanent. This is true in spite of the fact that PEs may also be structural in a literal sense; that is, they may have material manifestations (such as scores or vinyl records). Hence the relationship between PEs and improvisation can be understood through the analytical framework of work/text/performance introduced in Chapter 1. In this regard PEs form a crucial site of intersection between ontology and processes of inscription, a zone that musicians negotiate physically, cognitively, and socially. When a jazz musician improvises on a "structural understanding" of a "song," that understanding is refracted through the notated versions of the song that the musician has encountered and recordings she has heard, the ways in which she has practiced and performed the song in the past, other renditions of the song she has heard, and beliefs and assertions about this piece of music.

Finally, it is important to distinguish preexistent elements from "structural" or "cognitive" elements of music in a broader sense. Although PEs, like many aspects of musical design and their cognitive representations, can be embedded hierarchically

---

[12] Larson (1987, 1999) makes this point especially clearly.

[13] To wit, treatments of these terms as equivalent are extremely common in musical analyses; theorists often mix terms such as "the structural soprano" and "the essential melody" quite freely.

so as to function on multiple levels, they are more than just style guidelines or mental grammar rules. More specifically, they cannot be atemporal; they always have implications as to how a performance should or can unfold. A raga, for instance, is not simply a scale; it also has associations with a particular season and time of day, performance style, melodic patterning, and—crucially—how a performance should develop. These temporal ramifications help counterbalance the contingence and diachronicity of improvised performance; by making it possible to know some elements of large-scale design at the outset, they enable musicians to plan synoptically rather than simply following a thread through a labyrinth.[14]

When preexistent elements function in this way, they also serve as *constraints*. I previously addressed constraints in Chapter 2, situating them with respect to liveness and interface design. The limitation or specification of certain parameters is a fundamental aspect of improvisation as well. In relation to technology, the same constraints that facilitate direct control and the clear communication of liveness also enable improvisational fluency. In addition, improvisational constraints have specifically musical ramifications. Commonsense understandings of preexistent elements as constraints find expression in descriptions of improvisations as "on" or "over" an element such as a figured bass or chord progression, or "against" the limitations of a particular tune. Pressing (1998) in particular discusses this aspect of PEs in depth. As previously quoted, he defines the referent as "a set of cognitive, perceptual, or emotional structures (constraints) that guide and aid in the production of musical materials" (52). He further elaborates five specific ways in which referents promote fluid performance: they furnish material for embellishment, allowing the performer to devote less "processing capacity" to selecting and creating materials; they can be analyzed pre-performance; particular variations or manipulations of them can be rehearsed pre-performance; in group situations, they function as a coordinating factor because they are shared; and they act as in-time structuring devices. The effect of these functions, he notes, is to "free up more processing resources for perception, control, and interplayer interaction, increasing the chances of reaching a higher artistic level" (ibid.).

Perhaps the most obvious and global constraint of improvised musical creativity is the requirement that it proceed inexorably forward through time. Improviser and composer Steve Lacy, quoted by Borgo, highlights this limitation: "In fifteen seconds, the difference between composition and improvisation is that in composition you have all the time you want to decide what to say in fifteen seconds, while in improvisation you have fifteen seconds" (Borgo 2005, 124). At first glance it seems

---

[14] With regard to improvisation research more generally, the fact that some aspects of large-scale design *are* known or determined prior to performance in many musical traditions is an important corrective to potential overemphasis on contingence.

remarkable that a general condition of performance should begin to appear as a restriction particular to improvisation. The emergence of this effect, however, is one consequence of the increasing mediation of musical performance, and especially of the way in which recordings and their associated technologies seem to interrupt the flow of time.

It should also be noted that the phenomenon of improvisational constraints can be construed both negatively and positively. References to limitations, restrictions, and the like emphasize what something is not (or cannot be), while the concept of affordance (addressed in Chapter 2) draws attention to the ways in which an outcome or practice is *specified*. The latter sense nevertheless clearly pertains to a sense of productive constraint.

Moreover, the dualities at work here—restriction and productivity, limitations and freedom—reveal the meaningful terms of an axis of significance. Issues of control form a distinct stream within discourse on improvisation among scholars and musicians alike. Time and again, performers describe an ideal state in which agency and intentionality begin to disappear. Berliner highlights this tendency, noting a tension between "musical actions calling for a passive performance posture and others calling for precise artistic control" (Berliner 1994, 219). One musician whom he interviewed evocatively explained that "there is such a thing as letting the music take you, if you are willing, or if you are open enough" (ibid.).

An important aspect of such statements is the link they establish between control and subjectivity. In order to improvise successfully, musicians often seek to release their agency—in other words, to lose themselves. Decisions and the actions they entail become intuitive and immediate rather than conscious and considered. In the ideal performance environment, notes Robert Henke, "you don't need to think; you just do."

Composition, Improvisation, and Performance in DJ and Laptop Sets

> A live mix is a little like cooking. Little elements to put in the mix, you know? . . .
> What I'm doing is I'm putting some things in the pot, and then this is the live mix. And then it's
> not really possible to recreate exactly the same thing at home.
> —PACOU, interview with the author, July 20, 2006

In comparing live performance to cooking, Pacou suggests that certain elements—the ingredients—precede the performance itself. Through the process of mixing, they enter into novel and special relationships with each other, resulting in a unique, larger entity. What sorts of ingredients constitute EDM performances, and what do they become? To what extent does a "recipe," or predetermined plan, guide the performance? Which elements are composed beforehand, and how and to what extent do these elements change within performance? What kinds of "texts" are used, and how do their potentialities play out within a set? In this section I address these questions through two sets of detailed analyses, one focusing on the work of laptop duo Sender Berlin and the other on that of Detroit techno DJ Jeff Mills. I situate each of the performances that I analyze within a network of creative events, discussing it in relation to other sets by the same musician(s) and to particular compositions within it.

First, however, I wish to explore the prehistory of these kinds of performance by briefly addressing some of the improvisational ways in which the composition or "production" of EDM originates. For most electronic dance musicians, the production of recordings in the studio and real-time performance share many approaches and activities. In particular, "production," the word that musicians typically use to denote the process of creating and recording a track, often involves considerable improvisation. Musicians frequently begin or develop compositions by setting in motion a pattern such as a loop or sequence, allowing it to repeat indefinitely, and improvising in relation to it while recording the results. In the words of Robert Henke, "something is going on, and if the result is pleasing, I capture it." This approach creates a continuous flow of sound, unfolding in repetitive cycles, that mirrors that of performance. Indeed, some musicians compare this process explicitly to performance; Pacou, for instance, noted that he starts with a drum loop and then adds complementary patterns, as if he were mixing sounds in a DJ set. He records in short bursts of up to thirty minutes and then edits his material, choosing what he wants to keep and making appropriate adjustments.

Electronic dance musicians often refer to improvising while recording as "jamming." Henrik Schwarz, for instance, described the process that led to the passage shown in video example 1.7 ◉ as the result of jamming on stage, while Apparat explained that the reduced track that forms the basis of video example 1.6 ◉ was the result of a "jam session" in the studio. (Both passages were discussed from an ontological standpoint in Chapter 1 under the heading "Reduced Tracks.") Within popular music and jazz more generally, "jamming" is an interesting insider concept, one that refers to a particular subset of improvisational activities. In an EDM context, it specifically describes music making that occurs freely and continuously (i.e., without revision), against or "above" certain technological and musical constraints. When one is jamming, the tape (or other recording device) is rolling, and the music is repeating in constant, potentially endless loop-based cycles. One cannot revise: it either works or it doesn't. Musicians experience the predictable presence of the constraints—in combination with the fact that "jams" usually have lower expectations of perfection than performance or composition more generally—as a source of freedom. In EDM "jamming" suggests informality, a connotation that it shares with other styles. It does *not*, however, refer to group improvisation, as it does in jazz and many rock contexts.[15] In EDM, one jams "with" the performance interfaces, and with ever-present recorded sound.

Within production, a sequence of free playing followed by a refining phase is characteristic, although musicians vary in terms of how early they begin to edit. Arrangement, the stage in which they define the formal layout of a track, typically occurs later in the process; most musicians regard it as more analytical and less intuitive. Apparat, for instance, explained that he finds arrangement more challenging, as he prefers a loop-based, improvisational approach to generating material. Recognizing the need for formal clarity, however, he strikes a balance between these competing factors: "For me it turned out to be the better idea to start arranging as early as possible, but I'm still the one who starts with the loop. I mean, you have to have the idea of the song before you can start arranging it. But as soon as I have the idea I force myself with the arrangement." Sender Berlin also begin with loops (and, like Pacou, with drum loops in particular). In their case, however, improvisation continues during the arrangement process. After writing an amount of material that they consider sufficient for an interesting track, they set their patterns in motion; as the loops repeat, they bring them in and out of the texture and apply effects, recording all the while. They subsequently save and refine the results that they find pleasing.

Occasionally, material recorded in a single take while playing around or jamming in the studio makes it into a set without further editing. More common, however, is another kind of interplay between performance and production, in which musicians incorporate newly developed material into their live sets before it has been substantially edited or arranged. They do so in order to "test" it before a live audience— partly in order to see what sort of response it generates, and partly to hear how it sounds in a club environment. This approach is obviously particular to laptop

---

[15] For discussion of jam sessions in jazz, see Berliner (1994, 192). Although discourse on jamming in rock and jazz seems to emphasize group improvisation and informality as its defining features, it should be noted that a continuity related to that mentioned above is also implied: a situation, the "jam," is ongoing, and participants are invited to join in. Another dimension of jamming has a specifically African American connotation of intertextual reference: to "jam on" something is a way of "signifyin(g)" on its meanings, in the sense most famously defined by Henry Louis Gates, Jr. (1988). I thank Ives Chor, John Covach, Walter Everett, and Chris McDonald for their contributions to a discussion on the meanings of "jamming" that I initiated on the "Pop Analysis" listserv.

performance (rather than the DJ set), since its musical constituents do not have to be encoded in material form prior to performance.[16]

Many EDM musicians incorporate equipment designed for studio recording, such as drum machines and synthesizers, into their performances. As a result, a curious tension between "playing" and "programming" can emerge. Musicians such as Pacou, who favors a highly extemporized approach and vintage devices such as the Roland TR-909 drum machine, often avoid programming their drum machines and synths prior to a performance; instead, they prefer to manipulate them on the spot during their sets. DJs occasionally make use of these devices as well (although this is rare); when Jeff Mills performed at the Detroit Electronic Music Festival in May 2007, and again at the Tresor club in Berlin in October 2007, he played a TR-909 during certain segments of his sets. At these moments he was not simply supplementing a recorded track, but rather creating an entirely new fabric of sound using only the drum machine.[17] Musicians' choices in such contexts are completely improvised, involving no prior planning. Although they view their actions on the drum machines and keyboards as "playing" their equipment, from a technical point of view what they are doing is very similar to how they would "program" these machines in the studio. In this way an essentially compositional action ("programming") becomes suffused with the qualities of an improvisational, performative behavior ("playing").

Although extemporaneous musical performance is not necessarily characterized as "improvisation" within some musical cultures, electronic dance musicians do think of their actions in this way. They frequently use the term *improvisation* and its cognates in descriptions of their performances and their compositional work. Moreover, their characterizations of improvisational performance tend to define it as against something else. Pacou, for instance, described his own approach in contrast to another musician whom we had both seen perform in Berlin shortly before our 2006 interview. That musician told me, shortly before he played, that he preferred to have a track list established beforehand, because he wanted to know where the set was going and didn't want to make a mistake. During his performance, I spoke to

---

[16] It is possible that "testing" of this sort is becoming a part of some DJ sets, however: I have increasingly noticed certain producer-performers using a CD turntable to play some of their unreleased tracks, though none have suggested to me that they do so in order to evaluate the viability of a track or that they return to work on it further after playing it in this way. (Also note that when they so employ a CD, they see it as a supplement to the standard analog turntables and vinyl records rather than as a replacement for them.) A historical precedent for this practice is the use of "white label" records, which record companies furnish to DJs in advance of full-scale production in order to get a sense of how well they will play to audiences.

[17] Mills' use of the TR-909 should also be understood as harkening back to the early days of electronic dance music—and not simply to the fact that these machines were used to produce the music. Historical accounts of the rise of house and techno DJing frequently mention certain performers (such as Frankie Knuckles at the Warehouse in Chicago) incorporating Roland's analog drum machines into their sets. See, for instance, Brewster and Broughton (2000, 307).

Pacou, who asked me, rhetorically, "What's live about what he's doing?" During our interview, he made this specific comparison again:

> Every time, every live act will sound different. That's the thing: for me it's very important to have a degree of improvisation on the stage. I don't want to have this thing like [*name deleted*] the other night, everything preplanned to the last beat and the last little ... I don't want to have that kind of thing. I prefer to have it hands-on, and, you know, being able to change it around.

In this quotation, Pacou contrasts improvisation with pre-planning. The suggestion is that making decisions during the performance imbues it with an essential liveness that is missing from overly pre-planned sets. Note, however, that Pacou does not oppose improvisation and composition. In this regard his perspective is similar to that of many other electronic musicians. In the sections that follow, I open analytical windows into the interplay of these two activities through examination of specific performances and the tracks that form them.

Analysis 1: "The original track, it's every time in the back of the mind" (Sender Berlin, Live Performances, 2006 and 2007)

In 1995, Hendrik Vaak, Torsten "Stassy" Litschko, and Alexander Lukat formed the group Sender Berlin, choosing their name from the transmitters that had brought West Berlin radio to the divided city. They came to prominence at Tresor, the most famous techno club of the post-Wall era, where they were frequent performers at the weekly "Headquarters" events for lesser-known but promising artists. They released their first album, *Spektrum Weltweit*, on Tresor's label in 1999; it was followed by *Gestern, Heute, Morgen* (Tresor Records 189) in 2002 and *Unequal Arts* (unGleich Records 19) in 2005. They have also released several twelve-inch recordings during their career, and they established their own label, unGleich Records, in 1999.

Vaak and Litschko are the primary members of Sender Berlin; they compose all of the group's recorded material. Lukat serves in an auxiliary role, as a DJ who "warms up" the crowd prior to Vaak and Litschko's live PAs.[18] At present, their performances involve a laptop computer, the program Live, and several additional pieces of hardware. On the whole, they use an amount of technology that ranges from moderate to high, with a fondness (similar to Pacou, another former Headquarters artist with whom they have collaborated) for "classic," vintage instruments.

---

[18] In fact, since meeting Sender Berlin in 2005, I have not seen Lukat perform with them at all. In the analyses that follow, therefore, I will use "Sender Berlin" to refer to the recorded compositions and performances of Vaak and Litschko. In addition, only Vaak and Litschko participated in interviews.

FIGURE 3.1 Korg MikroKONTROL MIDI controller 🖳

I have filmed two of Sender Berlin's performances, at Maria in Berlin on July 15, 2006, and at Tresor in Berlin on December 14, 2007. Each employed the same basic setup, with only small differences; the description that follows is based on the earlier event at Maria.

In the center of the performance table, closest to the musicians, is a Korg Mikro-KONTROL (Fig. 3.1). This device is a MIDI controller, comparable to those described in Chapter 2 (see esp. Figs. 2.2–2.4). Note that the MikroKONTROL is *not* a synthesizer; rather, its keyboard functions solely as a control organ, along with touchpads, sliders, knobs, and a joystick.

To the right of the MikroKONTROL (viewed from the perspective of the musicians as they face the audience) is a Pioneer EFX-500 (Fig. 3.2). The left half of the EFX-500 enables effects such as delay and echo, assignable in various rhythmic increments and across different frequency bands, while the right side uses a continuous, rotary interface (similar to that of a turntable, though smaller) to control ring modulation and other transformations. Above the MikroKONTROL is a DJ mixing board, which is provided by the club in which they are performing. To the right of the mixing board is a Roland TR-909, a classic analog drum machine.[19]

---

[19] Sender Berlin did not use the 909 in the December 2007 performance, but their setup was otherwise as described above. Further detail on the 909 and its sibling, the TR-808, is available in Butler (2006, 64–65).

FIGURE 3.2 Pioneer EFX-500 effects unit (photo courtesy of Pioneer Electronics [USA] Inc.)

The final device, to the left of the laptop, is a Korg MS-20, an analog synthesizer manufactured between 1978 and 1983 (Fig. 3.3). At the time of its creation, the MS-20 was comparable to the MiniMoog, in that portability was one of its chief assets; it featured both patch-cord (modular) and hard-wired (internal) synthesis pathways. In the present day the MS-20 belongs to a larger technological network in which Sender Berlin participate. In their home studio they use a "virtual" MS-20—a replica of the sound and appearance of the original, but in a digital version that appears on their computer. Such "virtual synths" are not uncommon; in an unusual twist, however, Korg has also produced a modern MS-20 hardware controller, identical to the original in appearance (including patch cords), for use with the software. Part of a line called the "Legacy Collection," this new MS-20 is *not* a synthesizer, but rather an 84 percent scale physical replica of the original. For Sender, the original device is preferable in performance, while the modern update is better suited for recording.

A distinctive and interesting feature of Sender Berlin's approach is its collaborative nature. In recent years, research on improvisation has placed increasing emphasis

FIGURE 3.3 Korg MS-20 🎧

on group interaction,[20] sometimes to the point that it is portrayed as a defining quality of improvisational practice. This newfound prominence represents a corrective
shift or reaction to the priorities of earlier work in the area, which tended to foreground the virtues of exceptional soloists while neglecting the significant inter-
changes occurring between musicians. It is important to note, however, that the
degree to which interaction is present and the ways in which it occurs are specific to
the style in question.[21]

On the whole, electronic dance music falls somewhere in the middle of the inter-
actional spectrum. Most EDM producers and performers work individually. During
the recording process, producers write and record music by themselves (usually in
home studios), with audio engineers and other figures becoming involved only
during the final stages, after the compositions are effectively complete.[22] Performances, including both DJ and laptop sets, are typically solo as well.[23]

This is not to say, however, that interaction is not an important part of EDM practice. In performance it occurs primarily between the audience and the musician, in
ways that determine both musical and affective outcomes.[24] Even during solitary
composition, moreover, the external nature of the technologies involved often leads

[20] Monson (1996) and Sawyer (2003) are among the foremost sources in this regard.

[21] Consider, for instance, the long tradition of solo improvisation within classical organ performance. Not only
does the musician not seek or respond to feedback from other people in this context, she or he typically does
not even face the audience and is often removed from their line of sight. One could hardly imagine a less "interactive" manner of performance.

[22] Generally speaking, musicians seek external assistance only for technical processes such as mastering and record
pressing. Moreover, some producers (such as Pole) do their own mastering as well.

[23] One exception is the occasional "tag-team" DJ set, in which two DJs alternate on separate turntables.

[24] I discuss this interaction with respect to liveness in Chapter 2.

musicians to think of their interaction with technology as a kind of collaboration. This perspective emerged, for instance, in a 2005 interview with Mijk van Dijk. For van Dijk, collaboration can involve direct engagement with other musicians as well as solitary interaction with machines, and the two possibilities are equally viable:

> MARK BUTLER: So in general it seems like you're saying that whether you're working by yourself or with someone else, the basic thing is, you start with one sort of idea…
>
> MIJK VAN DIJK: Yeah.
>
> MB: And there's some kind of response to that idea.
>
> MVD: Response by other people, or by myself, jamming with that idea.
>
> MB: OK.
>
> MVD: And searching…Sometimes the idea is very clear, and I know exactly where I want to go, what kind of atmosphere I want. Sometimes I just have this fascinating beat, or bass line, and I'm wondering, "So how could this sound?" And you leave this going on, and you try…I call it "asking my friends"—which are the synths.

Vaak and Litschko, however, collaborate more obviously and traditionally as well: they always compose and perform as a team. In their live sets they distribute technological responsibilities in consistent ways: Vaak controls the laptop and the MS-20, Litschko controls the effects unit and the 909, and the two share the mixing board and MIDI controller more or less equally. They also consistently said that Litschko is responsible for "rhythms" in performance, whereas Vaak controls "sounds"; by this they mean that Litschko has primary control over percussion sounds, while Vaak deals with synths, bass lines, and other elements in which pitch is a principal feature. Litschko is also the main generator of effects, although Vaak often provides verbal input to him about them. For instance, at several points in the performances I observed, Vaak leaned over and spoke to Litschko in order to suggest (as he later explained) that a particular sound could use more effects. Because Vaak selects and deploys loops within Live (thereby controlling "sounds" in another sense), he is effectively the leader of the performance. In general, however, the two share control as much as possible, and Litschko occasionally makes small changes on Vaak's equipment.[25]

---

[25] With regard to the balance of control, it is also worth noting that any change to the sliders on the mixing board and the MikroKONTROL—which both performers manipulate—can affect the fundamental criterion of whether a sound is present or absent in the mix (as well as its overall volume). More precisely, the MIDI controller (the MikroKONTROL) governs elements on the computer in Live, while sliders on the mixing board control the output of the various audio channels.

27:57	01. Litschko releases jog dial
	05. Litschko removes left hand (LH) from vertical fader of mixer
	23. Vaak places right hand (RH) on MikroKONTROL
	25. Litschko places RH on EFX-500 knobs
27:59	29. Vaak places RH on vertical fader
28:02	20. Vaak's RH is visible on mouse. (Was probably placed there earlier, but view was obstructed.)
28:05	05. Litschko removes RH from EFX-500 knobs
	11. Litschko places RH on EFX-500 jog dial
28:06	06. Litschko places LH on MikroKONTROL. (Vaak also briefly speaks to Litschko.)
28:07	10. Litschko places LH on mixer
	16. Vaak places LH on vertical fader; moves up and down
28:11	17. Vaak releases LH from vertical fader
	20. Litschko releases LH from mixer
	25. Vaak's RH becomes visible on MikroKONTROL
28:13	06. Vaak places RH on vertical fader; moves up and down
28:14	19. Litschko places LH on mixer EQs
	22. Vaak removes RH from vertical fader
28:15	04. Litschko removes LH from mixer EQs
	17. Litschko returns LH to mixer EQs; continues to remove/return
28:16	12. Vaak places RH on vertical fader; moves up and down
28:18	25. Vaak removes RH from vertical fader; Litschko removes LH from mixer EQs
28:19	17. Litschko moves RH from jog dial to knobs of EFX-500
28:20	13. Litschko places LH on EFX-500 knobs
	17. Vaak places RH on vertical fader; moves up and down. (This continues through 22:16.)
28:21	05 and 26. Litschko removes LH from EFX-500 knobs
28:22	27. Litschko removes LH from EFX-500 knobs, final time
28:23	04. Vaak continues manipulating vertical fader, but with LH
	09. Vaak places RH on MikroKONTROL
	22. Litschko places LH on jog dial
28:25	29. Vaak removes LH from vertical faders; Litschko removes LH from jog dial
28:26	22. Litschko LH reaches for mixer but pulls hand back
28:27	28. Litschko removes RH from EFX-500 knobs
28:28	21. Litschko places RH on 909 knobs
	26. Vaak places RH on mixer
	30. Litschko begins to place LH on 909 also (continues adding and removing)
28:36	29. Litschko removes LH from 909 for last time
28:37	12. Vaak removes RH from mixer
28:38	04. Litschko places LH on MikroKONTROL
	10. Vaak places LH on vertical fader
	23. Litschko removes RH from 909
28:39	11. Litschko places RH on mixer, lower knob
28:40	14. Litschko removes LH from MikroKONTROL and RH from mixer; Vaak removes LH from vertical fader. Vaak's RH now visible on mouse

FIGURE 3.4 Action list, Sender Berlin at Maria, Berlin, July 15, 2006, 27:57–29:11

Note: Timings are given in minutes, seconds, and frames, at a rate of thirty frames per second. All timings are based on the author's digital video recording.

28:41	05. Vaak removes RH from mouse
	28. Litschko places LH on MikroKONTROL
28:42	02. Litschko places RH on MikroKONTROL
28:43	13. Vaak places RH on vertical fader; moves up and down
28:44	28. Litschko removes LH from MikroKONTROL
28:46	01. Vaak places RH on MikroKONTROL
	13. Litschko removes RH from MikroKONTROL
	28. Litschko places RH on 909
28:47	24. Vaak removes RH from MikroKONTROL
28:48	14. Vaak places LH on MikroKONTROL
28:49	07. Litschko places LH on MikroKONTROL
28:50	12. Vaak places RH on mouse; Litschko removes LH from MikroKONTROL
28:51	09. Litschko places LH on mixer EQs
28:52	05. Litschko removes RH from 909
	23. Litschko places RH on jog dial
28:53	09. Litschko removes RH from jog dial
	23. Litschko places RH on vertical fader; moves up and down
29:01	00. Vaak removes RH from mouse
	11. Vaak places RH on a vertical fader; moves up and down. (Litschko's RH remains on a different vertical fader but does not move at this time.)
29:02	22. Vaak places RH on mouse
29:06	29. Vaak removes RH from mouse
29:07	11. Vaak briefly reaches for vertical fader with RH; Litschko pushes other vertical fader down
	26. Vaak returns RH to mouse
29:08	25. Vaak removes RH from mouse
29:09	07. Vaak places RH on vertical fader; pushes up as Litschko pushes down
	13. Vaak removes RH from vertical fader
29:10	09. Vaak removes LH from MikroKONTROL; Litschko removes LH from mixer EQs
	16. Litschko removes RH from vertical fader
29:11	07. Litschko places RH on 909
	28. Litschko places LH on 909

FIGURE 3.4 (*Continued*)

Video example 2.5 gives an excellent demonstration of the complexity and precise coordination entailed in Vaak and Litschko's performance interactions. 🎧 In Chapter 2, I noted how the intricacy of their movements helped imbue the performance with an aura of liveness; here, I present a detailed account of their specific actions. Within the seventy-four seconds shown in the excerpt, Vaak and Litschko manipulate their interfaces almost constantly, sometimes at a rate of several actions per second. When the example begins, at 27:57 into the performance, Litschko's left hand is on one of the mixing board's vertical faders, while his right-hand thumb is turning the jog dial of the EFX-500. Vaak's hands are momentarily free; he has just finished making several adjustments to another vertical fader. Figure 3.4 lists the ensuing actions in as complete a form as possible.

FIGURE 3.5   Sender Berlin at Maria, Berlin, July 15, 2006, 29:09, frame 7

Several moments stand out in particular. At 28:11, both musicians remove their hands from the mixing board with near split-second coordination; this is the first of several successive moments of release.[26] The next, at 28:18, is visually clear but sonically neutral. At 28:25, however, the performers' actions create the most intense musical effect thus far: Litschko lets go of the jog dial, Vaak releases a vertical fader at the same exact moment, and a new snare-drum pattern enters the texture.[27] Finally, at 28:40, the pattern peaks, as three hands are lifted into the air: Litschko's left from the MikroKONTROL, his right from a knob on the mixer, and Vaak's left from a vertical fader. From here, the musicians' physical gestures—and specifically their arms—become increasingly intertwined. At 29:09, frame 7, for instance, Litschko's right hand is on one of the mixer's vertical faders, while his left hand reaches over it to adjust the EQs. Both of his hands, meanwhile, are above those of Vaak, who also has his arms crossed: his right hand reaching under his left arm (his left hand has remained on the MikroKONTROL since 28:48) to push a *different* vertical fader up while Litschko pushes his down. In addition to the video example, Figure 3.5 shows this moment as a still frame.

---

[26] In this and the next two video examples, timing captions in the bottom right corner mark the moments referenced in my analysis.

[27] The spacing of these changes in seven-second increments is not coincidental; this duration corresponds to the four-bar level, which these actions reinforce and clarify.

Two brief additional passages offer further insight into the musical and communicative processes at work in Vaak and Litschko's performance interactions. At 32:02, near the end of the track heard in video example 2.5, Litschko can be seen releasing the jog dial, clearing the texture of an effect that he has allowed to build up (see the beginning of video example 3.1 ●). During the next thirty seconds, the two musicians gradually remove sounds from the texture, creating a breakdown. The audience appreciates the change and participates: at 32:15 a fan can be heard whistling along with the beat, and a few seconds later synchronized clapping begins. Near the end of this thirty-second passage, Litschko increases the effects once more, creating a crescendo that leads into an abrupt switch to a new track. Subsequently Vaak focuses his energy on channel 4 of the mixing board, pushing it repeatedly up and down. At 32:48 his timing coordinates with the snare-drum rhythm; this synchronization is evident with close attention. When I asked about this passage, he explained that channel 4 controls the volume of effects within the mix; during this passage, Litschko is manipulating the snare sound with effects, which Vaak is making audible at precisely those moments when the snare makes an attack. In video example 3.2 (37:50–38:47), the musicians continue to coordinate effects, but their cueing processes are more apparent. ● Near the beginning of the excerpt, Vaak speaks to Litschko. Then, at 38:34 he taps the slider for channel 4 in a relatively unobtrusive way, and Litschko pushes it up shortly thereafter. The audience expresses their appreciation throughout the passage.

When watching Sender Berlin perform, moments in which cueing is visually evident are rare. Time and again they seem to turn knobs, push sliders, and introduce new tracks in unison with no apparent premeditation. When I asked them how they were able to coordinate their actions so precisely, they emphasized the many years they have been playing together. However, they also portrayed the recorded track—which they themselves had composed—as a framing structure that enabled them to make these decisions spontaneously in real time. During our 2005 interview, Vaak explained how compositions and the compositional process relate to their performances, explaining that "from the making of the song, you know also the arrangement in the head: [*verbalizing the thought process he is describing*] 'OK: we play this sound, this sound, this sound; then we make the break.'" One year later, he elaborated this theme, while emphasizing the differences that arise within performance: "We never try to reproduce [the arrangement], but we know the track; we know the original.... The original track, it's every time in the back of the mind."

Although Sender Berlin's interaction with one another is most evident on the stage, it begins in the recording studio.[28] Their compositional approach is also pervasively collaborative. Vaak and Litschko usually write tracks together, although occasionally

---

[28] Throughout most of their career, it took place in their home as well: Vaak and Litschko shared an apartment in the Friedrichshain district of Berlin until December 2007.

one of them begins a track by himself and then solicits input from the other about it. Their recordings evolve over considerable time spans: each album, they explained, has taken about three years from the initial stages to recorded realization. (They described this process evocatively as their "production rhythm.") During the first two years, approximately, they develop material in the studio. At first it takes the form of incomplete or unfinished "sketches," which they often test by incorporating them into live performances. This allows them to evaluate the crowd's response to the material and to see how well it matches other parts of the set. Depending on the success of the test, sketch material might be discarded, altered, or incorporated into a track as-is. In this approach, performance functions as an integral part of the compositional process. The two activities interrelate dynamically rather than simply proceeding in succession.

All of Sender Berlin's performances center around their own precomposed tracks. In the rest of this section I consider three of their performances, both in relation to the compositions that form their bases and as improvisations. The Maria set discussed above, which took place on the evening of July 15, 2006,[29] will receive the most attention. However, an audio recording of another performance from the same period, at Cabaret Renz in Vienna on March 17, 2006, will provide substantial material for comparison. Prior to the Maria performance I had interviewed Vaak and Litschko in their home studio in July 2005. After filming the set I analyzed it in detail, and in August 2006 I conducted another interview in which we watched parts of the video together and discussed the performance. Since then I have asked them about several further details of the performance over email and in person. I later filmed one more performance, on December 14, 2007, at the Tresor club in Berlin. It contrasts significantly with the 2006 sets but still reveals many common elements.

Maria was a large club featuring two dance spaces; it typically drew a young, party-oriented crowd.[30] Given the time of Sender's performance, the dance floor was reasonably occupied, but not full; about 150 people were present throughout most of the set. The performance was part of a huge conglomeration of events known informally as "Love Week."[31] The other performance venue described here, Tresor, has

---

[29] Properly speaking, this performance actually occurred at 8:00 A.M. on the morning of July 16. (It was originally scheduled for 6:00 A.M., but the club pushed the schedule back.) It was midsummer in Berlin, and the sun had been shining brightly for several hours by the time Sender began. For those present, however, it was still part of "Saturday night."

[30] Maria closed in 2011. The venue is currently the home of the club Magdalena, which also features electronic dance music.

[31] Originally developing in association with the techno festival known as the Love Parade, which brought huge numbers of electronic musicians to Berlin from around the world, Love Week soon became quite independent, taking place annually even during years in which the Love Parade did not occur in Berlin. The main event has since become a nonevent; after a hiatus of several years, it last occurred in Berlin in 2006. See http://en.wikipedia.org/wiki/Love_parade (accessed June 15, 2008) for a useful overview. The performance by Pacou

the longest history of any current EDM-oriented club in Berlin. During the 1990s it was one of the most important sites for the performance and dissemination of techno music in the world. It opened in 1991, a few months before German reunification, in the underground vaults of a former Wertheim department store near Potsdamer Platz.[32] During the Wall era Potsdamer Platz had been part of the no man's land along the border, but it subsequently became the site of massive commercial redevelopment. The city eventually sold the land on which Tresor was located, and the club closed in April 2005. (When I visited Berlin in 2005 and 2006, Maria was hosting a regular Wednesday-night event called "Tresor im Exil.") In 2007 Tresor reopened in a huge former industrial building in the eastern part of the Mitte district, and Sender Berlin performed there in December of that year. Their time slot, from approximately 2:00–3:00 a.m., preceded that of the legendary Detroit techno musician Juan Atkins, the headliner for the evening.

At the time of our 2005 interview, Sender Berlin were wrapping up the recording of their third album, *Unequal Arts*, which was released later that year. By the time of the Maria performance they had been playing a live set based largely on the album for approximately six months. Because of this, they explained, the set had congealed to a certain extent, particularly with regard to track selection. Figures 3.6 and 3.7, which show the tracks played in each set along with their beginning and ending times and total durations, reveals that the summer 2006 performances in Vienna and Berlin involved an almost identical track list.[33] In contrast to the standard practice for DJ performances, therefore—and for the majority of laptop sets as well—track selection was not improvised in these two sets.[34] Figure 3.8 shows the source of each track played, which in the majority of cases is the album *Unequal Arts*. Figure 3.9, the fourth example given on the following pages, will be discussed shortly.

Two factors are especially pertinent here. First, for Sender Berlin, the "live set" itself—and not only each track within it—carries ontological weight. Over time it

---

described in Chapter 1 took place earlier on the same evening as the Sender set described here; it occurred in the club S036 and was on schedule, from 2:00–3:00 A.M.

[32] "Tresor" means "safe" or "vault" in German.

[33] I derived the track listings and timings of Figures 3.6 and 3.7 through extended close analysis and by familiarizing myself with all of Sender's recorded output. As with any other laptop set, a casual observer of one of these performances would have simply witnessed the musicians playing continuously for about an hour; track names were not announced and there were no breaks between tracks.

[34] Henrik Schwarz's approach to track selection illustrates the opposite end of the spectrum among laptop performers. In fall 2007 I observed him perform twice during the same week: on September 20 at Club 103 and on September 23 at Bierhof Rüdersdorf (on the grounds of the larger club Berghain). The two performances were very different, in terms of the order of tracks and the actual tracks played. (They also differed entirely from the June 2006 performance by Schwarz at Mutek in Montreal.) Of the two, Schwarz preferred the Rüdersdorf evening, noting "it was really great to play as there was a lot of positive energy there already when I was starting—so that's always a good start to play very open and do a lot of improvisation."

Track name	Begin time	End time	Duration	Cut or mixed into next track?
1. "Bon Voyage"	0:00	4:14	4:14	Mixed
2. "Theory's Dead"	3:41	9:50	6:08	Cut
3. "Unformatted"	9:50	17:04	7:14	Cut
4. "Brain Eater"	17:04	23:29	6:25	Mixed
5. "Dr. Sorge Is Watching the Planet"	22:29	28:31	6:02	Cut
6. "Griselda (Arenys del Mar Mix)"	28:31	35:58	7:27	Mixed
7. "Emotion Engine"	35:06	44:11	9:05	Cut
8. "Yellow Snowflakes"	44:11	50:55	6:44	Cut
9. "Zona de Curva"	50:55	1:02:14	11:19	Mixed
10. "Zona de Curva" (unreleased live version)	1:01:47	1:06:04	4:17	Mixed
11. "Back to Prime Time"	1:04:38	1:15:33	10:55	N/A

FIGURE 3.6 Track listing for Sender Berlin, Cabaret Renz, Vienna, March 17, 2006

Track name	Begin time	End time	Duration	Cut or mixed into next track?
1. "Bon Voyage"	0:50	3:27	2:37	Mixed
2. "Theory's Dead"	2:48	7:44	4:56	Mixed
3. "Unformatted"	6:57	11:47	4:50	Cut
4. "Brain Eater"	11:47	17:41	5:54	Mixed
5. "Dr. Sorge Is Watching the Planet"	16:11	21:13	5:02	Cut
6. "Griselda (Arenys del Mar Mix)"	21:13	27:57	6:44	Mixed
7. "Emotion Engine"	26:59	32:31	5:32	Cut
8. "Yellow Snowflakes"	32:31	37:20	4:49	Cut
9. "Zona de Curva"	37:20	46:14	8:54	Mixed
10. "Zona de Curva" (unreleased live version)	43:07	50:24	7:17	N/A

FIGURE 3.7 Track listing for Sender Berlin, Maria, Berlin, July 15, 2006

a. Track Listing for *Unequal Arts* (unGleich Records 19, November 2005)

Track name	Position in live sets	Begin time	Duration
1. "Bon Voyage"	1	0:00	2:55
2. "Zona de Curva"	9	2:55	6:05
3. "Emotion Engine"	7	9:00	4:54
4. "EE Minimized"	Not played	13:54	2:28
5. "Unformatted"	3	16:22	3:36
6. "Sender Berlin"	Not played	19:58	5:16
7. "Theory's Dead"	2	25:14	3:30
8. "International"	Not played	28:44	5:20
9. "Brain Eater"	4	34:00	5:16
10. "Griselda (Arenys del Mar Mix)"	6	39:16	5:07
11. "Back to Prime Time"	11	44:23	5:20
12. "We Have Time"	Not played	49:43	5:10

b. Other Sources

Track name	Position in live sets	Source	Duration
"Dr. Sorge Is Watching the Planet"	5	Album *Gestern, Heute, Morgen* (Tresor Records 189, 2002)	5:40
"Yellow Snowflakes"	8	12" Vinyl, *Yellow Snowflakes* (unGleich Records 15, 2004)	5:47
"Zona de Curva" (unreleased live version)	10	Private recording by Sender Berlin	Unknown

FIGURE 3.8 Source material for 2006 performances: (a) Track listing for *Unequal Arts* (unGleich Records 19, November 2005) (b) Other sources

Notes on *Fig.3.8a*: The tracks on this album are discrete; the album is not presented as a continuous stream of sound. Nevertheless, I have indicated when tracks begin in relation to the album as a whole, for the sake of easier comparison with the mixed sets.

Track 10 is a remix by Carl Past, a Vienna-based musician who also records on the unGleich label. The track has been released only as a remix.

comes to possess an increasingly stable identity, such that "the set" can be compared across performances. This stability maximizes in relation to each album release, so that the periods of strong compositional presence are also marked by greater consistency in performance. Second, even as they become increasingly determinate, each of Sender's "live sets" evolves principally through improvisational practices. The common

Track name	Begin time	End time	Duration	Cut or mixed into next track?
1. "Sender Berlin"	0:36	8:22	8:22	Mixed
2. "Unformatted"	6:49	13:31	6:42	Mixed
3. New track	13:00	16:45	3:45	Cut
4. New track	16:45	24:39	7:54	Cut
5. New track	24:39	31:11	6:32	Mixed
6. "Bon Voyage"	30:33	31:11	0:38	Cut
7. "Theory's Dead"	31:11	35:09	3:58	Cut
8. "Brain Eater"	35:09	36:40	1:31	Cut
9. "Dr. Sorge Is Watching the Planet"	36:40	40:25	3:45	Mixed
10. New track	40:18	47:09	6:51	Mixed
11. "Zona de Curva"	46:09	56:48	10:39	Mixed
12. "Zona de Curva" (unreleased live version)	51:59	55:47	3:48	Cut
13. "Yellow Snowflakes"	55:47	1:02:29	6:42	Cut
14. "Griselda (Arenys del Mar Mix)"	1:02:29	---	---	N/A

Note: Information regarding the exact duration of "Griselda" in this performance is not available; my videocassette ended at 1:02:38 and I was unable to film the few remaining minutes. Sender Berlin's performance did conclude with this track, however.

FIGURE 3.9 Track listing for Sender Berlin, Tresor, Berlin, December 7, 2007

elements of their performances emerge, they explained, through collective "jamming" together in their home studio. They also arise in relation to the process of experimenting with new material on stage, as described above. Whereas the two 2006 performances, close as they were to the release of an album, did not exhibit any works-in-progress, the 2007 set in Berlin—filmed approximately one and a half years later, and thus at a very different point in the production cycle—diverges significantly in this respect. As Figure 3.9 reveals, the Tresor performance featured four newly composed examples of "sketch material." In addition, Vaak and Litschko decided to begin the set with the appropriately titled "Sender Berlin," a number found on *Unequal Arts* but not played in the 2006 performances.[35] In other respects, the 2007 performance includes most of the tracks featured in the previous year's set (only

[35] When I first interviewed Sender Berlin in July 2005, they played this track for me in order to illustrate their compositional process. They had just finished recording it, and they said it was "too new" to have a name yet.

"Emotion Engine" and "Back to Prime Time" are omitted). The tracks are presented, moreover, in ways that feature the earlier "live set" as a distinct and identifiable construct: beginning at track 6 ("Bon Voyage"), four tracks from the 2006 set appear consecutively in their original order (although "Unformatted" is omitted, having been shifted to an earlier position). All four are much shorter than before, however; "Bon Voyage," for instance, lasts only thirty-eight seconds. The effect of this passage is similar in some respects to the "megamixes" of pop artists played in dance clubs featuring more mainstream music: the tracks are clearly meant to be recognized (and indeed, audience members cry out instantly when "Bon Voyage" and "Theory's Dead" begin), but in a way that briefly summarizes a body of work without dwelling on individual numbers. In other respects, there are many significant differences (several of which I discuss further below) in the realization of these older tracks. These alterations reveal a live set that both coalesces and transforms over long spans of time.

Within individual tracks, the most obvious area of difference across these performances is duration. Comparison of Figures 3.6 and 3.8 reveals that all of the tracks in the Cabaret Renz performance are longer than their first recorded versions.[36] Moreover, many are significantly so, with several durations around twice that of the original. In the 2006 Maria set (Fig. 3.7), only six of ten tracks are longer, and the differences between durations are generally smaller. Three tracks are actually shorter.[37] When the ten tracks that the 2006 sets share are compared (see Fig. 3.6 and 3.7), it becomes evident that seven of the Cabaret Renz tracks are longer, two are about the same, and one is significantly shorter. The shorter track (the unreleased mix of "Zona de Curva") closes the Maria performance, however, which is presumably why it is longer in this case. As a whole, the Cabaret Renz performance is about twenty-five minutes, or 50 percent, longer than its counterpart from Maria.

Following EDM conventions, each performance occurs as a continuous stream of sound, with no intervening silences between tracks. Transitions or connections from one track to the next therefore become key sites for intervention in performance. Sender connected tracks either with a sudden switch or by overlapping loops from the end of one track with the beginning of the next. The examples indicate these methods as either a "cut" or a "mix," respectively. In general, tracks are overlapped more often in the Maria set. In the Cabaret Renz performance, the overlapping is as follows (with connections indicated by dashes): 1–2, 3, 4–5, 6–7, 8, 9–10–11. In the Maria set, the pattern is 1–2–3, 4–5, 6–7, 8, 9–10. In sum, all the

---

[36] This measurement is not applicable to the unreleased version of "Zona de Curva," since it has no commercially available original version.

[37] These are "Bon Voyage," "Dr. Sorge Is Watching the Planet," and "Yellow Snowflakes." Note that two of these are non-album tracks.

tracks overlapped in the Cabaret Renz set are also overlapped in the Maria performance, and tracks 2 and 3 are connected as well. Track 8, which is not an album track, is freestanding in both cases.

Some of these differences were the result of factors specific to the performance context. Echoing other musicians whom I interviewed, Sender Berlin indicated that the variables of audience response and performance space played important roles in shaping an unfolding event. The acoustics of Maria, they explained, make it more difficult to hear subtle changes such as small adjustments to reverb or delay; as a result, they had to make bigger and more dramatic alterations in order for the audience to perceive a difference. In the course of our 2006 interview they made several direct comparisons between performances: at Maria, at eight in the morning, the remaining crowd was very "ravey," and Sender perceived their listening preferences to be rather circumscribed and closely associated with dance music clichés. Thus they avoided ending the set with "Back to Prime Time," a relatively calm number, because the audience at that point would have preferred hard bass drums. Interestingly, later the same day they played a set they described as "completely different": it took place at 2:30 in the afternoon, outside in the sunshine, and they played sitting down. They viewed the audience in the second location as much closer to their ideal type: open-minded, looking for more than a party, and musically in-the-know. As a result, they performed a longer and more improvisational set, more like the one heard at Cabaret Renz in Vienna.

Sender Berlin also took care to highlight the musical choices that led to differences in their performances. In particular they identified two main areas that are the focus of improvisational alteration: first, the formal disposition of each track; and second, the selection and application of effects. Both of these have far-reaching ramifications. The first, for example, encompasses the musical parameters of texture and duration in addition to form itself. Because sections begin and end when patterns enter and exit,[38] bringing elements into and out of the mix is the most important activity that performers undertake, and the one to which they devote the most attention. Their decisions regarding textural elements determine the specific constitution of each section, its duration, and ultimately the length and form of the track as a whole.

In the following paragraphs I illustrate a variety of ways these musical transformations play out in specific performances through in-depth analysis of a sequence of tracks that appears in both 2006 performances: "Brain Eater," "Dr. Sorge Is Watching the Planet," and "Griselda" (tracks 4, 5, and 6 of each set). I also compare the performed versions of each track to their album versions. Figures 3.10–3.12 graph the texture and form of each track as it occurs on the album, while Figures 3.13 and 3.14

---

[38] See Butler (2006, esp. 90–97) for further discussion.

represent the entire three-track sequence as it occurred in the Cabaret Renz and Maria performances, respectively.[39] Please view and listen to these examples online. Prior to reading the analysis, I suggest these means of acquainting yourself with the graphic format and the details represented:

1. View a graph of your choice. Become comfortable navigating the graph. Directions, along with an explanation of the notation, are provided on the website.

2. To the extent that you are interested in the details of the individual textural elements, familiarize yourself with these. Then listen to each recorded track while following along with its graph. Audio example 3.1 🜂 corresponds to Figure 3.10 🖥, audio example 3.2 🜂 to Figure 3.11 🖥, and audio example 3.3 🜂 to Figure 3.12 🖥.

3. Next, listen to the recorded performance from Cabaret Renz in Vienna while following along with the corresponding graph (audio ex. 3.4 🜂/ Fig. 3.13 🖥).

4. Study the graph of the performance from Maria in Berlin (Fig. 3.14 🖥).[40]

This set of instructions is directed toward a reader who wishes to engage with the examples as fully as possible. Other readers may be less concerned with details and may wish to focus instead on the broad outlines of the analysis. In terms of organization, it will be helpful to know that the argument is structured around the following analytical procedure: (1) discussion of a recorded track; (2) comparison of this recorded track to its renditions in the Vienna and Maria performances; (3) detailed comparison of the two performances in terms of their treatment of the track in question; (4) repetition of steps 1, 2, and 3 for each of the remaining tracks within the sequence; and (5) broader comparisons between the two performances as wholes.

The three tracks are representative of Sender Berlin's style in several ways. In contrast to the loop-oriented approach of musicians such as Pacou or Jeff Mills, they

---

[39] These examples are interactive versions of two graphical formats—the textural graph and the sound palette—which I developed for transcribing electronic dance music in *Unlocking the Groove* (Butler 2006). For detailed explanations of these notational systems, see pp. 179–81 of that work. Here, the textural graph is the primary component, with sound-palette functionality folded in through the mouseover action.

[40] The audio quality of my field-based video recording of this performance was sufficient for my own transcription, but is not in my opinion adequate for public presentation. Hence I have not included a recording of the entire passage shown in Figure 3.14. Short video clips from this performance do appear in other parts of this chapter, however.

tend to use longer patterns in which pitch plays a more developed role. In the majority of their tracks, the bass line is the most distinctive element, the strongest marker of musical identity. Their rhythms, and the grooves they develop, often involve a funky quality that is not especially common in the work of other Berlin artists in their milieu. At the same time, their tracks are extremely regular hypermetrically; they almost always involve multimeasure patterns at the four-bar level, and often at the eight- and sixteen-bar levels as well.

"Brain Eater," despite its rather sinister name, is mellow in affect, with a simple bass line involving just two pitch classes and three perfect intervals. At 124 BPM, the track is rather slow for techno. Its four-on-the-floor bass-drum pattern is supplemented with two variable hi-hat patterns and a percussive vocal sample, while the guitar and synth patterns help to articulate longer hypermetrical units. The most prominent feature of the track, however, is an alternation between two chords (E minor and F minor), which vary timbrally across eight-bar units. On the album, the chord loops occur in several variants: the basic pattern shown in the notated clip, another involving an envelope that "blooms" over each chord's duration, a third with staccato chords, and at least two additional combinations of these.

In performance, the chords are the main focus of effects manipulation. In the version of "Brain Eater" from the Vienna performance, for instance, Litschko alters the sound of the chords drastically with delay in passages such as measures 129–52. In the Maria set, meanwhile, "Brain Eater" is subjected to extensive timbral manipulation in a manner that emulates the sound of the Roland TB-303 Bass Line generator, the classic instrument of acid house. More specifically, Vaak "tweaks" the sound using the MS-20, which is connected to a "virtual" 303 on his laptop. This effect is first noticeable around measure 33 in the Maria performance; beginning around 17:11, the effect is both audible and visible. Such transformations are unique to each performance and clearly improvisational.

Comparing the textural graph of the Vienna performance of "Brain Eater" (Fig. 3.13) with its album version (Fig. 3.10) reveals both formal similarities and points of departure. Measures 17–32 of the album correspond to measures 9–24 of the Vienna version; other parallels occur between measures 73–80 (album) and 97–104 (performance) and between 97–112 (album) and 113–28 (performance). Perhaps most striking is the fact that measures 41–48 and 65–72 from the album appear in identical places within the set. On the whole, the performance follows the album most closely during earlier passages and gradually becomes more different. Measures 129–44 and 153–200 of the set, for instance, have no formal counterpart on the album, while measures 145–52 cite a much earlier part of it (mm. 65–72). Other portions noticeably extend cited passages in order to highlight an important sound, as during measures 65–96 of the set, which take a passage that lasted eight bars on the album (mm. 65–72, in which two versions of the chord pattern occur simultaneously) and extend it to thirty-two.

When the July 2006 performance at Maria is compared with the album and with the Vienna set, meanwhile, it reveals a rather different tendency (see Fig. 3.14; compare with Fig. 3.10 and 3.13). In its first half, it relates quite closely to both of the previous versions. For instance, the first eighty-eight measures of the Maria performance present material from the first seventy-two bars of the recorded track (in order, with just one section omitted).[41] Comparison of the two performances, meanwhile, reveals that measures 1–64 of the Maria set are based almost entirely on material from measures 1–96 of the Vienna performance (Fig. 3.13), the only significant departures being the use of different chord patterns and the omission of measures 25–40 of the Vienna material. In measure 89, however, something changes. From here through the rest of the track, the Maria performance differs radically from both of its predecessors.

As previously noted, the "arrangement" of a track is its formal and textural patterning. In performance, many musicians treat the recorded arrangement of a track merely as a point of departure or a loose guideline. Sender Berlin, by contrast, tend to regard it as a more essential part of the track's identity. Recalling their idea of the "original track" always informing performance, Vaak's comments take on new significance in relation to the musical relationships just described: "From the making of the song, you know also the arrangement in the head.... 'OK: we play this sound, this sound, this sound; then we make the break.' That you know because you have built this track." Vaak further characterized the recorded track as a "script." Although not to be followed exactly, the script is *inscribed*, in this case in memory. "So every time you make some new things. But you have in your head the script from the track," he noted. Figure 3.13 shows that Sender Berlin followed the recorded script of "Brain Eater" relatively closely during their Vienna performance, although they began to move away from it as the track progressed. The Maria set, by contrast (Fig. 3.14), corresponded even more faithfully to the script at first, but after presenting the track's basic material it moved away into uncharted, improvisational territories.

The next track in this sequence, "Dr. Sorge Is Watching the Planet," derives from Sender Berlin's second album, *Gestern Heute Morgen*, which was released in 2002. As such, it predates most of the other material in the live performances by three years. Its inclusion blends the old with the new in several ways: most notably, the version played in the live sets is almost entirely different from the album version. The earlier and later mixes of "Dr. Sorge" share just two elements: the bass line, which oscillates between the pitches C and A, and riff 1, a percussive sound that fills in the textural

---

[41] Specific correspondences between album and performance are as follows: mm. 17–32 of the album are a near equivalent to mm. 9–24 of the performance (the only discrepancy being a variant chord pattern), and mm. 49–72 of the album a near equivalent to mm. 25–48 (with varied chords in mm. 33–48 of the set and additional bass-drum withholdings).

background (see Fig. 3.11; compare with "Dr. Sorge" as represented in the two performances). In other respects, the album version of the track is rather funkier: in contrast to the four-on-the-floor pattern that pervades the live sequences discussed here, it features a syncopated bass drum in combination with snare-drum backbeats. Because of the bass-drum pattern's rhythmic gaps, the album version feels affectively "slower" than the performed renditions, which is ironic given that the tempo of the original is actually faster. Existing language for rhythm and meter (both colloquial and theoretical) provides no means for describing such a perception; I will refer to it as the "rhythmic demeanor" of the track. The album version also includes three synth patterns, the second of which is the most interesting and prominent.

In the performances of "Dr. Sorge," these synths are removed altogether. The bass drum matches the steady quarter-note beat of the surrounding tracks, and new percussion sounds complete the texture with additional even rhythms. The most important new component, however, is riff 2, a distinctive and funky loop that becomes the focus of a great deal of timbral play; in the performances it acts almost as a second bass line.

The Vienna and Maria versions of "Dr. Sorge" start off on the same trajectory. In both cases, riff 1 enters the mix near the end of "Brain Eater." After "Brain Eater" has been removed from the mix, the formal sections of the two performed versions of "Dr. Sorge" begin to correspond closely: measures 33–48 (Vienna) with measures 49–64 (Maria), measures 57–72 (or 65–72) with 65–72, and measures 73–80 with 73–80. As is evident from this listing, the two tracks begin in slightly different places (because the Vienna performance has a shorter overlap with "Brain Eater"), but their formal patterns converge in measures 65–80 (because the Maria set states each section for a shorter amount of time). From measure 81 on, however, the performances follow their own paths. The second half of each version is largely devoted to improvisation on riff 2 using effects; as in "Brain Eater," there are many delays and 303-like sounds. In addition, Sender Berlin frequently foreground their manipulation of riff 2 by "soloing" it; these passages are evident in the textural graph as passages in which only one line is present.

"Dr. Sorge" functions as a transitional track in both sets. In particular, Vaak and Litschko foreshadow the next number by interpolating its distinctive piano riff. (This begins with the upbeat to mm. 93 and 85 in the Vienna and Maria sets, respectively.) In the Maria performance, a similar process occurs from the other side as well. Although "Brain Eater" effectively ends when the mix jumps from its bass line to that of "Dr. Sorge," one sound from "Brain Eater"—synth 1—actually continues through all of the following track (see Fig. 3.14). Though not particularly prominent, its presence functions as a lingering reminder of the previous track's unfolding.

A third and quite explicit connection between tracks occurs at the moment of transition between "Dr. Sorge" and "Griselda." In both sets, riff 2 from "Dr. Sorge" is isolated for a final time as the track comes to an end. Its closing pitch, A, is drawn out for a full measure, which is followed immediately by the bass line of "Griselda," also heard solo and beginning on A. The timbral similarity of the two sounds assists in the process; one becomes aware of the shift only retroactively. An abrupt switch or "cut" from one track to another—a technique that usually *disrupts* the unity of a track—is thus used to forge a connection.

One unexpected result of the changes introduced in performance is a recurring hypermetrical discrepancy. Arising in the middle of "Dr. Sorge" in both cases, it stands out from the otherwise highly regular multimeasure patterning. In the Vienna performance, the discrepancy seems to arise from the combination of multiple tracks. It is first noticeable at measure 107, when the textural changes (and the riff 2 soloing in particular) move from the downbeat to the middle of the four-bar hyper-measure. The piano, however (as shown by the arrows), continues to articulate the previous four-bar divisions. Beginning at measure 127, it joins the other instruments on the new hypermetrical downbeat. All textural components briefly return to the original downbeat in measures 153–60, but they quickly switch back to the displaced location thereafter. In the Maria set, by contrast, differences occur not between the elements of two tracks but rather between the rate of textural change and the previously established four-bar patterning. Beginning at measure 138 and continuing through the end, all patterns are shifted forward by one bar.

These changes in multimeasure patterning are clearly related to the improvisational tweaking of riff 2. In each performance, the passages in which this sound is foregrounded vary in length depending on how long each effect is applied. At times they are drawn out more than others, and the musicians treat this flexibly. In the Vienna set they eventually adjust or "correct" the "Griselda" piano riff so that it does not create conflicting hypermetrical downbeats between the two tracks; in the Maria set this is unnecessary given the consistent alignment between them.

The third track that occurs in the sequence, the Arenys de Mar mix of "Griselda," has the longest and most complex bass line of the three (see Fig. 3.12). Aside from this distinctive sound, two main aspects of the track stand out. The first of these, the articulative piano and chord sounds, are pervasively present throughout. The piano sound, which as described above is also used to link "Dr. Sorge" to "Griselda," is an outstanding example of a highly condensed kernel of musical identity. Every time it appears, it synecdochically refers to the track from which it is drawn in two succinct beats. The second prominent feature of "Griselda" is its synth lines, which occur in four variants, each more elaborate than the one before. The fourth synth pattern, moreover, is itself subjected to increasing embellishment as its repetitions unfold.

These features of the synth lines are highly suggestive of improvisation within the recording process.

In contrast to the first two tracks in the sequence, however, the performances of "Griselda" seem to involve relatively little improvisation. They are quite uniform, both in relation to the album version and to each other. They follow the album, for instance, more or less section-by-section. Although there are once again signs of increasing differentiation beginning around the midpoint of the performed track, they are much less pronounced in this case (see Figs. 3.13 and 3.14; compare with Fig. 3.12). Some of the more intense sections, such as measures 65–80 and 101–44 from the album,[42] seem to be extended within performance, but the main differences are relatively small; they lie with the hi-hat variations and the bass drum withholdings. Perhaps this lack of alteration arises from the way in which the recorded track in some sense obviates improvisation: it already involves a great deal of variation and embellishment, and there is little room left for the hypermetrical articulations that are added to the other tracks.

Shifting focus from the treatment of individual tracks to comparison of the entire three-track sequence ("Brain Eater"/"Dr. Sorge"/"Griselda") across the two performances, we see that one structural commonality is a tendency for greater improvisation to occur in the second half of a track. In the beginning of each track, the musicians seem to feel a need to construct or otherwise build it up. Once its identity is established, however, improvisation can begin in earnest; at this point they can put down the script. In addition, with each performance the three-track sequence works as a segment of increasing intensity. Note, for instance, the tempo increase of 4–5 BPM from each track to the next. These alterations are technologically unnecessary (as previously mentioned, Live can easily and automatically coordinate the tempo of an entire set), suggesting that a musical justification is at work. The three tracks also progress in terms of textural density. This growth occurs naturally with "Griselda" in the third position, but with respect to "Dr. Sorge" it requires intervention through the introduction of external elements.

Within each track there is usually one principal arena of improvisational manipulation. The most common of these is the 303-based tweaking of effects, though bass-drum removals play an important role as well (just as they would within a DJ set). It should be noted that almost all of these removals are done live, by pulling a channel slider down, even when they correspond to details of the recorded versions or occur in the same places across performances. Litschko's manipulation of other percussive elements is clearly improvisational and creates unity across the three

[42] Compare with mm. 57–96 and 113–200, respectively, in the Vienna performance.

tracks. The most notable of these is an open hi-hat sound, which I have shown in the textural graphs of "Brain Eater" and "Griselda" with a pattern of upward-leaning diagonal slashes. The same pattern occurs as the principal hi-hat sound in the live versions of "Dr. Sorge." As such, it functions as a unifying element within each performance; it is likely a preset sound that Litschko adds directly from the 909 drum machine.

The ways in which Sender Berlin use the 909 and the other interfaces in their performance configuration also foregrounds the relationship between improvisation and liveness. For electronic dance musicians these domains are thoroughly interrelated. Pacou's remarks on the differences between improvised and preplanned sets are telling in this regard, and worth considering once more:

> Every time, every live act will sound different. That's the thing: for me it's very important to have a degree of improvisation on the stage. I don't want to have this thing like [*name deleted*] the other night, everything preplanned to the last beat and the last little…I don't want to have that kind of thing. I prefer to have it hands-on, and, you know, being able to change it around.

In this statement Pacou clearly connects the presence of improvisation within performance to a number of qualities of liveness, including "hands-on" control and the uniqueness of the event. Note also how he situates improvisation "on the stage." In terms of location, this is a direct contrast with his comparison to cooking earlier in this chapter, in which he notes that "it's not really possible to recreate exactly the same thing at home." In both remarks he situates liveness in a public arena, in a sphere in which performance can be imbued with a special presence through musical creation in the moment.

For electronic dance musicians and their audiences, these connections between liveness and improvisation become visible through and on interfaces. Even as they generate unfolding compositions, musicians employ their hardware to communicate that not only "performance" but also "improvisation" is taking place. Three brief passages from Sender Berlin's 2007 performance at Tresor in Berlin illustrate these processes at work in ways that relate to the analyses presented above.[43] In video

---

[43] As the following comments (and a perusal of Fig. 3.9) will reveal, the Tresor performance includes all three tracks analyzed above, with "Brain Eater" and "Dr. Sorge" once again heard consecutively. For reasons of space, I have chosen not to discuss the tracks' appearance in the 2007 set in the same level of detail. I will, however, offer a brief summary. First, "Brain Eater" lasts just forty-eight measures. During this time it is largely reduced to its bass line, which is combined with drum sounds from "Theory's Dead." Subsequently, "Dr. Sorge" is also shortened, to a duration of 114 measures. It features all of the sounds heard in the 2006 Maria set (including the interpolations from other tracks) except for riff 1 and the "scratch" sound. It also presents a previously unheard

example 3.3, Vaak turns the knobs of the MS-20 in order to alter the bass line of "Brain Eater" in the manner of a Roland TB-303. ⬤ Video example 3.4 shows a solo passage featuring riff 2 from "Dr. Sorge." ⬤ The pattern repeats four times, gradually increasing in timbral intensity. Litschko zeroes in on the mixing board, turning a knob with great passion and effecting a strong hypermetrical downbeat. In the release that follows this moment, the musicians step into the role of listeners, letting go of their interfaces and dancing to the sounds they have created. Video example 3.5 shows an even more intense manipulation of a single sound, in this case the signature riff from the unreleased mix of "Zona de Curva." ⬤ Litschko draws the passage out while adding shimmering effects, all the while turning the dial and knobs of the EFX-500 in a markedly visible manner. He lets go with a flourish of his arms, the bass drum and the other instruments return, and he briefly claps and dances along with the sound. The audience yells in appreciation, both during the suspenseful buildup and after its release. Each of these moments functions as a meaningful rupture in the otherwise continuous performance. By providing moments of perceptible process, these passages serve as windows into the musicians' technological and creative approach. Ultimately, all those present can not only hear but also see that they are spontaneously creating something unique to this event.

Analysis 2: Preexistent Elements in DJ Performances (Jeff Mills, "The Bells")

Jeff Mills, born in Detroit in 1963, is one of the most famous DJs in the world, as well as a leading techno producer. He established his reputation as a DJ in the 1980s on the Detroit-based radio station WJLB, where he played sets on a show hosted by Charles Johnson ("The Electrifying Mojo"). Performing under the name "The Wizard," Mills combined the pace and virtuosity of hip-hop DJing with track selections from techno and house; he has long been known for changing records very rapidly, and he frequently employs complex tricks such as beat juggling. With "Mad" Mike Banks, he founded the techno "collective" of producers and DJs known as Underground Resistance, though he has since been active primarily as a solo artist. As a producer he established the label Axis Records, the music of which is characterized by a hard, fast, and minimal techno aesthetic. Axis also functions as an umbrella label for the smaller imprints Purpose Maker and Tomorrow Records. Mills has also released several well-known albums and twelve-inch singles on the Berlin-based techno label Tresor Records.

---

synth line. A two-bar hypermetrical discrepancy arises after the first riff 2 solo. New material enters after "Dr. Sorge," interrupting the previously established link with "Griselda," although the latter track returns to conclude the set.

FIGURE 3.15 Jeff Mills, "The Bells," twelve-inch vinyl (author's copy) ⬛

"The Bells" is one of the most popular tracks of Jeff Mills' career. It was first released in 1997, on a Purpose Maker twelve-inch entitled the *Kat Moda EP* (PM-002). This version is still in print, in addition to a tenth anniversary re-release (PM-020). Jeff Mills continues to feature "The Bells" within his DJ sets, as do many other techno DJs.

As these comments indicate, "The Bells" is, among other things, a product. I ordered it online from a record store in Detroit and received it in the mail, along with other records from the Purpose Maker imprint and several Underground Resistance stickers. The twelve-inch vinyl on which it was inscribed came in a simple black sleeve, the only adornment a themed Purpose Maker photograph on the label in the center of the record (Fig. 3.15).

"The Bells" is also a musical composition, one that exemplifies Jeff Mills' style extremely well. It begins, in a typically fast tempo, with just two textural elements: a four-on-the-floor bass-drum beat with a "hard" timbre, and a noisy, syncopated synthesizer riff that alternates tuned and detuned sonorities.[44] (Please refer to online textural graph, Fig. 3.16. ⬛ Textural graph of Jeff Mills, "The Bells," twelve-inch version) Recordings of "The Bells" are widely available online via sites such as YouTube and

---

[44] "Detuning" is a technique used in EDM and hip-hop production in which sonorities are rendered slightly out of tune in order to promote a dissonant and "noisy" aesthetic.

Spotify.) The track continues to build a basic percussive groove during the first thirty-two measures, paving the way for the entrance of the sound for which the track is named: the "bells" that begin in measure 33. Although the timbre of this riff is obviously synthesized rather than acoustic in origin (it is not sampled from the sound of an actual bell), it is clear and resonant, and it acts like a bell: it peals out a short call, and then repeats itself in an echo. This bell motive, within the track "The Bells," therefore not only incorporates but also thematizes repetition; its behavior reflexively indicates its content.[45]

In measure 65, a new sound, a bass line, begins to fade into the texture. It is motoric, chugging along in continuous sixteenth notes that recall the synthesized disco of producers such as Giorgio Moroder (best known for his work on Donna Summer's "I Feel Love"). Given that the bass line is an essential part of most techno recordings, its arrival here—nearly two minutes into the track—is rather late. After its emergence, the bells make a final appearance (mm. 81–88), and then the track drops back down to the opening textural configuration (riff 1 and bass drum, mm. 93–96). From here the texture builds up once more, achieving a high plateau in measures 105–20. In measure 145 the two initial patterns appear a third time, signaling the beginning of the outro.

Within the track as a whole, these changes articulate a formal pattern that is widespread in electronic dance music. From a sparse introduction, the track gradually adds sounds until a full, characteristic texture is achieved (mm. 1–88). The second main section (mm. 89–144, fifty-six measures) begins with a "breakdown," in which the texture is scaled back considerably, followed by another buildup to a core.[46] The track concludes with a brief outro (mm. 145–64, twenty measures), which mirrors the intro in its sparse texture.[47]

The musical details of "The Bells" are a classic instance of Mills' stark, stripped-down, and repetitive aesthetic. The entire track contains just seven sonic elements: the bass drum, riff 1, the hi-hat, the handclaps, the bells sound (for the purposes of this list I treat the original and its echo as one element), the bass line, and an

---

[45] Alternating between a prominent riff and an altered version thereof also strongly evokes a common performance technique, dating back to disco and hip-hop of the 1970s, in which DJs would alternate between two copies of the same record in order to extend a favorite passage. "The Bells" is certainly not the only EDM recording to reference this technique; the best known, "Sharevari," by A Number of Names, was also one of the earliest techno tracks, dating back to 1981. For a discussion and analysis of "Sharevari," see Butler (2006), 153–55.

[46] Although the breakdown is most obvious in mm. 93–96, its precise beginning point can be traced back to the removal of the bass line in m. 89. Measures 137–44 present a similar ambiguity thanks to a thinning of the texture; in this case, however, it is easier to group this passage with the preceding measures because the bass line continues.

[47] See Butler (2006, 221–25) for a discussion of archetypical formal shapes in EDM tracks.

atmospheric hissing sound that I have called "steam." These in turn form a relatively small number of textural combinations. There is one main riff and one bass line. Loops repeat in short durations—only quarters and half notes, except for the repetitions of riff 1 at a two-bar level.[48] Hypermeter occurs over relatively brief durations: the two-bar patterning formed by the bells and its echo beginning in measure 33 is the first clear hypermetrical articulation (notice how easy it is to count half notes in fours during this passage). Subsequently, measures 49–56 suggest a single four-beat hypermeasure (with the "beat" comprising two regular measures), as do measures 81–88. In general, however, meter is most palpable within the measure. Although there are regular eight-bar textural changes, most of these longer spans are relatively undivided.

These comments address "The Bells" as a musical construction. I have described it on the basis of the sounds that emerge when the record is played back without alteration, viewed through the lenses of musical analysis and particular kinds of transcription. Yet the track is clearly something more than just these sequences of sonic configurations. What is the *work* that we call "The Bells"? Fans of Jeff Mills demonstrate a marked tendency to ontologize "The Bells," consistently treating it as a "song" despite the numerous ways in which it resists working as one. The hook that defines "the bells," for instance, is hardly lyrical; its four attacks sound out just three pitches over a two-beat span. This extreme concision intensifies the looped repetition that characterizes techno riffs more generally. The bells sound is also tonally ambiguous.[49] Moreover, as a signature riff it is surprisingly scarce; it appears in just one portion of the track (mm. 33–88) and never returns. Indeed, as a primary hook, riff 1 would seem to have better credentials: it occupies much more of the track, including the beginning and end, and recurs several times. Questions of unity also arise with respect to the bass line: when it finally enters the texture in measure 65, it seems almost as if it belongs to another track.[50] Although the introduction of a bass line completes the track in a certain sense (because one expects a techno track

---

[48] This two-bar level is in fact rather weakly articulated; one must listen quite attentively to notice how the pitch pattern fluctuates. Because of the clear repetition of the rhythm pattern, the one-bar level is much stronger.

[49] In set-class terms, it forms (014), a favorite of the Second Viennese School. This is not to suggest, of course, that Mills and Schoenberg share compositional approaches or aesthetics (indeed, Mills' repetitive practice is diametrically opposed to Schoenberg's published views on repetition), but rather simply to note the presence of this interesting and widespread pitch-motivic cell within a radically different context. It is also worth noting that the tonal ambiguity of the bell motive applies to the track more generally; although the notated transcription might seem to point toward A minor as a key center (if one generously ignores the bass line's emphasis on B), in the track as heard each pitched motive seems to occupy its own closed sphere of repetition. Deemphasizing tonal concerns in favor of rhythm and timbre is typical of the hard-techno style in which Mills works.

[50] This effect becomes especially noticeable in mm. 105–36, in which the bass line more fully dominates the texture.

FIGURE 3.17   Flier advertising Jeff Mills' performance at the Tresor club in Berlin, October 6, 2007, 📀

to have a bass line), the way in which Mills divides the track between bells-domi-nated and bass-line-dominated sections creates an effect of two large chunks of ma-terial that do not relate in an obvious manner. These factors undercut the conventional formal shape suggested by the track's ebb and flow of texture; in thematic terms, "The Bells" is more a collection of striking ideas than a single unified form.

When Mills plays "The Bells" in a DJ set, however, his fans have no problems at all recognizing it; it is easily his most famous track. I have observed him perform as a DJ on two occasions: at the 2007 Movement Festival in Detroit (May 28, 2007) and at the Tresor Club in Berlin (October 6, 2007; see Fig. 3.17). On the latter occasion, I was fortunate to be able to watch him from a few feet away on stage. I have also

studied many audio and video recordings of his performances from commercial releases and the Internet. He plays "The Bells" in all of the performances I have encountered. Judging from the intensity of the audiences' responses (the energy of their
dancing and other movements; their screaming, shouting, and other vocalizations), it
usually marks a peak moment for them.[51] A collective roar almost always rises up at the
moment the track is recognized: typically this occurs when riff 1 appears, although
there is usually a second, louder wave of recognition when the bell motive first enters.

All of these behaviors are common at high-intensity moments; what is perhaps
more surprising is that audience members also *sing* "the bells." In addition to singing
along with the motive, they often sing it *before* Mills has played it. This pattern of
vocal anticipation is evident, for instance, in a 2007 performance from the Netherlands.[52] Although he does not bring in the bells sound until 3:17 into the clip, an audience member repeatedly sings it before then; examples occur at 0:40, 1:36, 2:06,
and 2:18. I noticed similar behavior during Mills' 2007 Tresor set as well. The Dutch
fan also excitedly shouts "Bells!" at 1:10, during an extended period in which Mills is
teasing the audience by withholding the bass-drum beat.[53] When audience members
sing in anticipation in this manner, they perform more than just their recognition of
the song; they also locate the track's identity, boiling it down to its essential two-beat
motive.

A process of ontological consolidation also occurs in the version of "The Bells"
played by the Montpelier Orchestra.[54] Arranged by French composer Thomas
Roussel, this rendition places much greater emphasis on bells and the bell motive
in several ways. First, the orchestration includes actual bells; in an introductory
section (0:00–0:38), they ring out various tones, leading gradually into a rhythmically augmented statement of the motive (it occupies a full measure rather
than two beats). At 1:37 the eponymous motive, in its original version, erupts

---

[51] Internet sites such as YouTube contain many clips of Mills performing "The Bells." For an especially high-
quality, dynamic example, see http://www.youtube.com/watch?v=_FXJHwDUX2k (from a 2007 performance in Poland; accessed July 21, 2008).

[52] This performance, which is viewable at http://youtube.com/watch?v=leUd4rcLh5Q (accessed July 23, 2008),
took place on September 28, just eight days prior to the Berlin performance I attended. It was part of the
"Awakenings Detroit Weekend," which took its name from the fact that Detroit musicians were featured; the
Awakenings series of events take place in the Netherlands. See http://www.awakenings.nl/index.php?lang=en
(accessed July 23, 2008). I thank Suzanne Bratt for bringing this particular performance to my attention.

[53] For an extended discussion of withholding the beat as a DJ technique, see Butler (2006, 91–94).

[54] The recording I describe here comes from a concert that took place on July 2, 2005, at the foot of the Roman-
built Pont du Gard bridge in southern France. Sixteen of Mills' compositions were performed by the Montpelier National Orchestra, conducted by Alain Altinoglu, with Mills on percussion and drum machines. The
event was part of the twentieth anniversary of the naming of the Pont du Gard as a UNESCO world heri-
tage site. A combined CD/DVD of the event has since been released by Tresor Records (Tresor Records 223,
2005).

against a full orchestral background; the crowd screams loudly, as if they were at a club rather than an orchestral concert. Roussel also preserves the echoing behavior of the bells: violins play the bell motive, and xylophones (and subsequently clarinets) its echo. The bass line, which was hard to relate to the bells in the original version, now occupies a much smaller percentage of the track: an interlude in which brass instruments play a simplified version of bass line 1 a and b appears in just two brief eight-bar passages, at 2:34–48 and 3:47–4:01. In the interim, the bell motive reappears (as it never did in the original) in the orchestra. Its last appearance occurs in a closing section, in which the bells sound out an augmented version of the motive eight times in succession.[55] Through these changes, the track becomes thematically unified, both musically (the melodic patterning is much more tight-knit) and semantically (it is more persistently and explicitly focused on the theme of ringing bells). Roussel undergirds this increasingly tight organization with tonality. His version of "The Bells" is clearly in A minor: the first and last bell tones are on the tonic, and the last sound we hear is an A minor chord in the strings.[56]

As these phenomena reveal, the musical work "The Bells" not only exists but also *lives* in ways that cannot be reduced to a singular or stable arrangement of sounds. For techno fans, "The Bells" is more than just an object that one can purchase and listen to at home; it is an entity that fully comes to life in musical performance.[57] In the stylistic context of techno, in which the majority of records are treated more as generic "tools" for DJs than as freestanding compositions,[58] the recognition and naming of a small number of seminal tracks functions as an important act of musical identifica-

---

[55] Like the previous augmented version of the motive, this statement is also made to occupy a full measure; however, it is melodically simplified (it is reduced to three notes, F–A–G#), and the rhythm is altered to form a 3+3+2 pattern.

[56] It is up in the air as to whether the increased unity, which brings the track into conformance with classical conventions, improves or diminishes "The Bells." Although the new approach to formal organization clarifies matters, it could be regarded as overly obvious. The disunity of the original is not easy to interpret, but it also poses a challenge that draws listeners in. One might argue, of course, that the orchestral version is simply adapted for its context—and this may be true. However, questions of value remain: Was "The Bells" modified according to classical aesthetic standards in order to imbue it with high-art prestige? A definitive answer to this question would lead us into overly tangential territory; for present purposes, it is most important to notice how this version corrals and solidifies the track's identity.

[57] See also Madrid's discussion of performances in the EDM style known as Nor-tec (Madrid 2008, 152–54). Madrid makes similar observations about product/process relationships between recorded EDM tracks and performance, writing that "it is in the unpredictability of performance, which gives the computer musician plenty of opportunities to improvise, that the music acquires meaning" (154). Where our approaches differ slightly is in the attention given to products; I have argued that the products of EDM are central to its musical creativity and warrant attention equal to that given to processes, but Madrid tends to favor the latter (while still clearly acknowledging the role of products within performance).

[58] For a contextualization of techno records as DJ "tools," see Butler (2006, 204).

tion. The musical identity of "The Bells" also inheres in Mills' conceptions of it. To the extent that Mills, as a DJ, improvises on a structural understanding of "The Bells," his perception is filtered through an additional layer of knowledge, one derived from his status as *composer* of the record he is playing. In this regard, "The Bells" takes on a dual status as preexistent element within DJ performances by Mills in particular.[59]

One may also understand the composition "The Bells" through the lens of performance apart from its rendition in DJ sets. The improvisational manipulation of sound that many EDM producers introduce into the compositional process often reflects the kinds of alterations that occur within DJ practice. At several points in the recording, for instance, Mills withholds elements of the texture during an anacrusis, returning to a full texture on the subsequent (hyper)metrical downbeat: see measures 24, 47–48, and 64. The echoed version of the bell motive also evokes the ways in which DJs alter timbre using the EQ controls on their mixing boards. Though it is not possible to say with certitude whether Mills actually improvised these changes, they strongly recall various kinds of improvisatory transformations that occur within DJ sets. From the perspective of an audience member, it may be impossible to tell whether certain kinds of alterations originate in the production of the record or the DJ's performance.

As a DJ tool, "The Bells" may also be understood to suggest various possibilities for performance. Texturally sparse passages such as measures 93–96 and 145–48 invite the DJ to overlay the track with other records. Long undivided spans (e.g., mm. 105–20) encourage textural and timbral variation, or possibly the mixing in of a new track. Perhaps most significantly, the thematic disunity described above makes sense in the context of a DJ set. For listeners who are not intimately familiar with the track, the entrance of the seemingly incongruous bass line could easily suggest a new record entering the texture; the distinctive new sound evokes a kind of *faux* mix. A sensitive DJ could react to this thematic differentiation in several ways: he might preserve the apparent rate of change by mixing in an additional track (a real one, that is) about sixty-four measures after the entrance of the bass line, or he might deemphasize the bass line as a component of the track (and increase the relative

---

[59] Situations in which DJs play their own records are not uncommon in electronic dance music. In the case of Mills, the prominence of "The Bells" within techno helps it proliferate into alternate versions such as orchestral arrangements and other renditions. For instance, the performance from the Netherlands described above was apparently "live" (it is so described in comments on YouTube, although I cannot personally confirm this claim)—in other words, performed using the studio equipment of a live PA rather than played back on vinyl. Given that Mills is the composer of the track, one would expect this performance to take on an aura of originality: we are hearing a recreation of "The Bells" in its original format rather than a record. In fact, however, he departs dramatically from the recorded release, playing a version that is nearly twice as long, with many extended breakdowns.

presence of the bell motive) by mixing out around measure 89 or 93,[60] or he might even play a second copy of "The Bells" on the other turntable in order to bring about a reprise of the signature motive.

"The Bells" can therefore be understood as an inscribed form: a meeting of text (encoded vinyl) and work (meaningfully formed musical identity), with particular implications for its use within performance. Having addressed the first two terms of this trichotomy in detail, it is to the third that I will now direct my attention. One of the framing questions proposed earlier emerges as especially important for considering how this preexistent element functions within performance. Namely, to what extent does the inscribed form of "The Bells" specify the sonic result when it is played within a DJ set? In order to address this question, I turn to a detailed consideration of the function of "The Bells" within a specific performance by Jeff Mills.

In 2004, Axis Records—Mills' primary label—released a DVD entitled *Exhibitionist*, which features him performing four DJ mixes. Although there are a few other commercially available video recordings of DJ sets, they offer little to those interested in seriously examining what and how the DJ is performing; their purpose is usually to promote a particular DJ as a star figure, and they focus on flashy visuals rather than the music being played. *Exhibitionist* is therefore both unusual and highly useful: it shows Mills DJing clearly, in normal lighting and at close range, and it includes a track list for each set.

My analysis focuses on the second mix on the DVD, entitled "Purpose Maker Mix" (see video example 3.6, ©2004 Axis Records ◖). Figure 3.18 is a track listing for the mix (provided in the liner notes), which consists almost entirely of releases on Mills' Purpose Maker imprint.[61] Figure 3.19 supplies more detail about an approximately eleven-minute portion of the set, spanning from "Alarms" through "Scout," in which "The Bells" appears. The abbreviations in Figure 3.19 refer to four types of actions: putting the record on the turntable (PUT); adjusting the mixing board to bring the record into the mix (REM, for Record Enters Mix); taking the record out of the mix (ROM, for Record Out of Mix); and taking the record off the turntable (TOT, for Takes Off Turntable). I have designated the three turntables A, B, and C, respectively, beginning with the one to Mills' left.

---

[60] "Mixing out" refers to the process of removing a currently playing record from the mix.

[61] The only exceptions arise in tracks 10–12 of the DVD. Here, the camera moves away from Mills into another room, where it shows the Detroit-based duo Random Noise Generation performing a live PA. They play three tracks, and then the focus returns to Mills. Because of this interlude, the Purpose Maker mix is not a single uninterrupted set; however, the portion on which I focus is part of a continuous span of fourteen and a half minutes. Presumably the set was limited to releases from a single label (and to works by Mills) in order to simplify licensing; with the exception of the Random Noise Generation tracks, only one of the four mixes on the DVD—the eponymously titled "Exhibitionist Mix"—contains tracks by other artists.

1. "Automatic"
2. "Skin Deep
3. "Native High"
4. "Alarms"
5. "Casa"
6. "Tango"
7. "The Bells"
8. "Reverting"
9. "Scout"
10. "U-Move," Random Noise Generation
11. "PMP (Power, Money, and Pain)," Random Noise Generation
12. "Reign," Random Noise Generation
13. unreleased
14. "Call of the Wild"
15. "Cubango"
16. "Gift from the Hills"
17. "Ticket to Thrillville"
18. "Reach"
19. "Ride"
20. "Java"
21. "Circus"

FIGURE 3.18 Jeff Mills, *Exhibitionist*, "Purpose Maker Mix," Track Listing
Note: All tracks except 10–12 by Jeff Mills. Total duration: 45:21.

Turntable	PUT	REM	ROM	TOT	Track
B	2:58	4:24	7:17	7:18	Alarms
C	4:46	5:23	8:15	8:22	Casa
A	6:02	7:03	9:26	9:27	Tango
B	7:27	8:49	11:05	11:18	The Bells no. 1
C	8:41	N/A	N/A	11:15	Unknown (not played)
A	9:35	9:54	12:14	13:09	The Bells no. 2
B	11:21	11:33	13:57	*	Reverting
C	11:41	N/A	N/A	12:28	Unplayed rec. no. 2
C	12:33	13:20	N/A	*	Scout
A	13:19	14:14	N/A	*	Transitional record†

FIGURE 3.19 Jeff Mills, "Purpose Maker Mix," 2:58–14:32
Notes: `Still on the turntable at 14:32, when the camera moves to the Random Noise Generation set.
†No title is given for this record on the track listing. It is heard only very briefly, just as the focus of the camera and the audio mix shifts to the Random Noise Generation set.

The passage described can be viewed in video example 3.6. ◉ All four DJ actions are observable in the video; PUT and TOT are self-evident, while REM and ROM sometimes require a degree of deduction. Although it is usually possible to hear a record entering or exiting the mix, it is helpful to watch Mills' use of the vertical faders in order to determine the exact moment at which the entrance or exit takes place.[62] His mixing board contains four channels; the first is empty, and turntables A, B, and C are assigned to the second, third, and fourth. Mills uses the vertical faders to bring tracks in and out of the mix; he uses the horizontal cross-fader only for cutting rapidly back and forth between two tracks.

The portion of the set involving "The Bells" begins at 7:27, when Mills places a copy of the record onto turntable B. His intentions here are clear; after removing "Alarms" from the turntable at 7:18, he allows only nine seconds to pass before replacing it with "The Bells." What we are hearing at 7:27, however, is a combination of "Casa" and "Tango"; "The Bells" has not yet entered the mix. In the ensuing passage, Mills makes various adjustments to the sound and speed of these records. Around 8:00, he begins to fade "Casa" out of the mix very gradually, completing the process at 8:15. Thereafter he immediately begins cueing "The Bells" (that is, adjusting its tempo and beats so that it synchronizes with the currently playing record). At 8:29, he continues cueing with his right hand while searching for a new record in his crate with his left hand. He places this record onto turntable C at 8:37 and quickly flips it over.[63]

Within moments, however, Mills' attention returns to "The Bells." In contrast to his meticulously slow fade of "Casa," the new track bursts into the mix (8:49). He chooses measure 17 of "The Bells" as the moment with which to begin. In so doing, he preserves the sixteen-bar multimeasure patterning of the track, while also allowing a moderate amount of time to pass before the signature motive begins.

The portions of "Tango" and "The Bells" that he overlays complement each other well. See Figure 3.20, which shows the sounds present in the first two measures of their combination (mm. 65–66 of "Tango," sounding against mm. 17–18 of "The Bells"). The same patterns continue through measure 39 of "The Bells," which corresponds to measure 87 of "Tango." This is the last measure that we hear of the latter track. By superimposing these specific portions of the tracks, he creates a combination in which exactly one bass line is present. In addition, the sixteenth-note hi-hat pattern in "Tango" helps fill out the rhythmic surface of the mix; the

---

[62] In cases where a track fades in or out, I give timings for REM and ROM based on the exact moment at which the fade-in begins or the fade-out concludes, respectively.

[63] Mills never plays this record and eventually removes it from turntable C at 11:19. I discuss the implications of this set of actions subsequently; for now, it is sufficient to note that turntable C will not figure into analytical considerations during the portion of the set in which this unplayed record is on it.

"Tango," mm. 65-66

sounds with

"The Bells" no. 1, mm. 17-18

FIGURE 3.20 Combination of "Tango" and "The Bells" (8:49–9:26)

Notes: For purposes of comparison, all pitches are notated as they appear in the original tracks. In the "Purpose Maker Mix" they sound approximately one semitone higher than written, owing to the accelerated tempo at which Mills plays them. The downbeat pitches of the "Bird Call" sound vary between G♯ and F♯, as follows: G♯, G♯, F♯, G♯, G♯, F♯, G♯, F♯ (mm. 57–64); G♯, G♯ (mm. 65–66, as shown above); F♯, G♯, F♯, G♯, F♯, G♯ (mm. 67–72). Upbeats are always F♯. All other textural components repeat as notated.

"bird call" sound supplies a distinctive element in a range that is otherwise largely unoccupied; and each track presents one high atmospheric sound (the "steam" sound in "The Bells," and a string-like high A♯ in "Tango").

The events that follow the entrance of "The Bells" continue to reinforce multi-measure patterning. At the upbeat to measure 25, "The Bells" sounds out the withholding that occurs here in the original; this helps demarcate measure 73 of "Tango," at which point the bird calls cease. Eight bars later (m. 32 of "The Bells"; m. 80 of "Tango"), Mills creates a partial withholding within the mix by lowering the vertical faders. He raises them up again to emphasize the downbeat of measure 33, the point at which the bell motive is first heard. Crucially, he begins to pull "Tango" out of the mix just as the motive begins. Moreover, he stops "Tango" fully after its eighty-seventh measure; in measure 88, the distinctive bird-call sound returns, an event that surely would have interfered with the prominence of the bell motive.

During the following twenty-eight seconds (9:27–9:54), only one record, "The Bells," is playing. At 9:54, a sudden and noticeable change occurs, although we continue to hear "The Bells." Listeners who know the track well will realize that something impossible has just occurred: the track has jumped instantaneously, without a break, from measure 56 to measure 5. Close scrutiny of the video, along with knowledge of certain DJ techniques, reveals the sleight-of-hand: Mills has combined "The Bells" with another copy of itself, now playing on turntable A. I will describe the two records, according to the order in which they appear, as "The Bells" no. 1 and no. 2. Figure 3.21 (online 🖳) presents a textural graph of the passage in which they are combined, beginning with the lead-in to the combination (mm. 41–56 of "The Bells" no. 1).

After bringing in the second copy, Mills alternates rapidly between the two versions of "The Bells." In a passage lasting a little over a minute (9:54–11:07), he switches records twenty-two times. He does so with the cross-fader: in contrast to the majority of DJs, who use this device for mixing between tracks, he reserves it almost exclusively for cutting. Figure 3.21 shows his cross-fader actions on a line between the notated textures of the two records. "R" and "L" stand for "right" and "left."[64] Careful attention to the graph and the video, moreover, reveals yet another trick up his sleeve. At 9:56, in a move so fast that it almost escapes notice, he resets "The Bells" no. 1 by picking up the arm of the record and returning the needle to the beginning (to observe this motion, I recommend watching the video example at a slower speed if possible). His action places the two copies in very close proximity; they are now just six bars apart. For the rest of the excerpt he alternates between them, mostly treating copy no. 2 as a home base and no. 1 as a site of contrast or departure. His actions here highlight the records as platforms for performance. Using their surfaces and the cross-fader as interfaces, he produces new rhythms—musical entities that do not

[64] In order to preserve legibility, I do not alter patterning in the textural graph when a move to the other record lasts for less than one measure. See, for instance, mm. 17–20 of "The Bells" no. 2 (mm. 11–14 of "The Bells" no. 1): technically each "R" in this passage should enact a brief move to record no. 1 and a corresponding erasure of the patterns in record no. 2. Just once (m. 12 of "The Bells" no. 2), Mills also cuts with the vertical fader, using it to create a quick rhythm pattern on the "and" of each quarter-note beat.

1. Mm. 17–56 (copy no. 1)

2. Mm. 5–12 (copy no. 2, with brief interjections from copy no. 1 [m. 4] during m. 10)

3. Mm. 7–10 (no. 1)

4. Mm. 17–23 (no. 2)

5. Mm. 18 (no. 1)

6. Mm. 25–28 (no. 2)

7. Mm. 23–24 (no. 1)

8. Mm. 31–34 (no. 2)

9. Mm. 28–29 (no. 1)

10. Mm. 37–88 (no. 2, with four beats from no. 1 [mm. 40–41] during mm. 47–48)

Total duration: 124 measures

FIGURE 3.22 Excerpts from "The Bells" played in *Exhibitionist*, "Purpose Maker Mix," 8:49–12:14 (compare with Figs. 3.21 and 3.16)

exist in either record. In so doing he transcends the boundaries of "The Bells," exposing performance as something more than the reproduction of a preexistent element.

Ironically, because of the way in which Mills jumps back and forth between records, we almost never hear the two copies at the same time, even though they are playing simultaneously. Instead, the two copies echo each other, thereby extending an essential dynamic attribute of the track to a higher level of musical organization. Now it is not just the motive that echoes, but also the track itself. Moreover, this effect is intensified by the fact that "The Bells" no. 1 is only a short distance behind "The Bells" no. 2. Figure 3.22 lists the measures of "The Bells" that we actually *hear* in the "Purpose Maker Mix," with numbering based on the original track. As this information reveals, each time "The Bells" no. 2 states a few measures of the track, "The Bells" no. 1 follows with a smaller portion, usually from the passage just heard (this pattern begins with the second item on the list). Consequently, the echoing is *formal* in a quite specific way. Duration is also a part of this process: the statements of no. 1 are always shorter than those of no. 2, and therefore clearly subsidiary (like an echo in relation to its source).

Because Mills' cutting in this passage is so fast, and the resulting musical passages so brief, we experience the longer spans in which a record plays uninterrupted as releases from the otherwise frenetic pace. The mix settles into one such passage beginning at 10:47; from here, "The Bells" no. 2 plays continuously all the way from measure 37 through measure 88. Record no. 1 does make a brief appearance around 11:03, where it doubles the bell motive for four beats, but this is the last we hear of it.

DJs often use the double-copy technique in order to make a favorite track last longer. In fact, the practice of playing a track on two turntables in order to alternate between its best parts is often cited as an antecedent of the remix.[65] In this performance,

---

[65] See, for instance, Brewster and Broughton (2000, 136–37).

however, the total duration of the passage in which "The Bells" is heard (about three and a half minutes) is actually *shorter* than the original track, despite the inclusion of multiple copies. Mills does extend "The Bells" in a broader sense, however. Because of the way in which he selects and distributes material, we now hear seventy-eight measures containing the bell motive. This forms 63 percent of the 124-bar passage, whereas the forty-eight measures of bells found in the unmixed record constitute only 30 percent of that version.

Moreover, almost all of the material Mills plays comes from the first eighty-eight measures of the track. In particular, material from the portion of the track prior to the entrance of the bass line (specifically, mm. 5–64) accounts for 81 percent of what we hear. Because of repetitions, this material is played back over a span of one hundred measures. During this time frame the linear ordering of the record is continually disrupted. After the downbeat of measure 65 is breached, however, the remaining 19 percent (twenty-four measures) of the "Bells" passage unfolds without alteration. Measure 65 also coincides with the entry of the next track, "Reverting," into the mix.

The way in which Mills reapportions the material of "The Bells" functions as a decisive rejoinder to the question of unity within the original track. Indeed, the very lack of unity within the preexistent element seems to invite a response of unification, for both the "Purpose Maker Mix" and the orchestral version of Montpelier share this tendency. In his mix, Mills gives the bell motive and its accompanying material a much larger percentage of the track, while also reducing the scope and prominence of the bass line. Measures 65–88, the only passage in which we hear the bass line, are clearly transitional: "Reverting" is fading in by this point, and as it gains in strength "The Bells" begins to fade out. As soon as the latter is gone, "Reverting" presents its first two distinctive sounds (see Fig. 3.23); prior to this, the new track contained only relatively generic drum sounds.

However, in contrast to the Montpelier version, which brought the track into conformance with classical ideals of thematic and tonal unity, Mills revises "The Bells" in ways that reflect the aesthetics of DJ practice. Unity arises, paradoxically, through extreme fragmentation of the preexistent element. Its linear ordering is not enhanced, but rather subjected to constant disruption. Whereas Roussel (the Montpelier arranger) contained the disruption of the bass line by turning it into an interlude,

FIGURE 3.23 "Reverting," cowbell and riff patterns (begin 0:43 in original track; 12:11 in "Purpose Maker Mix")

Mills uses its effect to positive ends: it is precisely at the point where the bass line enters, causing us to wonder whether a new track is beginning, that he actually introduces a new track. In this way, disunity sparks growth.

Although the "Purpose Maker Mix" is without a doubt a remarkable performance, one might wonder about the extent to which it is also an improvisation. First, there is an unusual limitation, in that Mills plays tracks from only one label. At the same time, a major constraining factor—the audience—is absent. Both points are relevant to the question of track selection, and they might be taken to suggest that he may be playing a series of tracks chosen ahead of time. However, although it is not possible to answer this question definitively,[66] Mills' actions, along with various other considerations, indicate that a set list is unlikely. First, he can often be observed digging in the record bin behind the turntables. The camera never shows the bin closely enough to see his actions precisely, but it is clear that he is not simply picking up the next record from a prearranged stack. In the Detroit and Berlin sets mentioned above, I *was* able to see what Mills was doing behind the turntables; generally he would shuffle through a number of records before taking one (or sometimes two). He also moved both forward and backward through the crate. Though these actions might suggest either searching for a specific record or perusing a selection of records in order to see which might work, they clearly indicate a process of decision making within the moment.

Another series of actions occurring in conjunction with the "Bells" portion of the "Purpose Maker Mix" lends even stronger evidence for track selection within the performance. At 8:37, as I briefly mentioned above, he places a new record onto turntable C. As soon as it hits the surface of the table, he turns the record over. The track that he sought here cannot be identified, however, for Mills never plays it. He comes closest in 9:10–15, when he touches the record briefly as if to cue it; the vertical fader for C is also up during these few seconds, but no new sounds enter the mix.

At 9:27, Mills tries to remove the unknown record from turntable C with his right hand (while simultaneously taking "Tango" off turntable A). He fails, although he does at least stop the platter from spinning. By 10:50 he seems to have changed his mind: he sets turntable C in motion again, puts the needle down, and moves his hands as if he is about to cue the track. From 11:09 through 11:15 he actually tries to cue the track, but then he instantly abandons this idea and removes the record, successfully, from turntable C at 11:16 (while also removing "The Bells" no. 1 from

---

[66] Curious readers will undoubtedly wonder why I have not interviewed Mills, as I have done with the other musicians whose work I discuss. I have in fact sought interviews with him on more than one occasion, but they have not yet materialized.

turntable B). This series of reversals demonstrates decision making—and mind changing—at lightning-fast speed within the moment.[67]

Indeed, the speed with which Mills operates raises one remaining question regarding the degree of improvisation involved. As I have watched him perform, I have often wondered how he could possibly be improvising when he changes the music so rapidly. More quantitatively, a quick reexamination of Figure 3.19 will reveal that he often executes fundamental actions in time intervals of fifteen seconds or less. (This observation concerns the four basic actions only, excluding the additional variables of cueing, EQing, and digging for records.) The speed of his DJing, however, is the skill for which he is most well known; it is for this reason that he is called "The Wizard." Moreover, other improvising musicians also make decisions at very fast speeds; consider, for instance, all the series of decisions and actions that might unfold in just thirty seconds of a jazz solo. The difference here is that the musical choices I have described are physically observable and (with close attention) trackable in time.

For Mills, DJing is second nature, something he does regularly around the world, and a skill he has refined over more than twenty years. There is no reason, therefore, for him to need to select tracks ahead of time. In a worst-case scenario, had he been dissatisfied with the outcome of this filmed performance, he could have done another take. As it stands, the performance is clearly presented without editing (other than changes of camera angle) or touch-ups (which certainly would have been possible); anomalies such as the unplayed record are allowed to stand. The set list included with the DVD is also simpler than what Mills actually plays; it does not indicate, for instance, that "The Bells" appears on two turntables, and similar discrepancies arise in other parts of the set not discussed here. The constraint of a single label, meanwhile, is not as artificial as it might initially seem; after all, the label is his own, and most records function generically in this hard techno style. In comparison to other sets of his that I have observed (all of which involved records from multiple labels), the sound is quite similar.

On the basis of this evidence, the "Purpose Maker Mix" can easily be regarded as a recorded improvisation, although without an audience present it is more demonstrative than collaborative. More specifically, it is a real, continuous performance (not a "virtual" performance like those imagined to underlie most studio recordings, as discussed in Chapter 2), and that performance is improvised. Besides track selection, specific musical aspects that may have involved improvisation are (1) the overall direction of the energy level; (2) the inclusion of moments of recognizability or familiarity; (3) how much of each record is played; (4) which parts of each record are played; (5) how records are combined (and this includes whether they overlaid or

---

[67] Another unplayed record (presumably a different one) is introduced onto turntable C at 11:41, although Mills removes it sooner, and permanently, at 12:28.

juxtaposed, each of which involves too many variables to describe exhaustively); (6) the speed at which each record is played, a choice that affects pitch as well; (7) textural and timbral alterations involving EQs; and (8) other alterations with effects. Perhaps the most apparently improvisatory segment is the passage in which he cuts back and forth between the two copies of "The Bells"; though it is certainly possible that he has rehearsed this particular record combination (and presumably used it in other performances), the rhythms he generates by alternating between the two records are clearly unique to this performance.

Finally, one might also consider, with respect to the subject of Chapter 2, the extent to which this performance is "live." As a visual text, it invites us to watch without participating, a condition that is rare within dance-music culture. The title of the DVD is certainly apt: Mills himself is on exhibit. We see him manipulating his interfaces at incredible speed; he adjusts controls such as the EQs almost continuously, without visibly pausing to think, to the point that the instruments begin to seem like an extension of his body. As an object of our gaze, we experience him as a prodigy, as a mastermind, as a virtuosic dynamo, and perhaps even as a cyborg.[68]

The "Purpose Maker Mix" is not an "event" in the same way as Mills' performance at Tresor in Berlin was; it does not have "vibe" in a traditional sense because of the absence of an audience. Yet the frequent ruptures in the recordings, such as the lowering of the faders at 9:12–15, the many cuts from one track to another, or the various withholdings of the beats (even those found in the original records), open up spaces through which pours the live and immediate. In conjunction, the vertigo-inducing pace at which he operates, along with various unexpected changes of course (the never-played records, for instance), keeps us breathlessly within the moment. We see Mills work, and it is clear that we are watching a performance as well.[69] Through his actions in time, a recorded, "fixed," preexistent element—"The Bells" as both text and work—becomes live and fluid.

---

[68] Theories of cyborg subjectivity and the posthuman have sometimes been applied to EDM performance, although the number of studies is smaller than one might expect. Madrid, for example, describes a Nor-tec performance involving cyber-collaboration. Artists Falcón and Plankton Man, performing before an audience in Paris, were joined via cyberspace by Terrestre in Tijuana. According to Madrid, "technology allowed Terrestre to transcend his physical body in cyberspace and to extend it with the virtual prostheses that the Internet and the sonic and visual mediation of Plankton Man and Falcón provided. At that moment (while the performance took place), Terrestre became a posthuman cyborg capable of exerting influence over dancers thousands of miles away" (Madrid 2008, 161). Robert Henke, cited extensively throughout the present study, has also performed collaboratively in this manner on a number of occasions. For other EDM sources involving cyborg theory, see Pini (1997), Rietveld (2004), Marsh (2005), and Sellin (2005). For two extensively cited works addressing cyborg subjectivity more generally, see Haraway (1991) and Hayles (1999).

[69] Mills is not as physically demonstrative as many EDM performers, however: he does not make large movements, he dances only slightly and occasionally, and he rarely looks out. These tendencies hold even when he performs for a physically present audience.

In Retrospect

The creative work of Sender Berlin and Jeff Mills—the networks of performances and compositions described herein—reveal diverse and complex relationships between sonic outcomes that are specified in time ("improvised") and those specified ahead of time ("composed"). Sender Berlin's performances center around their own precomposed tracks. Each recorded track serves as a framing structure or "script" for a portion of the performance, providing a basis for improvisation and precise coordination. Many details of the performed sonic outcome are determined through improvisation, including the form of the tracks played, their texture, the durations of sections within tracks and of tracks as a whole, their hypermetrical organization, the selection and application of effects, and the transitions or connections between tracks. At a broader level, the "live set" itself is an ontological construct for Sender Berlin. It grows and changes through improvisational practices ("jamming" in the studio and on stage), but develops an increasingly stable identity over time. In general, Sender Berlin demonstrate a pervasively collaborative creativity—not only in performance, in which some tasks are divided and others shared, but also during composition. Interactivity between musicians and audience inheres in both of these realms as well. Composition is shaped by their practice of testing early material before potential audiences in performance, especially during the early stages of album development. Within performance, Sender's perception of the kind of audience present, their responses, and the acoustics of the performance space affect the ways in which their improvisation unfolds. Through performative gestures, musicians convey not only "liveness" but also "improvisation" to their audience.

Jeff Mills' performances as a DJ consist entirely of precomposed entities. His DJ sets typically involve a mixture of his own recorded compositions and records by others; the set discussed here presents some unusual restrictions by limiting performance to his own records on the Purpose Maker imprint. The recorded track "The Bells" serves as a platform for improvisation. Although its sonic outcome would appear to be highly specified prior to performance, his transformative use of technology opens and reconfigures its structure in dramatically unexpected ways. Accordingly, the details of the inscribed form specify the sonic result only partially. Their qualities, however, do seem to suggest directions in which performance might go. Most strikingly, the bifurcated structure of the recorded track, along with the distinctiveness and recognizability of its signature motive, seems to invite a response of formal consolidation. There are implications of how "The Bells" might be combined with other tracks as well, while from the other side, its design suggests traces of improvisation within the recording process. In contrast to the Sender Berlin performances, the Purpose Maker mix shows little evidence of prior planning. Instead, details ranging from track selection to timbral and textural manipulation appear to have developed improvisationally. Although the absence of an audience on *Exhibitionist* is unusual, Mills' other performances reveal an interactive dimension to "The Bells"; as one of his most well-known tracks, its appearance within his DJ sets invites audience recognition, appreciation, and interaction.

For these musicians, laptop and DJ sets serve as ways of reimagining, recontextualizing, and transforming the preexistent elements found on recordings. These technologically mediated forms of musical creativity reveal the increasing irrelevance of the polarities that continue to inform our understanding of performed and recorded compositions and improvisations. They take the ubiquitous ontology of recorded music as a given. Recording is not the opposite of performance, just as improvisation is not the opposite of composition. Recordings can be *prior* to performance. They can come unfixed. Recorded compositions can be the very formative material *of* improvised performances.

4 Looking for the Perfect Loop
MUSICAL TECHNOLOGIES OF MEDIATED IMPROVISATION

IN SPEAKING ABOUT "technology," a central theme of this work, I have thus far used the term in a practical, straightforward manner. Chapters 1–3, and especially Chapter 2, referred to a wide range of devices locatable in physical objects, reflecting a common understanding of technology as "machinery, equipment, etc., developed from the practical application of scientific and technical knowledge."[1] This sense of technology also encompasses the systems of knowledge that develop around such objects; when one speaks about the technology of sound recording, for instance, one refers not only to tape recorders, microphones, and the like, but also to the techniques and practices through which they are applied. Within the extremely broad sphere of technology, I have focused in particular on the technologies involved in recording, reproducing, and performing musical sound. I have emphasized the ways in which technology mediates relationships between musicians and sound and

---

[1] *Oxford English Dictionary*, 2nd ed. Interestingly, although technological invention is one of the most ancient of human activities, and the term itself dates back to Hellenistic Greek, the word *technology* appeared in English only in the seventeenth century. At that time, moreover, it was rare and its meanings rather different from those we employ today: it referred to the terminology of a particular area or skill, a discourse or treatise on that skill, or (following its Greek root) a systematic treatment of grammar (ibid.). The present emphases on mechanical and applied sciences developed later, around the time of the Industrial Revolution.

between audiences and performers, as well as the affordances and constraints of various specific technologies.

In this final chapter I wish to think about technology in a broader, more extended sense. The groundwork for such a project lies in the ideas of Michel Foucault, who presented an influential reenvisioning of "technology" in his late work. Specifically, Foucault articulated a fourfold division of human technologies:

(1) technologies of production, which permit us to produce, transform, or manipulate things; (2) technologies of sign systems, which permit us to use signs, meanings, symbols, or signification; (3) technologies of power, which determine the conduct of individuals and submit them to certain ends or domination, an objectivizing of the subject; (4) technologies of the self, which permit individuals to effect by their own means, or with the help of others, a certain number of operations on their own bodies and souls, thoughts, conduct, and way of being, so as to transform themselves in order to attain a certain state of happiness, purity, wisdom, perfection, or immortality.[2]

Foucault's ideas—and especially the concept of "technologies of the self" (which reflects his broader interest in the historical development of subjectivity)—have influenced several significant pieces of musical scholarship. For example, sociologist Tia DeNora, in an ethnography of the ways in which fifty-two women consume music in their everyday lives, reaches the conclusion that "music provides a rich array of cultural resources for self-constitution and reconstitution over time" (DeNora 1999, 53). Specifically, she finds that the women used music as an important means of mood and energy regulation and modification, and that they "turn to music as a device for ongoing identity work and for spinning a biographical thread of self-remembrance" (31). Judith Peraino, in turn, has used all four of Foucault's technologies as bases for her book *Listening to the Sirens: Musical Technologies of*

---

[2] Foucault (1997b [1982], 225). Foucault also presents these four technologies in an essay from the preceding year, although he initially describes them as "techniques" (Foucault 1997a [1981], 177). (In both works he tends to use the two terms somewhat interchangeably, though he favors "techniques" in the 1981 piece and "technologies" in the treatment from 1982.) Here he outlines "three major types of technique" corresponding to the categories of production, sign systems, and power, and then suggests a fourth type, "technologies of the self." His definition for this last kind of technology closely parallels that quoted above. By contrast, Jonathan Sterne, while building on a number of Foucault's ideas, makes a careful distinction between "technique" and "technology." He defines technique as "a learned skill, a set of repeatable activities within a limited number of framed contexts" and asserts that the "*technologies* of listening" that he examines "emerge out of *techniques* of listening" (Sterne 2003, 92; original emphases). The musical technologies that I describe in this chapter are not techniques in the sense of a skill or activity, but rather mechanisms that *afford* the skills, activities, and outcomes of improvised performance. I situate affordance in the context of this chapter later in this introduction.

Queer Identity from Homer to "Hedwig" (2006). Her chapter on technologies of production, for instance, examines how recorded music served as a medium through which sexual identity was formed and contested in two American queer communities during the 1970s: women's music, around which a distinctive lesbian, feminist subculture developed; and disco, which was essential to the constitution of urban gay male subculture during that time.

The themes of *Playing with Something That Runs* also suggest connections with the notion of "technologies of production," in that I share a deep concern with the "transformation" and "manipulation" of things—in this case, sound recordings (recall Foucault's mention, cited above, of technologies that "permit us to produce, transform, or manipulate things"). The path that I wish to follow, however, is not Foucauldian in any strict sense. Instead, I take Foucault's broad constitution of technology as a point of departure. The focus of this chapter is on *musical* technologies. My concern here is not with "music technology" in the mundane sense; I am not referring to physical objects, computer programs, or MIDI. Instead, I am developing a notion of musical technologies that describes aspects of sonic organization. I seek to imagine these technologies as principles of design affording certain kinds of performative interaction, rather than as structural units to be discovered and explicated. Musical technologies are an essential means through which the kinds of performance that characterize EDM are realized. They enable novel, contingently developing improvisations to be formed through the creative transformation of recorded musical objects. By structuring musical temporality in distinctive ways, they allow musicians to effect these transformations within the dynamic environment of live performance. Their implications for the unfolding of an event constitute an energetic field of possibility that musicians navigate.

The musical technologies to be described are seven: repeating, cycling, going, grooving, riding, transitioning, and flowing. By denoting each as a gerund, I seek to emphasize the active, dynamic ways in which they operate. After briefly presenting each technology in the context of this introduction, I develop them in depth throughout the chapter. Although individual technologies will initiate particular sections, other technologies will commingle with them. Instead of sharp delineations between sections and technologies, the chapter will feature a spiral organization: even as new ideas develop, key ideas will return. This aspect of its design is not coincidental but rather mirrors a broader argument I will make concerning the way in which performance in EDM channels musical energetics through time.

In contrast to the previous three chapters, which engaged extensively with concrete materials derived from field research and musical analysis, this chapter operates at a more theoretical level. Its project is not so much to explore specific examples but rather to develop a broad theoretical apparatus for conceptualizing DJ and laptop performance. As a final chapter it is decidedly forward-looking rather than retrospective.

The framework that it puts forth is not cultivated in order to wrap the intellectual project up into a single coherent package but rather to offer productive ways of thinking through the questions that it raises.

The most important of the seven technologies—and indeed, one that facilitates nearly all the others—is repetition. Repetition is an immediate, prominent, and pervasive feature of EDM, to the extent that it is often treated as a defining characteristic of the style. In the United Kingdom, the perceived repetitiveness of EDM is now part of the legal code: the Criminal Justice and Public Order Act of 1994, which outlawed certain kinds of raves, defined them as open-air gatherings of one hundred or more persons involving amplified music that is "wholly or predominantly characterised by the emission of a succession of repetitive beats."[3] Another kind of repetition may be seen to arise in the production, distribution, and performance of EDM, as each of these modalities is completely dependent on sound-reproduction technologies.

To imagine repetition as a specifically *musical* technology, one must first differentiate it from its long-standing associations with technology in a more mundane sense: in short, to distinguish repetition as an *effect* of technology from repetition *as* technology. The origins of the former school of thought date back to Walter Benjamin's 1936 essay "The Work of Art in the Age of Mechanical Reproduction," which in spite of its age is still widely cited as an authoritative statement on twentieth-century technologies. Benjamin, it should be noted, does not actually use the word *repetition* within this document. (Nor does he discuss music; his concerns lie chiefly with visual media.) His focus, rather, revolves around the status of an artwork's uniqueness—its "aura"—in relation to its newly emergent mass reproducibility. "That which withers in the age of mechanical reproduction," he writes, "is the aura of the work of art" (Benjamin 1969 [1936], 221).

Just five years later, Adorno extended these Benjaminian themes onto the terrain of music—specifically popular music—while simultaneously eschewing the hopefulness that Benjamin sometimes displays toward the radical possibilities of technological transformation. In its place Adorno proffers a withering pessimism. Defining popular music as low Other from the outset of his essay, Adorno frames it as a commercial product within a mass-market economy—an attribute that he regards as negative. The "fundamental characteristic" of popular music, standardization, affects it at all levels, including not just its means of distribution but also its form and musical details (Adorno 2002 [1941], 437–38). He links repetition in particular

---

[3] Criminal Justice and Public Order Act, 1994, c. 33. As many have noted, this definition is exceedingly broad and capable of applying to a plethora of musical styles. In its historical context, however, it was meant to ban a particular kind of electronic dance music event: the open-air raves that were spreading throughout the English countryside during the early 1990s. The Act as a whole encompassed many measures, with the legislation against raves forming one section.

to the means through which popular music was promoted during the Tin Pan Alley era ("plugging"). Moreover, he sees a strong connection between the system of standardization and questions of individual agency. He repeatedly frames popular music's fans as passive tools in a collective mass, as in this description of "rhythmically obedient" listeners:

> This obedient type is the rhythmical type.... Any musical experience of this type is based upon the underlying, unabating time unit of the music—its "beat." To play rhythmically means, to these people, to play in such a way that even if pseudo-individualizations—counter-accents and other "differentiations"—occur, the relation to the ground meter is preserved.... [T]he standardized meter of dance music and of marching suggests the coordinated battalions of a mechanical collectivity.
>
> (ibid., 460–61)

For the most part, however, Adorno's essay addresses repetition only indirectly.[4] Moreover, he speaks of musical repetition only briefly and intermittently.[5] Perhaps most surprisingly given his concern with industrialization, Adorno fails to address the role of recording technologies and other mass media in popularizing and disseminating music. This task was left to those who inherited his intellectual legacy. Attali, for instance, posits a "repetitive economy" that arises through the operation of recorded music as a commodity (Attali 1985 [1977]). His treatise uses "music" writ large as a rubric to develop a theoretical account of various historical and socioeconomic stages in the history of humanity.

When we imagine repetition as a *musical* technology, one with particular affordances for the musicians and dancers who engage with it, we can begin to see it as opening up possibilities rather than closing them off. It emerges as something other than a side effect of industrialization, and as more than an aspect of musical design. As a core musical technology, it is also crucial to the ways in which performances are fashioned.

As the most important of the seven musical technologies discussed in this chapter, repetition receives the most in-depth treatment. It is the focus of three sections. The first ("Repeating in Context, I: The Scholarly Field") situates repetition intellectually, delineating principal themes of research on the subject. Attention to work in psychoanalysis and Afrodiasporic studies in particular reveals that negative readings of repetition often devalue it in favor of progress and growth, whereas purportedly

---

[4] Contemporary reception, however, shows that the essay is widely regarded as dealing with repetition; it is extensively cited in accounts of the subject.

[5] This is not the case in his essay "Stravinsky and the Restoration," which I discuss later in this chapter.

favorable accounts often move away from their object of inquiry through a questionable maneuver in which repetition is "rescued" by revealing hidden difference. The second section ("Repeating in Context, II") focuses more specifically on electronic dance music, specifying the musical attributes that define it as a repetitive practice. Only a certain subset of music involving repetition is understood as "repetitive"; what leads listeners to such a perception? The third section, "Repeating in Time," takes up a charge to conceptualize repetition as a crucially temporal phenomenon. It therefore brings repetitive practices into dialogue with duration, pulse, periodicity, meter, entrainment, and other key concepts of musical time.

To frame repetition as a musical technology means to think of it not simply as some general musical attribute, but rather as a way of actively structuring time, music, and performance. The word *repeating*, which appears in the title of each section on repetition, is intended to draw out this sense of ongoing behavior or action-in-progress. Antecedents for such a usage appear in at least two published accounts of repetition. In the English translation of Attali's *Noise* (1985; trans. Brian Massumi), "repeating" appears as the next-to-last in a series of gerundive chapter titles: Listening, Sacrificing, Representing, Repeating, Composing.[6] As noted above, Attali's concerns lie with the ramifications of sound-reproduction technology rather than musical repetition per se. By contrast, in his 2001 dissertation Eugene Montague repurposes "repeating" as a technical term describing a specific kind of relationship between musical listening and movement. Montague's choice of language emphasizes the processive, contingent qualities of this phenomenon.[7] Whereas "repetition" may imply "a completed, finished construction," repeating provides "a recurring creating of the potential for movement"—an "ongoing, always renewing, determining of a specific future" rather than a product given at the outset (ibid., 46–47).

After the three sections on repeating, a fourth section addresses two technologies: cycling and going. I seek to theorize musical cycles as inherently temporal rather than spatial. By uncovering their kinetic dimensions, I reveal cycles as dynamic configurations of musical energy that push performance forward. In their goal-directedness they involve "going" as well. This emphasis on dynamism extends into the following section, "grooving." Here I build on the burgeoning area of groove theory in order to

---

[6] This rhetorical device appears only at a background level, however. Within the actual chapter the word *repeating* scarcely appears; the more conventional "repetition" is the preferred form instead. This distinction holds within the original French as well, albeit in a slightly more complicated manner. The chapter title, "Répéter," can mean either "repeating" or "to repeat." As in the English, however, Attali primarily uses "la répétition" within the chapter itself.

[7] These emphases clearly reflect the foundational role that Christopher Hasty's theory of meter plays in Montague's work. Attali may also have been an influence, at least in terms of how Montague titles his chapters: "listening," "theorizing," "dancing," "performing," and "playing (with music)."

tease out the specific components that make up this musical technology. An analysis of a set of grooves used in performance by the musicians Phon.o and Bernhard provides a practical illustration of the principles involved.

The subsequent section addresses a technology that I call "riding." Riding denotes a particular way of experiencing music as technologized process. This means not only that physical technologies are a central part of musical performance and listening, but also that these processes are imagined through technological lenses. Riding further offers a distinctive configuration of teleology in relation to subjectivity.

As a musical technology, "transitioning" entails a formal principle rather than a compositional segment. It is a mode of generating perpetual forward motion and growth that simultaneously avoids a sense of striving toward a defined goal. Transitioning works in tandem with flowing, the other technology addressed in the final section. "Flowing" refers to an essential quality of process within performance. When sound flows, it does so continuously and indefinitely. As with riding and transitioning, flowing develops via technology and is understood through technologized metaphors.

Like the physical and electronic technologies explored in Chapter 2, each of these musical technologies allows, invites, or suggests certain kinds of actions. These are its affordances. The site of possibility here is not the interface, however, but rather the unfolding musical improvisation. These musical technologies facilitate the freeing of recorded sound within performance and its creative refashioning through improvisational actions. These actions include, among others, overlaying rhythmic patterns; maintaining a uniform tempo; altering the texture; deconstructing and transforming the formal arrangement of recordings; creating structural articulations by removing and reintroducing the bass drum at strategically chosen moments; altering ongoing (repeating) sounds with effects, thereby creating climaxes (and generating liveness); and producing a continuous flow of sound from discrete objects. To reveal how musical technologies afford such actions is a principal goal of the discussion that follows.

Repeating in Context, I: The Scholarly Field

Despite its central role within musical communication, repetition is one of the most undertheorized of all musical phenomena. Work on the topic has grown in recent years, but the amount of music scholarship that directly addresses it in depth remains surprisingly small. As modest empirical evidence, note that in late 2009 a subject search for *repetition* in the *Répertoire International de Littérature Musicale* (*RILM*) yielded just 149 results—in all languages. It is not a stretch to surmise that the near silence, until very recently, from theory and musicology with regard to repetition suggests that it has not simply been ignored, but rather actively *excluded* from scholarly validation. The resultant lacuna likely stems from repetition's associations (with "low" cultural forms and with the music of minorities and non-Westerners) and from the various anxieties that have crept up around it. In particular, the unease surrounding repetition has connected it to large-scale technological mediation and to an attendant loss of agency and individuality, and in some cases to compulsions and other psychologically problematic behavior.

The effects of this scholarly undertheorization of repetition are several. First, our descriptive language for repetitive phenomena is impoverished. With regard to music in particular, scholarship tends to employ "repetition" and its derivative word forms to refer to a wide range of attributes and practices, many of which repeat quite differently. (As but one of many possible examples, the motivic repetition that Carl Schachter or another Schenkerian analyst might identify in the middleground of a graph is fundamentally different from the repetition that Lerdahl and Jackendoff 1983 ascribe to metrical accent.) Second, and related to the previous point, the terminology that is used to describe repetitive phenomena is often applied indiscriminately. Third, the various *musical* phenomena that fall under the rubric of "repetition" have not been clearly differentiated.

The literature on repetition that *does* exist—and here I include a number of influential studies that do not address music at all—can be divided roughly into six areas: (1) psychoanalytically inflected critiques (principally Freud 1961 [1920], but to a lesser extent also Adorno 2006 [1958]); (2) accounts that focus on the perceived effects of technologies of reproduction (Benjamin 1969 [1936]; Adorno 2002 [1941]; Attali 1985 [1977]); (3) work on repetition within African and African American expressive practices (Chernoff 1979; Erlmann 2000; Gates 1988; Monson 1996; Potter 1998; Rose 1994; Snead 1981); (4) philosophically oriented accounts (Deleuze 1994 [1968]; Kivy 1993; Rahn 1993); (5) research on minimalism in music (Cumming 1997; Fink 2005; Leydon 2002); and (6) theoretical or analytical work on repetition as an aspect of musical design (Garcia 2005; Horlacher 1992, 1995, and 2000; McClary 2007; Middleton 1983, 1990; Montague 2001; Schoenberg 1984 [1950]). Within the latter subdivision, a burgeoning interest in "groove" is increasingly evident; this originates in the earlier work of Keil (1966, 1987, and 1994 with Stephen Feld) but has recently been developed significantly by Benadon (2007), Butterfield (2006, 2007), Danielsen (2006), and Timothy Hughes (2003).[8]

---

[8] The list of sources in this paragraph, though quite broad-ranging, has undoubtedly omitted some works that other authors would wish to include. Any omissions, however unintentional, are my own. It might also be noted that some of the works listed resonate with categories additional to the ones in which I have placed them.

The following section explores certain recurring concerns and emphases within these areas. My goal is to set the stage for the more specific account of repeating as musical technology that I develop in the next two sections. Because that account explicitly aims to reveal repetition as (1) musically productive and (2) intrinsically temporal, this section highlights scholarship that offers points of departure for conceptualizing those dimensions. The first area to be considered, psychoanalytic theory, is significant because it sets a largely negative tone that is perpetuated in a great deal of subsequent work on repetition. The second area, African and African American studies, attempts to conceptualize repetition in positive terms. In so doing, however, it reveals a paradoxical tendency to characterize the repetition that it values as ultimately embodying *difference*, thus moving away from the very object it aims to describe.[9]

The fact that repetition is a more general form of human behavior has musical implications. Sonic events are often understood as behaviors, as actions attributable to musical "agents."[10] When such an agent repeats, questions are raised about its motivations for doing so. Possible motivations for repeating human behaviors have been addressed most explicitly in the psychoanalytic literature. The most influential source in this area, Sigmund Freud's *Beyond the Pleasure Principle* (first published in 1920 as *Jenseits des Lustprinzips*), associates repetition with early childhood, arguing that in this context it serves positive functions of learning and play: "the child repeats even the unpleasant experiences because through his own activity he gains a far more thorough mastery of the strong impression than was possible by mere passive experience" (Freud 1961 [1920], 45–46). Mature subjects, however, do not consciously desire repetition; for them, "novelty is always the necessary condition of enjoyment" (46). All the same, adults—particularly those suffering from traumatic neuroses—do tend to repeat certain past experiences unknowingly. Freud labeled this pattern "repetition-compulsion" (22). The repetition-compulsion has the character of a drive (*ein Trieb*), which Freud defines as "a tendency innate in living organic matter impelling it towards the reinstatement of an earlier condition" (47). As such it is inherently regressive in character, and ultimately associated with the death-drive, the primary counterpart to the life-sustaining tendencies of the libido.

Freud's ideas resonate within a number of influential musical critiques. The most obvious and strident of these appears in the work of Theodor Adorno, particularly "Stravinsky and the Restoration," a lengthy chapter within his *Philosophy of New Music*

---

[9] These tendencies have also been noted in an account of scholarship on repetition by Garcia (2005).

[10] For an early work on musical agency see Maus (1988); for a recent account see Leman (2007).

(2006 [1958]).[11] Adorno repeatedly characterizes Stravinsky's compositional technique as psychologically regressive. "As a virtuoso composition of regression," he writes, "*The Rite of Spring* wants not simply to surrender itself to regression but to gain mastery over it through copying it" (113). In this statement (as is typical of his essay more generally), Adorno moves quickly between compositional and psychoanalytic perspectives, suggesting that Stravinsky's musical techniques effect a kind of meta-regression, one in which the content of the *Rite* is also its means. The linkage to mastery via copying (itself a form of repetition) reveals the Freudian influence even more strongly. Nor does Adorno shy away from remarking on repetition as a *musical* phenomenon, portraying it as static and antidevelopmental in statements such as this:

> The elementary case of rhythmical variation, in which repetition consists, is that the motif be so constructed that if it suddenly reappears without a pause after its conclusion, the accents fall on other notes than at the beginning. . . . Accordingly, the melodic cells stand under a spell: They are not condensed but rather impeded in their development.
>
> (ibid., 114)

All of this, of course, is opposed to Schoenberg, whom Adorno presents as the epitome of musical "progress." Schoenberg's most well-known treatise on musical development, his essay "Brahms the Progressive" (1984 [1950]), is less overtly Freudian than Adorno's work but still psychologically inflected. In particular, obsessions creep up around themes of growth and development, and repetition plays a key role within these moments. Schoenberg is not opposed to repetition *carte blanche*; he acknowledges its role within well-organized and intelligible musical expression (399). At best, however, he regards it as a technical aid to musical communication, one that composers should strive to minimize through variation and growth. As with Freud before him and Adorno after, he associates repetition (in this case, explicit repetition on the musical surface) with infantilism: "An alert and well-trained mind refuses to listen to baby-talk and requests strongly to be spoken to in a brief and straight-forward language."[12] The ideal form of composition, "musical prose," should consist of "a direct and straightforward presentation of ideas, without any patchwork, without mere padding and empty repetition" (415). Throughout the essay Schoenberg is much more explicitly concerned with the details of musical technique than are other writers

---

[11] In addition to Adorno's Freudian critique, a small number of recent authors have theorized repetition through a Lacanian psychoanalytic perspective. See especially Cumming (1997) and Schwarz (1993). Both authors focus primarily on minimalist music and subjectivity but also address repetition.

[12] Ibid., 401. Notably, "baby talk" resurfaces as a section caption within Adorno's essay "On Popular Music" (Adorno 2002 [1941], 450–51).

on repetition. In the midst of the numerous musical examples, however, appear surprisingly frequent aesthetic evaluations. Typically they evince a strongly Modernist cast. After presenting (and praising) a series of excerpts from *Le Nozze di Figaro*, for instance, Schoenberg asserts that "organization based on different and differently shaped elements proves to be a vision of the future" (413). In such moments, when he valorizes change, progress, and "the future," Schoenberg reveals what is really at stake.

Schoenberg's position foregrounds difference and change; although recognizing the need for comprehensibility and coherence, he contends that the unifying elements within compositions must constantly grow and transform. What if sameness rather than difference were the favored term in this equation? A positive account of repetition has been one apparent goal of scholarship on African and Afrodiasporic expressive practices (including but not limited to music). This area of research is particularly relevant for electronic dance music, which originated in African American contexts in Chicago, Detroit, and New York. The most influential account of repetition in this field is Henry Louis Gates, Jr.'s, *The Signifying Monkey* (1988). Gates asserts his central claim near the outset: "Repetition and revision are fundamental to black artistic forms, from painting and sculpture to music and language use. I decided to analyze the nature and function of Signifyin(g) precisely because it *is* repetition and revision, or repetition with a signal difference" (Gates 1988, xxiv; original emphasis). For Gates, repetition unleashes a chain of "re-" words that resonate throughout the work: repeat, revise, rename, refigure, reverse. When these phenomena function expressively within black American culture, they are always relational; more precisely, they hinge on "a relation of difference inscribed within a relation of identity" (45). Signifyin(g) is the ultimate example, in the way it tropes and transforms the meaning of the ordinary word "signifying." For Gates, meaningful repetition always involves difference.

A number of other scholars have confirmed the role of repetition as a central, prominent organizational principle of African and Afrodiasporic expressive forms. Perhaps the strongest statement comes from Veit Erlmann, who asserts that "at the broadest level, African performance and all diasporic musical styles that flow from it are characterized by repetition" (2000, 85). James Snead, in an essay that gives a broad account of repetition in European and Afrodiasporic cultural expression (and that predates Gates's book), contends that black music "draws attention to its own repetitions" (1981, 151).[13] In a similar fashion, Tricia Rose refers to the ways in which black musical styles "privilege" repetition (1994, 71).

An important contribution of this work involves the specific, positive claims it has made about the ways in which repetition functions within these traditions of

---

[13] Snead primarily addresses philosophy and literature, but he also speaks briefly to music within his essay.

artistic communication. Ingrid Monson, for example, details a "musical texture in which repetition is both fundamental and a source of variety" (1999, 36); she links this mode of organization to improvisation, commenting on "the musical logic of layered periodic repetitions that structure processes of improvisation observable in the African diaspora" (49). Snead makes a similar point, albeit with a less sophisticated notion of the basis for performance: "Without an organizing principle of repetition, true improvisation would be impossible, as an improvisator relies upon the ongoing recurrence of the beat" (1981, 150). John Miller Chernoff, in the earliest of the works cited here, argues that African musicians use repetition to bring out the "rhythmic tension" of particular configurations (1979, 111). In so doing, they magnify the power inherent in the music and reveal "the *depth* of the musical structure" (112; original emphasis).[14] Erlmann, in turn, frames repetition in African music as a broadly based *practice* (as opposed, for instance, to a technical procedure). Drawing on Gates' argument that signifyin(g) foregrounds the signifier over the signified, Erlmann contends that this repetitive practice emphasizes "how things are being done"—in other words, "manner rather than matter" (2000, 86).

Among these scholars' significant achievements is a broad-based body of scholarship that values rather than discredits the role of repetition in music. At the same time, certain issues emerge within this work. First, the ways in which certain authors have connected repetition to blackness has led in some cases to charges of essentialism. Erlmann, for instance, states that "the question of repetition has been reduced by authors such as James Snead and Tricia Rose to a sine qua non of black identity."[15] Russell Potter also criticizes Rose's work for "seeming to concede that African traditions *are* indeed more repetitive" (1998, 37; original emphasis). In his response to such perceptions, however, Potter takes matters to the other extreme, tipping the scale of repetition versus difference strongly toward the latter side. He claims, in effect, that whatever appears "the same" in Afrodiasporic music is in fact always already different. Such arguments reveal a recurring tendency, perhaps already latent in the dynamic but tenuous balance between repetition and difference in Gates' work, to move away from repetition even as one seems to approach it.

If emphasizing the differences articulated within repetitions tends to retreat from repetition per se as a subject of inquiry, such a tactic also makes it hard to conceptu-

---

[14] Although Chernoff's work, with its detailed attention to musical design, predates the paradigm shift that took place in ethnomusicology beginning in the 1980s, it is still cited admiringly by leading scholars; see, for instance, the aforementioned works by Erlmann (2000, 86) and Monson (1999, 33–34).

[15] Erlmann (2000, 86). This remark, which is part of a larger point about associations between musical and racial difference, is balanced with a criticism of the perception of repetition as "the mark of cultural regression and commodification" by Adorno and other Marxist commentators (ibid.).

alize "literal" or "exact" repetition. Questions arise with regard to value. Some kinds of repetition—those with "signal differences"—become "good," while others are treated as problematic or not worthy of mention.[16] If, as for Gates, all meaningful repetition involves difference, how can exact or literal repetitions function meaningfully? Technologically mediated styles such as EDM do not allow us to rationalize exact repetition out of existence. Rather, they insistently and repeatedly raise it as an issue for consideration.

Snead, describing one way in which cultures may compromise between unmitigated repetition and unceasing novelty, posits "the notion of progress within cycle, 'differentiation' within repetition" (1981, 149). Although this formulation appears similar to the "relation of difference inscribed within a relation of identity" that underwrites Gates' theory (1988, 45), Snead's reference to cycles introduces the crucial variable of *time* into the equation. Gates, by contrast, does not invoke temporality at all. The kind of repetition with which he is concerned is essentially atemporal, centered on texts that various authors revise. Although this does involve temporality indirectly, in that revision occurs in different time periods, this fact is not a particular focus of his theory. To the extent that Signifyin(g) might serve as the basis for a theory of repetition in *music*—an essentially temporal phenomenon—this distinction is crucial. To fully comprehend how repetition functions as a *musical* technology, we must uncover its specifically temporal dimensions. I take up this task shortly in the section entitled "Repeating in Time." First, however, the next section continues to explore broad questions around repetition by exposing the components of repetitive practice in electronic dance music.

Repeating in Context, II: Electronic Dance Music as Repetitive Practice

> **Warning: "Lost" and "Djarum" contain repetitive beats.**
> We advise you not to play these tracks if the Criminal Justice Bill becomes law. "Flutter" has been programmed in such a way that no bars contain identical beats and can therefore be played at 45 or 33 revolutions under the proposed law. However we advise DJs to have a lawyer and musicologist present at all times to confirm the non-repetitive nature of the music in the event of police harassment.
> —AUTECHRE, *Anti EP* (Warp Records WAP54), text from sticker placed on record jacket, 1994; original emphasis[17]

---

[16] See also Garcia (2005, 2.20), in which "exact duplication or repetition *tout court*" is described as the "Other" of repetition with difference.

[17] Images of the sticker and the record can be viewed at http://www.discogs.com/viewimages?release=157 (accessed March 22, 2010).

In 1994, the British IDM duo Autechre released the three-track *Anti EP* in protest of the Criminal Justice and Public Order Bill, which became law later that year. As noted in the introduction to this chapter, the statute famously attempted to define the music heard at raves as "characterised by the emission of a succession of repetitive beats." Although Autechre's gesture may appear tongue-in-cheek, and the British definition hardly holds up to music-theoretical scrutiny, the singling out of repetition as a target for legislative intervention and protest certainly reveals just how strong responses to this aspect of musical design can be.

Indeed, although the text of the Criminal Justice and Public Order Act keeps its description of the music played at raves quite open, repetition is one of the few defining attributes that it specifies precisely. It does not indicate that the music involved is almost always electronic (instead referring to it simply as "amplified"); nor does it mention that this music is used for dancing (though it does indicate that EDM involves the "emission" of beats). The emphases that characterize this definition highlight the fact that EDM is well known—some might say notoriously known—as "repetitive."

Given EDM's many distinctive features, why is it so strongly associated with repetition in the public imagination? Repetition is evident in all musical cultures; in fact, it is a necessary component of human expression. Music without some degree of repetition is extremely scarce, almost to the point of nonexistence; the few examples that have been devised, such as Schoenberg's early athematic works (the third of the *Drei Klavierstücke*, op. 11, and the fifth of the *Fünf Orchesterstücke*, op. 16, entitled "Das obligate Rezitativ"), have an experimental or hypothetical character. Hence it becomes apparent, as James Snead has written, that cultures distinguish themselves not so much by the presence or absence of repetition in their expressive practices but rather by the attitudes they exhibit toward it:

> Culture as a reservoir of inexhaustible novelty is unthinkable. Therefore, repetition, first of all, would inevitably have to creep into the dimension of culture just as it would have to creep into that of language and signification because of the finite supply of elementary units and the need for recognition in human understanding. One may readily classify cultural forms based on whether they tend to admit or cover up these repeating constituents within them.
>
> (Snead 1981, 146)

Snead is speaking about culture in a broad sense, but his claim easily extends to music cultures in particular. And in the music-culture of EDM, repetition is markedly on display. Although it is hardly the only musical style to have been characterized as repetitive, it distinguishes itself by the extent to which it actively thematizes repetition, treating it not only as a fundamental structural principle but also as a deliberate aesthetic strategy, a feature of the music that is meant to be noticed and interpreted.[18] It is at this point that EDM emerges as "repetitive." This section attempts to uncover the musical means through which it does so and to reveal what EDM can show us about repetitive repetition more generally. Undergirding this discussion is the premise that "repetition" and "repetitive" are not simple linguistic relatives. The noun can easily be understood as neutral, as a straightforward label for a very broad phenomenon, whereas the adjective usually carries strongly pejorative connotations. It seems, paradoxically, that only certain kinds of repetition are repetitive.

Repetitiveness inheres first in the basic musical materials of DJ and laptop performances: loops, drum patterns, and bass lines. Nothing is stated once and then varied; everything that is present repeats many times. Change mostly occurs quite gradually and is based on the entry and exit of textural components rather than clear formal divisions. Within tracks (to the extent that tracks are present within performance), there are sectional types; however, there is no set number of each type, certain types may be omitted, and the order and length of sections varies.[19] This approach to form is an important difference between electronic dance music and certain other styles that employ repeating grooves. The clear verse-chorus form that is the basis of rock, rap, and a host of related styles structures repetition more diffusely, in that verses and choruses often use distinct grooves and larger verse-chorus repetition introduces differentiation through sectional division. Sectional repetition is a prominent feature of jazz and the blues as well, with repeating harmonic progressions serving as the primary articulating element.

Repeating grooves occupy a distinctive position within the texture of electronic dance music. In brief, they *are* its texture. In other prominently repetitive styles, grooves serve as foundations: their invariance serves as a backdrop or ground against which a "figure"—a vocalist, a solo guitarist, a saxophonist, a master drummer—can act more freely, foregrounding difference and change.[20] In a DJ or laptop set, by contrast, repeating patterns are the very substance of the music. Reactive differentiation finds expression in the bodies of dancers; their movements are the figures in this musical fabric.

Technology—namely, technology of sound production and reproduction—also plays a role in the way in which EDM manifests as "repetitive." Drum machines and sequencers allow sounds to repeat with mechanical precision, in terms of both timing and exactness. Many EDM rhythms are "quantized"—that is, spaced with mathematically

---

[18] Indeed, a great deal of repetition goes unnoticed as such. Danielsen (2006, 160–62) explores this point, drawing from the work of David Lidov (1979).

[19] See Butler (2006, 221–24) for further discussion of sectional types. The types given there are intro, buildup, core, breakdown, and outro.

[20] My use of "figure" and "ground" here follows the early insights of Philip Tagg on rave (1994).

perfect evenness and consistency.[21] Machines have a unique capacity to sidestep the minute timing variations—described in scholarship with such terms as "microtiming," "expressive variation," and "microrhythm"—that tend to inform human performance. This forms a significant point of distinction in relation to other styles that foreground repetition to a comparable degree. I am thinking in particular of funk, a style that is historically linked to EDM as an important antecedent for styles such as Detroit techno.[22] Funk has been widely characterized as highly repetitive, yet numerous minute timing variations are an essential part of its expressive configuration. Danielsen, for instance, has recently theorized funk strategies such as the "downbeat in anticipation": a particular way of playing the beginning of each measure on top of the beat, with a "highly accurate inaccuracy" (Danielsen 2006, 78).

It is important to realize that the strictness I have described is not simply a by-product of technology; rather, it is an intentionally cultivated creative strategy. Electronic dance music is not simply made with machines; in several ways it aspires to *sound like* machines.[23] In the ways in which they repeat, EDM compositions actively *model* technology. Here, perhaps, is the point at which "repetitive beats" may attract the censorious attention of the law and other guardians of public order. The beats referred to in the Criminal Justice Bill were presumably not the kind that theorists of meter have described; nor were they just any of the many recurring patterns in the music. More likely they were the bass-drum beats of a drum machine: the trace of EDM that enters the ears when one walks past a club from outside, or when rowdy English ravers disturb one's rest. The musicians who compose with these beats pay a great deal of attention to their timbral qualities, shaping their attack, decay, and overall tone until the desired effect is precisely achieved. Once a drum-machine or computerized beat has been programmed and set in motion, however, its continued repetition is, at least in theory, infinite.

These repetitive beats foreground the fact that when repetition is produced through mechanical means, the structuring of time can expand beyond typical human scales. DJ and laptop performances always run continuously for at least an hour, if not several, and the larger performance context of which they are a part—a night of clubbing—lasts for the course of an evening or longer. Technology thus

---

[21] This is generally true even with swung rhythms, as various degrees and styles of swing can be applied via algorithms. Nonquantized rhythms may arise via sampling, which frequently draws on recorded performances, and playing patterns as a means of input.

[22] See for instance Sicko (1999). Funk was also a source of influence for disco, and vice versa.

[23] My point here is not that EDM imitates the actual sounds of machines, such as motors or helicopters. Although this is sometimes the case, this fact is not particularly interesting. Rather, I am suggesting that techno and other genres "sound like" machines by presenting us with musical patterns that *act like* machines, and by cultivating aesthetic qualities that we associate with machines (such as precision, speed, and the like).

extends the physical capacities of human performers, although continued human involvement—including, of course, that of dancers and clubbers—means that the experience is not limitless. Rather, the night out stages a productive encounter between technologically facilitated and humanly produced repetition.[24]

Thus, even though EDM is hardly the only "repetitive" musical style, it does display a distinctive orientation toward repetition, which listeners respond to when they describe it in this way. Its repetitions are meant to stand out; they insistently and repeatedly proclaim their presence. What does it take for repetition to draw attention to itself in this way? What conditions lead to the perception of particular instances of repetition as "repetitive"? What can EDM show us about how this occurs?

First, repetitive repetitions are usually *immediate*. In other words, no time interval comes between the presentation of a musical element and its restatement. In terms of affect, immediate repetition differs quite significantly from recurrence after a period of absence. For this reason, I prefer to use "recurrence" to describe the latter phenomenon, although in common usage "repetition" and "recurrence" are often treated as synonyms. (Indeed, "recurrence" itself can encompass a wide range of qualitative variance depending on the amount of time intervening between statements.) Distinguishing between immediate repetition and subsequent recurrence might seem fussy, or perhaps too obvious to warrant protracted comment, but it is important to do so because in practice they are treated quite differently within analytical and critical accounts of music.[25] For writers whose work has been invested in validating the cultural status of "high" art (and in simultaneously distinguishing it from "low" forms of cultural expression), repetition has been valued in inverse proportion to its immediacy. "Hidden" repetitions as well as large-scale recurrences organizing long spans of time receive praise, while immediate repetition is either not deserving of comment or a cause for critique.

Second, "repetitive" repetitions are more often than not *exact*. Conceptualizing exact repetition appears difficult, however, for ontological questions begin to surface as soon as the issue is brought up. What is exact repetition? Does it even exist? How is it to be distinguished from its presumed opposite, difference? These questions have been the focus of prolonged philosophical inquiry, as for example in Gilles

---

[24] One could also think of pulse-pattern minimalism, which arose in the decade following the emergence of recording-centric styles such as rock and which featured technologically produced repetition in many early instances, as offering similar experiences of technologized, extrahuman temporality. Fink in fact comments on the "vastly extended timescale and large amounts of 'hypnotic' repetition" shared by minimalist music and EDM's predecessor, disco, arguing that the two styles articulate libidinal desire in a highly similar manner (2005, 31ff.). A crucial difference, however, surely inheres in the centrality of funk to the musical energetics and bodily engagements of disco and EDM.

[25] Moreover, this difference in treatment usually takes place without comment, thereby revealing that unexamined assumptions are at work.

Deleuze's *Repetition and Difference*, in which the author seeks to radically reimagine the relationship between the two terms:

> We are right to speak of repetition when we find ourselves confronted by identical elements with exactly the same concept. However, we must distinguish between these discrete elements, these repeated objects, and a secret subject, the real subject of repetition, which repeats itself through them....In every case repetition is difference without a concept.
>
> (Deleuze 1994, 23)

The idea of exact repetition has been challenged in particular through phenomenological lenses. As a number of authors have pointed out, even if sound has been fixed through recording or other mechanical means, no two listening experiences will be identical. Danielsen, for instance, observes that "in music where every basic unit is exactly like the preceding one and where the basic units, if taken out of time and placed on top of one other [*sic*], are identical—for example because the music is performed by machines and not human beings—every repetition is still different, because the time in which it occurs is new" (Danielsen 2006, 162). To extend this, even if it were somehow hypothetically possible to hear a repeating sound source with absolute consistency (across subjects, repetitions, or listening occasions), one would nevertheless experience subsequent iterations as "the second time," "again," and so on. This in itself is a difference in experience.

Here, however, I am interested in a functional notion of exact repetition, one based on recognition of the fact that people continue to experience and understand repetition as "exact" even when it only approximates that ideal. From this perspective the ability of exact repetition to be dislodged philosophically or phenomenologically becomes less of a concern. If one starts from a position in which repetition across-the-board is treated as always already negative (as it is in a great deal of scholarship on the subject), then scholars who wish to recuperate the concept have an interest in portraying exact repetition in particular as a mirage. However, if exact repetition can be valued instead for what it does, it then becomes possible to appreciate its epistemological reality.

An additional challenge to exact repetition is the fact that performers always play "the same thing" slightly differently. This fact is often presented as a kind of defense for repetitive musics, as a way of showing that they actually involve a great deal of variety within their repetitions. Danielsen, for instance, notes that "if the listener is sufficiently attuned to details and other events on a micro-level, there is almost always something different in a given repetition" (2006, 159). She mentions a riff played by the response guitar in James Brown's "The Payback" as an example: "The funky wah-wah riff is extended so that the gestures gradually get bigger and looser, occupying more space and more time" (ibid.). As described above, however, the achievement of musical repetition through mechanical reproduction allows expressive microtiming to be removed from the equation. The facilitation of musical repetitions through technology emerges as a fundamental component of the anxieties that develop around the perceived "repetitive" nature of EDM and other highly mediated styles. This music is "exact" in a much stronger sense, one that is also less apparently human in its articulation of time.

The ways in which we seek to imagine sonic events as human behaviors, as actions that can be attributed to musical agents, is crucial to the third path through which repetitions may come to seem repetitive. To the extent that repeating is understood as a kind of behavior, the actions of the musical agent who repeats must also be understood as *justified*. "Repetitive" repetitions, by contrast, are often perceived as unjustified and quickly garner negative attention. Repetitions that seem unmotivated or unnecessary receive labels such as "redundant" or "excessive," inviting us to speculate about the character of the musical agent who acts in such a way. Is she merely ineloquent, or possibly self-indulgent? Perhaps he is acting out a compulsion or is otherwise disturbed. Though such perceptions are not the sole source of the negativity that permeates much of the discourse surrounding repetition, they certainly amount to a significant dimension.

A fourth element pertinent to repetitiveness is the rate at which musical material changes. In many cases in which music emerges as repetitive, a small amount of content is tied to a large amount of presentation time. The balance of these two variables, though not an attribute of repetition per se, can serve as a useful rubric for measuring the repetitiveness of any given instance of repetition. The threshold at which "repetitiveness" emerges will likely reflect a balance between shared cognitive capacities and the particular cultural and aesthetic values of individual listeners.

Repeating in Time

In the previous chapter, in an effort to move beyond the polarization of improvisation and composition, I suggested a way of understanding the relationship between musical creation and performance in which the former was situated along a continuum measuring the relationship of musical specificity to time. In this model, sonic outcomes specified fully before performance (ahead of time) lie at one extreme, and musical results specified only within performance (in time) at the other. This conceptual framework also allows us to comprehend the unexpected way in which repetition engenders improvised performance in EDM. In relation to the dialectics of fixed/fluid and product/process that have shaped so much thinking about improvised performance, repetition would conventionally fall on the side of products and fixation. Repetition is more strongly associated with identity than with difference; it is often understood as a re-inscription of the same. Moreover, within a system in which music circulates as a commodity, repetition appears to be the means through which EDM actually generates products (namely, recordings). As a *musical* technology, however, repetition works quite differently. As the next section explains, *how* electronic dance music repeats—and more specifically, how it repeats in time—is essential to the transformation and release of prerecorded objects within fluid, improvised performance.

The role of repetition in performance is a metonym for the broader relationship between music and time. Through music we enact our relationship with time in a special way. In particular, humans have repeatedly sought means to measure and control time's motion. Repetition in music provides a strong connection to this tendency, for in the context of an unfolding musical event it functions as a key technology for mastering time. Just as recordings seem to "capture" sound, repetition appears to harness time.

The first element of time that repetition harnesses is *duration*. Repetition of duration comes into play through *periodicity*. Although repetition and periodicity are strongly associated, to the extent that the two terms are sometimes treated as synonyms, periodic repetition is in fact a subset of the broader phenomenon. Several conditions must be met for periodicity to arise. First, the duration involved must be clearly defined. As Christopher Hasty explains in *Meter as Rhythm* (Hasty 1997), this cannot take place until the event with which it is associated has ended. Moreover, for a definite duration to be reproduced by a succeeding event, the reproduced duration must also have a definite end. This gives rises to a further condition: namely, a third event must begin at the anticipated moment of delineation (84–86). Figure 4.1, a reproduction of Hasty's graphic representation, depicts the processes at work. Here, C and C' are two events, each consisting of a sound (A and A') followed by a silence (B and B'). The duration of C becomes definite when C' begins. But is the succeeding duration a reproduction of the preceding one? For this question to be answered, a C" must follow at the right moment.[26]

In terms of periodicity, the entrance of a C" would show that one repetition has occurred, for there are two iterations of a duration that we perceive as equivalent.

---

[26] It should be noted that, despite the importance of Hasty's ideas to the account I am developing here, my treatment of these issues will develop rather different concerns, especially as regards the pride of place that I seek to give to repetition (a term that Hasty appears to avoid throughout much of his work). In fact, my use of "repetition" throughout this discussion actually represents one such difference in orientation; Hasty generally favors "reproduction" in his discussions of projection. Further comment on Hasty's stance toward repetition, and on how my understanding of repetition differs from that which he finds problematic, will follow shortly.

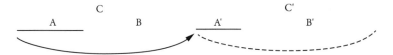

FIGURE 4.1. Projection from the standpoint of durational products C and C' (Hasty 1997, 84)

The articulation of these two durations required three beginnings. Periodicity in the fullest sense, however, involves something more: in particular, an expectation that an entity will continue to repeat. This would clearly require more than one repetition, for repeating must be established as an ongoing behavior. Although it is doubtful that scholarship could specify an exact number of repetitions needed for this expectation to arise (and surely the point at which it develops would depend on the norms of the musical style and the disposition of individual listeners), the quantity involved must at least be plural.

It is also important to realize that periodicity arises through the repetition of a duration and not the event itself. This distinction between durations and events is evident in Figure 4.1 above. The events labeled C and C' are composite, consisting of both sound and silence. Although the presence of both elements is clearly unnecessary for event-ness per se, the inclusion of the intervening silences makes Hasty's point much clearer. Otherwise, the reader might be prone to conflate the two sounds—A and A', themselves events in their own right—with their respective durations.

Certain kinds of commonly identified repetition—for instance, the repetition of a motivic pattern in a Schenkerian sense—are clearly not periodic, for they do not involve a definite duration (and its reproduction). Although periodicity obviously entails the perceived repetition of many kinds of patterns (melodic, harmonic, timbral, lyrical, and so on), as a phenomenon it derives not from the patterns themselves but rather from the repeating durations they articulate.[27] Moreover, through the way in which they repeat, these durations color the very elements with which they coexist.[28] Note as well that the discussion above clearly frames periodic repetition as *immediate*. Certain cases of

---

[27] It should also be noted that the sense of periodicity that is of concern here requires duration to be directly perceivable through listening. The periods of other repeating phenomena, such as the orbits of planets or the rotations of subatomic particles, are discernible through measurement but not perceivable through our aural capacities (though some—most famously the ancient Greeks—did believe that the motions of heavenly bodies made music).

[28] This claim about the experiential co-presence of musical dimensions that are often treated discretely derives from observations made by Mari Riess Jones and other cognitive psychologists about the dynamic manner in which we attend to music in time (Jones, Moynihan, MacKenzie, and Puente 2002; Jones, Johnston, and Puente 2006). I describe Jones's theory in detail shortly. Grant (2010) develops this perspective on temporal attending into a much broader claim about the function of meter in experiential contexts, arguing that meter should not be thought of as "one component or parameter of music; when present, it is fundamental to the perception of everything musical" (278).

immediate repetition might not develop into a sustained sense of periodicity (as for instance when a duration is presented twice and then abandoned), but perceptions of periodicity as ongoing will always arise through repeatings that are immediate.

Along with duration, the second element that repetition harnesses is *pulse*. In electronic dance music, pulse is steady, ever-present, and explicitly articulated. EDM shares these features with certain other minimal, repetitive styles, such as the repertoire that Robert Fink has described as "pulse-pattern minimalism." Fink uses this term to denote the music of Philip Glass, Steve Reich, and subsequent minimalists working in pulse-based styles (2005, 20) and to distinguish their practice from the drone-based work of composers such as La Monte Young. Both kinds of minimalism feature continuous, ongoing sound and bind small amounts of content to large amounts of presentation time. Pulse-patterned music, however, configures time with an extreme precision that drone-based minimalism largely shuns. It is this dimension that is of interest to us here.

More broadly, pulse is a feature of all music that exhibits meter. Within music theory, meter is widely understood as a hierarchical perception involving at least three simultaneous layers of regular pulsation: one corresponding to the beat or "tactus," a faster-moving layer that divides beats into twos or threes, and a slower-moving layer that corresponds to the measure. Electronic dance music and other repetitive pulse-patterned styles differ not in their overall relationship to this construct—EDM is, after all, metrical—but rather in the characteristic ways in which they deploy meter's basic elements. First among their signal features is a special relationship toward pulse. Pulse in these styles tends to be explicitly and fully articulated. In other traditions, pulse often goes unnoticed, and a substantial number of pulses may be omitted; it is up to listeners to infer them. Here, by contrast, the tendency is to sound *all* pulses within a given layer. In particular, the referential beat, which is a near constant presence, is usually played by a single dedicated instrument.

Higher-level groupings have important functions in pulse-patterned styles, but there are fewer of them. Wide gaps between higher and lower levels are characteristic. This tendency is evident in a range of styles, including many of Reich's compositions and the "minimal" and "hard" genres of EDM. In Jeff Mills' track "The Bells," for instance, short periodicities receive the greatest emphasis (see discussion in Chapter 3, especially Fig. 3.16 and corresponding analysis). The loops of the bass drum, hi-hat, and handclaps repeat in quarter-note increments, while the bell sounds and bass line articulate half notes. In fact, only one sound—riff 1—loops over a longer duration. The rhythm pattern formed by its attacks spans four beats (one bar), while the detuning of alternating chord pairs within it also weakly articulates an eight-beat span (two bars). The next longest duration, expressed via textural changes rather than loop lengths, occurs at the eight-*bar* level.

Because of this gapped relation between faster- and slower-moving layers, the sense of periodicity cultivated by electronic dance music may be attenuated in places where we would typically expect it to be strong. The most obvious of these is the measure; in minimal techno, for instance, it is not uncommon for a series of pulses to appear and be divided without articulating periodicity at the level of the measure. This strategy favors pulse at the expense of metricality. In other cases in which only two metrical layers are present, they may emerge as the beat and a grouping thereof, such that the music is heard as "in two" or "in three" in a general sense without differentiating between simple and compound meter.[29]

Gretchen Horlacher has written about similar tendencies in the music of Steve Reich. She notes how he foregrounds pulse, "often engag[ing] the lowest levels of counting" (2000, 269). With regard to his work *The Desert Music*, meanwhile, she describes a process in which he clearly establishes levels with periodicities of one, two, and twenty-four quarter notes while maintaining ambiguity with regard to the middle levels (ibid., 281–83). Robert Fink, in turn, claims "an intense, self-contradictory, fast-and-yet-slow experience of passing time" as a central component of minimalist aesthetics, asserting that "with minimalism,...the key feature of the experience is the *interpenetration* of fast and slow" (2005, 104–5; original emphasis). This play with temporal extremes seems to resonate outward into discourse on minimal music's effects. On the one hand, a great deal of music that has been singled out as "repetitive" has also been described as static, antidevelopmental, and lacking *telos*. On the other, many repetitive styles are characterized by an extremely active rhythmic surface, such that their fans among the general public would label them "fast."

In more practical terms, these aspects of temporal design have crucial implications for the ways in which performers and listeners (including listeners who are dancing) respond to and create music. First, the ever-present pulse provides musicians and dancers with a clear and constant base, both within individual tracks and throughout the performance as a whole.[30] Beyond that, however, they have a great deal of freedom; there is room for significant intervention on their part. The relatively indeterminate middle levels of meter, for example, work as spaces to be filled in by performers. They, rather than the composer, provide these essential periodicities, which are clearly among those to which people relate most directly. At the same time, because long-range goals are relatively well established, performers can direct musical growth and audience responses toward these signposts effectively. Above and beyond mere

---

[29] For further discussion of these phenomena, see Butler (2006, 111–13 and 129–30).

[30] The similarity of bass-drum beats across tracks within a genre is an important factor facilitating this continuity. Indeed, it is significant that musicians actually alter the tempo of tracks in order to preserve the continuity of bass-drum-as-thread, as the practice of beat matching demonstrates.

repetition per se, therefore, the distinctive qualities of EDM as a vehicle for real-time improvisation hinge on the particular ways in which pulses and pulse patterns repeat.

These emphases on the ways in which performers interact with musical technologies apply not only to pulse, but also to the broader phenomenon of meter. In particular, this interactive perspective suggests an understanding of meter as *practice*. That is, meter is not something that comes from outside us, a fixed musical attribute that we happen to encounter; rather, it is something that we *do*. In addition to listening and playing music, some of the most significant ways in which we construe and maintain meter are counting and moving in time (including, but not limited to, dancing). Through these actions we locate and express meter in and through our bodies.

Moreover, all of these behaviors may be understood as modes of attending. In cognitive psychology, models of meter as a dynamic mode of attending have become increasingly prominent during the past two decades. The work of Mari Riess Jones and a team of co-researchers at the Ohio State University Lab for Research on Attention and Rhythmicity has been particularly influential in this regard. Earlier theories had conceptualized metrical cognition in terms derived from information theory and computer science; they treated the mind as an information processing machine that compared the accent patterns of an incoming musical stream to an internalized "clock" in order to find the best metrical match (Povel and Essens 1985). By contrast, Jones and her team developed an event-based view of meter, arguing that "attending itself is a dynamic and temporally based activity" (Jones, Moynihan, MacKenzie, and Puente 2002, 314; see also Jones, Johnston, and Puente 2006). Jones' model takes the temporal dimensions of neural activity as its starting point, positing that internal oscillators within the brain will gradually synchronize to a regular external rhythm. Figure 4.2 illustrates this process, which in cognitive psychology has come to be known as "entrainment."

The black bars in this figure represent the attack points of musical tones, while the distance between these attack points is labeled "IOI," for "interonset interval." The series of waves beneath the bars represents corresponding attentional peaks. This type of attending-in-time is anticipatory. As the oscillators synchronize with the stimulus rhythm, anticipation becomes stronger (thus the higher peaks) and the ability to predict the next arrival more precise. Note also that attentional focus is distributed across a range, which the model terms an "expectancy profile." As shown in the pop-out detail, the expectancy profile peaks at a moment described as the "Expected Critical IOI." Notably, this profile has width; it is not a durationless time point. Rather, the dynamic attending model views expectation as "an active temporal anticipation" instead of "a grid point in a memory code" (Large and Jones 1999, 124).

An Entrainment Model

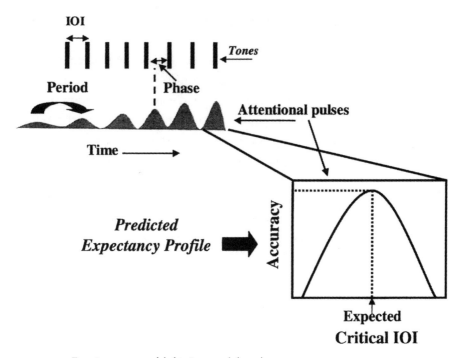

FIGURE 4.2. Entrainment, as modeled in Jones et al. (2002), 314

Finally, this dynamic, in-time mode of attending is not only temporal; it is also rhythmic and periodic. Large and Jones describe the attentional peaks as "pulses," and more specifically as "periodic attentional pulses" (123). In this way, cognitive behaviors come into synchrony with musical behaviors. Entrainment can thus be seen as another dimension of our active constitution of meter.[31]

Moreover, entrainment theory also shows how the process of attending to a periodic pulse can be dynamic and variable. Since periodicity, as we have seen, is a particular kind of repetition, we might therefore ask how temporal phenomena involving repetition can also possess these qualities. Of foremost concern among these phenomena is meter. The most comprehensive and detailed account of the ways in which music theory has situated meter with respect to repetitive phenomena is

---

[31] At the same time, the extent to which entrainment is subject to voluntary control is not yet clear (Jones et al. 2006, 91–92). This does not dispel my basic point, however: meter is still something that we do through attending, and not an external attribute that we simply discover. It is also important to differentiate entrainment as a general temporal phenomenon from meter as a more specifically musical phenomenon. London brings this point into dialogue with a view of meter as behavior when he writes (2004, 4), "Meter is a musically particular form of *entrainment* or *attunement*....Meter is more, however, than just a bottom-up, stimulus driven form of attending. Metric behaviors are also learned—they are rehearsed and practiced."

Christopher Hasty's monumental *Meter as Rhythm*. In this work Hasty attempts to rethink the very nature of meter. He is especially concerned with the separation of musical time into "rhythm" and "meter," a division that became paradigmatic within music theory by the mid-1980s.[32] As Hasty reveals, meter always comes out on the short end of this asymmetrical binary (Hasty 1997; see esp. 3–10). Because it can be described numerically, it ends up being conceptualized in terms that are primarily quantitative rather than qualitative. It is represented spatially, as a location on a time line, rather than temporally. It is portrayed as general rather than particular. Perhaps most importantly to Hasty's point, meter in this opposition is treated as already determined, as given. It is unvarying and always "the same." As a result, it begins to seem mechanical and inexpressive:

> Viewed in this way, meter, like a clock, runs unperturbed, continually and uniformly measuring a time in which a variety of events may occur—the genuinely rhythmic events that occupy the time meter measures off. And with this image it is difficult to avoid the implication of a rigid determinism. Once set in motion, meter can seem to run autonomously, driven by its own internal laws and fated from the beginning to reproduce its preordained set of time divisions.
>
> (1997, 5)

Hasty's effort to rethink meter so as to afford it the same novelty and particularity associated with rhythm has inspired a great deal of subsequent work. In attempting to move away from accounts of meter as inexpressive and unvarying, however, Hasty seems to scapegoat repetition. More specifically, he strongly associates periodicity with what he describes as "denial of tense": a spatialized conception of time in which past, present, and future are imagined as points on a line, and "now" is by definition a durationless instant (7). From such a perspective, time can be viewed synoptically, in marked contrast to how we actually experience it.

Hasty also connects this formulation and cyclic repetition: "The regularity of cycle is the recurrence of the same time span over and over again without regard to qualitative differences among returns and without regard to the number of repetitions," he writes (8). Moreover, he argues that a treatment of meter as cyclic will inevitably lead to an abstract, quantitative approach: "An analysis of meter in which meter is conceived as cyclic repetition will explicitly invoke the discontinuity of number and will result in the representation of rhythm as a systematic whole of coordinated periodicities in which all the parts are ultimately fixed in a scheme of

---

[32] The solidification of this division within rhythm and meter scholarship has sometimes been described as the "1980s consensus"; see for instance Temperley (2001, 60–61) and Grant (2010, 4–9).

changeless relationships" (10). In essence, he argues that the very concept of the cycle overwrites any heterogeneity that individual cycles might possess: "*the* cycle itself, as rule, is autonomous and logically precedes any such marking."[33]

Perhaps the strongest indicator of Hasty's ambivalence toward repetition is the fact that he avoids the word throughout most of his book. It does not appear in the index and is generally used only in discussions of other authors' views. In formulating his own theory, Hasty generally prefers "reproduction." His analytical work, meanwhile, seems to suggest that he developed his theory at least in part in order to deal with highly nonrepetitive, possibly nonmetrical styles: for instance, chapter 14 presents extended analyses of compositions by Webern and Babbitt (as well as early seventeenth-century works by Monteverdi and Schütz),[34] and his other publications focus almost exclusively on twentieth-century art music. Ironically, however, a large number of the scholars who have been drawn to Hasty's approach deal with strikingly repetitive styles.[35] This suggests that, regardless of one's stance toward it, repetition is a key issue for this way of thinking about musical time.

As a response to the opposition of rhythm and meter that had been solidified by the "1980s consensus," Hasty's refutation of meter as endlessly self-replicating makes sense. Today, however—in no small part due to the rethinking of musical time that Hasty's work cultivated—it seems both possible and important to develop an account of musical repetition that affords it the dynamism previously associated only with "rhythm." Temporal "activity" does not have to be inextricably linked to temporal "change," as Hasty seems to suggest when he describes rhythmic perception as "a coordination of our attention with what is active and changing" (68). Moreover, the ongoing repetition of a musical entity (such as a pattern of metrical accents) is not inherently "given"; pointing out that we expect a pattern to continue repeating is not the same as saying that this repetition is inevitable or infinite. Although theorists may have treated meter this way in the past, this attitude can now be challenged. It is time to discover how musical regularity and repetition can have character: to integrate repetition and particularity, much as Hasty did for meter.

---

[33] Hasty (1997, 8). The italicization of *the* is original, and important to his point: he is speaking of a view in which a piece of music is regarded as possessing a single homogeneous meter, expressed as a regulating cycle. His remarks about repetition more generally are also concerned with meter in a basic sense. By contrast, my emphasis throughout this chapter is much more focused on actual repeating patterns (thereby imparting a significant degree of particularity).

[34] The rest of the book does present many short examples from common-practice works.

[35] Relevant sources include Butterfield (2006) and my own work on electronic dance music (Butler 2001 and 2006). Gretchen Horlacher, who has written principally about Stravinsky but also on Reich, also uses Hasty's ideas in recent work (2001).

Cycling; Going

An endeavor of this sort must concern itself not only with repetition and perio-dicity, but also with the cyclical dimensions of EDM's repeating components. As has been previously shown, such components are a central feature of this music's design:

> [T]he fundamental unit of musical structure in EDM is a repeating pattern associated with a particular instrument, which fans and musicians describe as a "loop." Most tracks are composed primarily (if not entirely) of loops.... The primary indicator of loop-based structure is cyclical repetition: if the rhythm of a certain part of the texture varies freely, with no discernible pattern of rep-etition, it is probably not a loop....
>
> Although many popular-music styles with roots in African-American music make use of cyclical repetition, the pervasiveness of loop-based structure in EDM sets it apart.... [In EDM], the vast majority of rhythms unfold as con-stantly repeating patterns. As a fundamental structural idea, this cyclical repeti-tion manifests itself on multiple levels: not only in loops, but also in sequences, and ultimately within the structure of a complete track, as embodied in the form of a continuously revolving record.
>
> (Butler 2006, 90)

Existing scholarship, however, offers few tools with which to conceptualize the cycle as a musical technology. Discourse on cycles has too often cast them as atemporal, spatial, static, and timeless. They are frequently conflated with circles, which lack a clear beginning and end. By contrast, this section develops an account of cyclical design that is inherently temporal. My orientation throughout is broadly theoret-ical, focused on developing a conceptual framework. I posit an understanding of cycles as having clear points of origin, distinct phases with particular qualities, and goal-directedness. They engage in-time attending and are intrinsically dynamic, working as an impetus that propels performance forward. In the latter respect they involve "going" as well; although this technology appears primarily in the second part of the section, I treat "cycling" and "going" in tandem.

Scholarship on temporality in music has employed notions of "cycle" often enough but has rarely attempted to develop a theoretical account of the concept. Instead, the majority of research is descriptive, technical, or analytical in orientation. Ethnomusi-cology, the field that has most seriously engaged with cycles as musical constructs, offers a plethora of work describing cyclical designs in the music of a specific cultural group. Many ethnomusicological sources extend their musical observations through homology, arguing that musical cycles mirror cultural concepts of time, cosmology, and so on.[36] In music theory, which until very recently was focused almost exclusively on a particular canon of Western art music, the word *cycle* has mostly been employed as a technical term. In the area of metrical theory, for instance, Yeston (1976), Horlacher (1992), Krebs (1999), and others have used it to denote the amount of time required for two superimposed rhythmic layers with noncongruent lengths to align. In addition, some theorists have developed analytically oriented research focusing on cyclical designs in the music of specific composers.[37] This work is much smaller in quantity, however, than the corresponding style-specific literature in ethnomusicology. Most frequently, music theorists employ "cycle" to describe an atemporal technical process, as with the widely used "interval cycle."

A recent work that does offer a serious theoretical engagement with questions of temporality and cyclical design is Justin London's *Hearing in Time: Psychological Aspects of Musical Meter* (2004). *Hearing in Time* is the first book-length work by a music theorist to address meter from the standpoint of cognitive psychology. In particular, London develops a view of meter that is strongly informed by the entrainment theories of Jones and others (described in the previous section). "The guiding hypothesis of this book," London writes, "is that meter is a particular kind of more general behavior" (4). More specifically, "meter is a form of entrainment behavior" (6). And most precisely, "Musical meter is the anticipatory schema that is the result of our inherent abilities to entrain to periodic stimuli in our environment" (12).

London first links meter to cycles in chapter 4 of his book, in a section entitled "Cyclical Representations of Meter" (64–69). He develops a format involving circular diagrams, which subsequently appear in chapters 7–9 as well. The pair of examples reproduced below in Figure 4.3 is representative.

Both figures represent a meter consisting of nine pulses, although the beats within each cycle group these pulses differently. The first figure groups them isochronously into three beats; the meter of this example would be 9/8, 9/16, or 9/4. The second figure, however, groups the pulses asymmetrically into four beats consisting of two, two, two, and three pulses. London describes this type of meter as "non-isochronous" or an "NI-meter" (101–102). These non-isochronous, maximally even patterns correspond to the class of rhythms that I have elsewhere described as "diatonic."[38] Indeed,

---

[36] Fabian (2002 [1983]) provides an important critique of anthropological claims about time in non-Western cultures, arguing that such depictions are part of the broader colonialist underpinnings of the discipline. More specifically, he contends that these claims produce a "denial of coevalness," which he defines as "a persistent and systematic tendency to place the referent(s) of anthropology in a Time other than the present of the producer of anthropological discourse" (31).

[37] See for instance Horlacher (1992, 1995, and 2000).

[38] See Butler (2006, 82–85). The application of this term to rhythms was first suggested by Jay Rahn (1996).

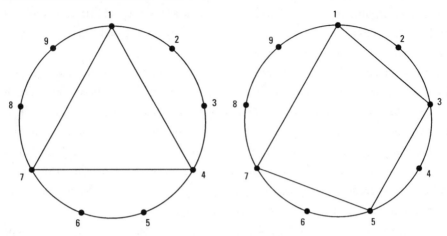

FIGURE 4.3. Circular meter diagrams from London (2004 [figures 7.1 and 7.2])

the way in which these diagrams support London's argument about the metricality of these patterns is one of the major strengths of this graphical format.

At first glance, London's circles appear quite different from previous theoretical representations of meter, which are almost exclusively linear. The hierarchical dot diagrams developed by Lerdahl and Jackendoff in *A Generative Theory of Tonal Music* (1983), for example, run in a continuous horizontal strip below the score. Hasty's projection diagrams also follow the score linearly; his approach would undoubtedly connect this aspect to the continuous unfolding of time.[39] In London's case, it turns out that the circle diagrams ultimately represent an abstraction about metrical structure rather than a claim about specific experiences of time. London is clear on this point: "If a meter is a stable, recurring pattern of attentional energy, it makes sense to represent this pattern with a circle, for in this way certain aspects of metrical structure will become apparent while at the same time freeing our representation of meter from any particular musical surface" (64). Although the circular design might seem to suggest movement in the form of a following or temporal attending that traces the perimeter of the shape, as well as qualitative aspects such the feeling of "coming back to" beat 1, the shape in this case turns out to be an icon of replication.[40] The circle does not represent a specific perception, but rather an abstraction of a composite perception that is seen to underlie an entire musical entity. This is in fact the very notion of meter as "*the* cycle" that Hasty critiques

---

[39] Hasty's diagrams are also frequently multiple and polyphonic in ways that Lerdahl and Jackendoff's approach does not support.

[40] It is also worth noting that the dots in the diagrams, which represent peaks of attentional energy, appear to reduce the width and shape of Jones's expectancy profile to a single point. London does try to circumvent this impression with prose, writing that "dots as markers for attentional peaks will have some temporal spread" (65).

(1997, 8, as cited in the previous section).[41] Therefore, despite its many insights, London's theory does not provide an experience-based account of cyclical temporality.

The centrality of graphical representation within London's account is indicative of a much larger trend. Spatial metaphors and images underlie a significant percentage (quite possibly a majority) of existing accounts of cyclically structured time. Although some authors, like London, are explicitly concerned with representation itself (see, for example, Benadon 2007 and Toussaint 2003), most employ the circle as tool for conceptualizing qualities ascribed to cyclical design.[42] The cycle is thus said to have no clear beginning or end, to move back regressively toward its beginning,[43] and to do the same thing over and over again. These associations lead to descriptions of cyclical time as static, and ultimately (paradoxically) as timeless. Perhaps most notably, many of these recurring claims about cyclical design closely mirror those found in musical and cultural accounts of *repetition*.

However, the most striking feature of these accounts of cyclical temporality is the pervasive binarism on which they are constructed. "Cyclical" time is almost always defined in relation to its perceived opposite, "linear" temporality. The terms of this storied opposition are of course predicated on the basic geometrical concepts of circle and line. Applied to musical time, the line becomes the emblem of teleology. In its most canonical formulation it symbolizes progress, narrative orientation, and the striving of an individual subject toward a goal. It also construes time as an endless, equable flow, according to Newton's paradigmatic conceptualization of "absolute" time.[44] Third, the *telos* toward which the musical subject strives is apparent throughout the composition, and relationships between present events and that goal are clearly defined. In opposition to this dynamic linear time, cyclical or circular time is depicted as a static, repetitive, and regressive Other. As with the rhythm/meter dichotomy, this binary is clearly asymmetrical. The cyclical is defined in negative terms, according to what it is not; indeed, the binary "linear/cyclical" is often glossed simply as "linear/nonlinear."

In order to conceptualize cyclical design in a way that allows it the same degree of temporal possibility afforded to "linear" temporality, it is imperative to recognize

---

[41] To be fair, London does nuance this view of meter in several ways. Within general classes of metrical types he identifies varieties that depend on tempo (chap. 4), and his "Many Meters Hypothesis" (chap. 9) permits a range of beat locations as a consequence of expressive timing. Nevertheless, these subtleties are largely absent from the diagrams themselves, which serve as the primary representations of cyclical design.

[42] London's circular representations are also strongly evocative of the clock face, one of the most extensively used icons of structure within music theory (although theorists more typically use clock faces to model pitch and pitch-class spaces).

[43] These first two claims are logical contradictions, of course, yet they frequently appear within the same argument; see, for instance, Goldsworthy (2005, 309–10).

[44] For an extended discussion of Newtonian time, see Grant (2010, 120–75). For a brief discussion in relation to cyclical temporality, see Hasty (1997, 9–10).

that cycles and circles are not equivalent. Most importantly, cycles are inherently temporal. Moreover, in contrast to circles, they are not intrinsically geometric. Astronomical cycles—a key source for defining and measuring temporal units—are at least elliptical, but many natural cycles do not involve circular motion; examples include sound waves, heartbeats, menstruation, and alternating electrical current, to name just a few possibilities. Rather, cycles in the sense that concerns us here may be thought of as a series of phenomena forming a process, one that returns to its original state on completion.

Significantly, the kinds of cycles that occur in musical time—for instance, measures, riffs, and loops—always have clear points of origin, a property that is lacking in circles. They may also be understood to possess distinct phases, each with its own experiential or qualitative dimensions. For instance, a measure of 4/4 meter, felt as a series of attentional pulses ("beats"), might display the following kinetic qualities:

1. Beat 1: strongest sense of orientation; position from which the rest of the measure's energy radiates
2. Beat 2: most commonly felt as reactive to beat 1 (an afterbeat), but may also be felt as leading to beat 3
3. Beat 3: second strongest sense of orientation; felt as reactive to beat 1 across a broader unfolding time span
4. Beat 4: most commonly felt as an upbeat—as leading toward the arrival of a new, anticipated downbeat—but may occasionally be felt as an afterbeat of beat 3

Attention to these qualitative aspects reveals how clock faces and other graphical representations fall short as descriptors of musical time. For instance, whereas the last fifteen minutes of an hour do not have any inherent qualitative difference from any other fifteen-minute segment within its duration—and a span of time such as 12:15–1:15 is equivalent, say, to 12:00–1:00—the span from one downbeat to the next in an ongoing meter is *not* equivalent to that encompassing beats 2 to 2 (and so on). Moreover, as these comments indicate, metrical cycles are also goal-directed: insofar as the duration of the measure and the placement of beats are sustained as anticipated outcomes, we feel that we are going somewhere, and we can also predict that goal. It is here where the technology of "going" begins to reveal itself.

In contrast, then, to the static, rootless, and nonprogressive qualities suggested by the conflation of circle and cycle, this view of cyclical temporality construes it as dynamic; as involving the past and the future as well as the "now"; as involving difference as well as sameness; and as crucially involved with in-time attending. Developing an account of the positive attributes of cyclical design is an important goal for music theory, which in its approaches has tended to link the cycle to the unvarying, automatic repetition ascribed to meter. (In theories based on a strict rhythm/meter division, this repetition is generally assumed; in the most prominent response to such theories [Hasty 1997], cycles are dismissed as models for metrical experience on the basis of their perceived repetition.) Musical time, however, is simultaneously recursive *and* forward-moving in important ways, and theories of time should address both aspects instead of favoring or excluding one at the expense of the other.

EDM uses the cyclical, recursive properties of musical time to great advantage, to the extent that cyclical design may be understood as an explicit, foundational structural principle of its musical practice. This does not mean, however, that EDM is somehow nonteleological, that musicians and dancers are uninterested in growth, motion toward goals, climax, and the like. Previous work has described the many ways in which musical design and performance practice create goal-directed progress across both moderate and large time spans.[45] These end-oriented processes interact with cyclical elements such as loops and sequences, which of course possess their own internal variegation, change, and growth. In this way, the teleology of EDM becomes multiply inflected.

How might such a teleology be conceptualized? Fink suggests the term *recombinant teleology*, explaining, "I borrow the terminology of gene splicing to emphasize the radical metamorphosis—through technology—of codes that were once thought 'natural' and immutable" (2005, 43). In practice, however, Fink mostly employs this term to refer to departures from "classical" teleology; his emphasis is on various combinations of cyclical and linear organization, leaving notions of "recombination" mostly in the metaphorical background.

This kind of temporal teleology might also be conceived of as *spiral*—in other words, as moving through cycles of varying sizes while also progressing forward. Jeff Pressing (1993) proposes just such a model as a way of reconciling "cyclic" time, which he associates with meter, with nonmetric or "linear" time (understood in his view as "scientific" or clock time). See Figure 4.4. One feature of a spirally conceived teleology that is appealing for electronic dance music is that it precisely mirrors the movement of a needle through the groove of a record: although the record rotates in a perfect circle, the groove moves slowly forward through a spiral. One less appealing feature is that Pressing's model does not account for differences between individual iterations of the cycle. It is thus an idealization, though it does usefully collapse the linear/cyclic dichotomy.

---

[45] See Butler (2006) for a detailed account of specific practices within dance music. Fink develops a similar argument at length, although his critique is focused more on constructions of desire and on problematizing portrayals of dance music as pure *jouissance* (2005, 31–47).

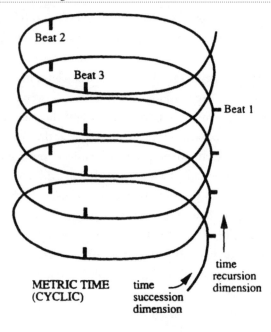

FIGURE 4.4. Pressing's spiral combination of linear and cyclic time (1993, 112)

Finally, there is one way in which the circle might still be productive as an icon of cyclical teleology. Imagine a circle that is not intrinsically closed but rather openable, like a necklace. Unclasped, it would reveal forward linear movement through a series of events. Closed, it would show the recursive dimensions of cyclical repetition. This model also works well because it involves clear beginning and ending points, in contrast to a seamless circle. In addition, it directs attention toward the circle's circumference. Other circular models are misleading in that they visually suggest that the interior plane of the circle may be a significant component of the graph. In fact, it rarely figures into consideration; the perimeter is generally the site of the modeling action.[46] Furthermore, because the necklace offers movement through both linear and cyclical paths, it avoids some of the contradictory claims made about exclusively "circular" patterning (for instance, that a circle moves "back" to its beginning, when more properly it is moving forward through a curve to an anticipated point of orientation).

Because musical cycles, as with repeating patterns more generally, possess temporal dynamism, they are integral to the way in which recorded sound is liberated

---

[46] The approach developed by Benadon (2007), which is based on polar coordinates, offers an exception.

within live performance. Rather than stopping time, the encircling of time's flow through the technologies of loop, riff, and sequence provides essential energy that propels the performance. The cyclical repetition of durations and tensional/accentual patterns, transformed through improvisatory intervention, fuels the forward motion of the event. Time thus harnessed is time freed.

Grooving

Musical dynamism and the effective shaping of time are essential aspects of "grooving" as well. As Anne Danielsen has written, "a groove does not stand still" (2006, 155). "Groove" is an insider term, which in recent years has increasingly been recognized as a distinct principle of musical design. Uses of the word typically involve one or both of two related ideas. The first of these is qualitative. For instance, when we speak about the way a song grooves, we are commenting on its shaping of time. I previously defined this sense of groove as "the way in which the rhythmic essence of music flows or unfolds" (Butler 2006, 5). In the program Live, groove as rhythmic quality is implemented in a highly practical fashion: the software includes a library of several hundred rhythmic profiles, called "grooves," which may be applied to any clip in a track (including samples as well as MIDI clips). Some relate to specific musical styles (hip-hop, rock), some to widely used EDM instruments (the Akai MPC-2000), and others to technical parameters such as degree of quantization or swing. Within the program, grooves actually constitute a specific file type (.agr).

The second commonly used sense of "groove" denotes a specific musical construct. For instance, one may speak of "the groove" of a song, which is a specific subset of its musical texture. Mark Spicer articulates this usage in the following definition:

> *Groove*: the complex tapestry of riffs—usually played by the drums, bass, rhythm guitar and/or keyboard in some combination—that work together to create the distinctive harmonic/rhythmic backdrop which identifies a song.
>
> (Spicer 2001, 10)

Repetition is also absolutely essential to groove in any sense. Lawrence Zbikowski defines groove as "a large-scale, multi-layered pattern that involves both pitch and rhythmic materials, and whose repetitions form the basis for either a portion or all of a particular tune" (2004, 275). Timothy Hughes further specifies that "a figure is not a groove unless it is *designed to be repeated*" (2003, 14; original emphasis).

The idea of a groove as a background pattern, as a repetitive and perhaps mechanical ground for freer, improvisatory "figures" performed by a soloist or lead musician(s), is pervasive; its relevance for a great number of musical practices cannot be denied. Monson, for example, describes this relationship as "the musical logic of layered periodic repetitions that structure processes of improvisation observable in the African diaspora: call and response over layers of repetition and departure" (1999, 49). Given the Afrodiasporic roots of rock and pop, such practices are likely traceable to various African drumming traditions in which an ensemble provides a constant fabric of interlocking percussion patterns against which a master drummer freely improvises. The relationship of rapped lyrics and "beats" (in this context, the instrumental groove) in hip-hop music works in a similar fashion, as for instance Robert Walser notes when he writes: "voice and instrumental tracks are placed in a more dynamic relationship in hip hop." Further, "the rhythmic placement of the phrases creates polyrhythmic tension up against the groove" (1995, 204).

Something similar is at work in one of the earliest and most well-known accounts of groove, that developed by ethnomusicologist Charles Keil. In a 1966 essay that is still widely cited, he develops a notion of "engendered feeling" that he sees as emerging through phenomena such as groove and swing. (Drawing on the work of the jazz scholar André Hodeir, he also links these phenomena to something called "vital drive.") For Keil, this feeling develops through a particular interaction between something strict and something free. He mentions "the tension generated by a complex relationship between meter and rhythm" (1966, 59), though his concern is less with "rhythm" in the sense of durational pattern and more with the microscopic timing deviations—now known more generally as "microtiming" or "expressive variations"—that create a sense of swing. He discusses jazz drummers who play "on top" of the pulse as well as those who "lay back" behind it (61), providing assessments such as "I hear Monk phrasing into or against the groove, while Miles is phrasing over or in-and-out of it" (65). Keil continued to develop these ideas in subsequent publications, proposing a new term—participatory discrepancies—to describe such expressive departures from regularity (Keil 1987; see also Keil and Feld 1994).[47]

EDM also develops a dialectic of human freedom in relation to temporal and mechanical regularity, through the improvisatory movements of dancers, and through the transformations and alterations that performers effect upon the unfolding soundscape. Participants in its musical culture value both sides of this equation,

---

[47] This later work, however, also displays an unfortunate essentialism, a tendency to reductively specify what music "is." This is evident for instance in the 1987 essay, which opens by proclaiming that "the power of music lies in its participatory discrepancies" (96). For more recent work that extends Keil's ideas and connects them to those of Hasty, see Butterfield (2006). Monson (1999) also mentions the "participatory qualities of repetition" (51) and frames riffs, repetitions, and grooves as "multilayered, stratified, interactive frames of musical, social, and symbolic action" (32).

however. The mechanical is not devalued but rather prized. Moreover, the groove does not play a background role in EDM; it is the primary formative material of the music itself. In keeping with these distinctive emphases, the following paragraphs focus not on departures from regularity but rather on the design of grooves as musical technologies. This prioritization also reflects my concern to show what is interesting about strictly regular and repetitive musical components.

The most extended music-theoretical treatment of groove to date appears in Timothy Hughes' 2003 dissertation on the music of Stevie Wonder. Hughes establishes the distinctive qualities of groove-based design at the outset of the work, noting that "the extensive repetition of relatively short musical segments ... requires a very particular construction" (15). More specifically, "a groove must be designed to function when played a single time, when following itself, when preceding itself, or all of the above" (ibid.). These considerations lead Hughes to develop a threefold taxonomy of groove types: the autotelic, which is "designed to lead the listener to expect its beginning to follow its ending"; wavelike grooves, which "are designed to create a sense of completeness at their end and then simply use repetition to generate a wave-like pulsation from completeness to incompleteness and back"; and a third type that is "designed to progress away from the beginning and then abruptly snap back when repeated" (ibid.). The guiding criterion here is teleology: the categories are structured around the ways in which they shape expectation and direct musical tendencies.

Establishing a range of teleological possibilities for grooves is significant in itself, given the reductive ways in which their shaping of time has generally been portrayed. Here, however, I will focus primary on the "autotelic" category, as this is the most prevalent type within Hughes's work, and also the most clearly delineated.[48] Hughes's first example within this category appears in his discussion of the song "Living for the City"; I have reproduced his transcription and analysis in Figure 4.5. In discussing this groove, which plays through nearly three-fourths of the song, Hughes emphasizes how the right hand moves in and out of phase with the left hand's constant pulse on F♯. The phases of the cycle involve a coordinated deployment of rhythm (the right hand begins in rhythmic unison, moves to the offbeats, and subsequently returns to the beat), harmony (movement away from and back to an F♯ major triad), and voice leading (upper-voice motion from F♯ to A and back again). At the end of the cycle, we strongly anticipate the return of the two-bar downbeat and the F♯ in the melody with its supporting harmony (2003, 28–30).

---

[48] The other two categories are less clearly distinguished, both from each other and from the autotelic. At times they seem to be presented as categories distinct from the autotelic, and at other times as subphenomena within it. Note also that the third category is not given a name during the initial presentation.

FIGURE 4.5. Transcription and harmonic analysis of Stevie Wonder, "Living for the City," primary groove (Hughes 2003, 29)

Hughes' account further reveals several distinctive features of autotelic grooves as a general class. First, their most important characteristic is the way in which they lead to their beginnings. This has come up previously, when I mentioned the paradoxical way in which cyclical designs are often said to lead "back" to their beginnings, even though they are moving forward in time. Danielsen, for instance (in an otherwise very dynamic account of grooves), employs this circular imagery when she writes, "When we are actually *in* a groove, the musical course is anything but open ended; it is experienced instead as a closed circle. The rhythmic dialogue leads back to its own beginning and the basic elements remain unchanged, almost as if they were decided beforehand" (2006, 237 n. 40). Hughes, however, is careful to avoid conflating temporal cycles with spatial representations. He offers a clarification:

> On paper, a repeat causes the sight-reader to look back to the beginning of the music being repeated—a spatial leap in an opposite direction....However, notation is not music, but rather a symbolic representation of music. Music itself is always experienced in a sequential, or linear fashion. So when we hear music repeated we hear it *move forward to its own beginning*....In analyzing how a groove works, it is always important to...analyze the moment of repetition—the seam between the occurrences—as forward motion from the end to the beginning.
>
> (Hughes 2003, 79–80)

In spite of the important corrective that this emphasis on forward motion offers, this account can be further clarified. A trace of spatial thinking is still detectable in the separation that Hughes maintains between concepts of "beginning" and "ending." Is the "end" of the groove shown above really the G♯ minor $\frac{4}{2}$ chord? Perhaps we might more usefully invoke ideas of "departure" and "arrival" here. In this way, we can see that the beginning of this autotelic groove is both a point of departure *and* (from the second iteration on) a moment of arrival. This simultaneity of arrival and departure is a fundamental element of cyclical design.

Related to both of the above points is a further property of autotelic grooves: they are not complete in themselves. The conclusion of the tensional process set up within the groove actually occurs outside its boundaries, at the moment when repetition begins (Hughes 2003, 32). This also reveals how the incomplete design of the autotelic groove works against the circle analogy, for a single groove cannot "come full circle" until it begins again. In spite of their prevalence, music theory has thus far only scratched the surface of these kinds of designs. Note, for instance, the contrast they form with the antecedent-consequent patterning that is taught to beginning theory students as the exemplar of normative phrase structure: in that system of design, the antecedent possesses its own cadence, distinct from the consequent; the boundary between the two is usually demarcated by some sort of diminution or cessation of motion; and in both phrases the real resolution occurs at the end rather than the beginning.

The notion of autoteleology itself is also worth examining. Hughes often glosses this kind of groove as "self-generating" (e.g., 15). This is not entirely accurate, however. The grooves do not generate themselves; a pattern such as that shown above could be resolved by any F♯ triad, and the piece could go on to something different. Rather, what these grooves generate is their own *telos*. A literal translation of the term is therefore the most precise.

I now wish to develop an analysis, one that will focus on a striking set of autoteleological grooves designed specifically for use within improvised performance. The grooves in question are *locked grooves*: short loops that are etched into records as perfect circles, so that they will repeat infinitely on playback.[49] In an earlier work (Butler 2006) I used the idea of locking—and more specifically, of *unlocking*—as a metaphor for the richness and openness of temporal experience within EDM. I also provided a brief technical definition of "locked groove" (ibid., 5). Here, however, I wish to explore the design of locked grooves in significant detail. By exploring the characteristics of locked grooves created and used in performance by two Berlin-based musicians—Bernhard Moosbauer and Phon.o (Carsten Aermes)—I will reveal how these DJ tools function as effective musical technologies.

The locked grooves that are used within electronic dance music share certain basic technical characteristics. First, because the circumference of the groove corresponds to the amount of time required for a record playing at 33⅓ rpm to complete one revolution, the tempo of a four-beat locked groove is always 133.33 beats per minute. Its total duration is therefore 1.8 seconds. The tempo and duration can always be altered using the controls on a variable-speed turntable, of course. Furthermore, it is possible

---

[49] Infinite playback is possible only in theory, however, as the physical surface of the groove will eventually wear out from the weight and friction of the needle.

to create a loop with a different number of beats (most commonly three), although the overall duration of the loop will remain the same. Such patterns are uncommon, however; the vast majority of locked grooves contain four beats.

Because locked grooves are grounded in the physical medium of vinyl, they are particular to DJ rather than laptop sets. In performance they are most typically used as supplemental elements; DJs mix them in with full tracks in order to augment and transform the overall texture. They are especially common in the techno genre, which is already minimal and repetitive.[50] In this context they effectively fit into the overall sound while simultaneously taking the structural principal of repetition to the ultimate level.

In comparison to these established practices, the approach favored by Phon.o and Bernhard is unique in two respects. First, they create entire performances using *only* locked grooves. Second, they compose and produce a significant number of locked grooves themselves. Each musician has an independent history, particularly Phon.o, who is internationally active. A labelmate of Apparat, he releases his own albums and twelve-inch singles and performs live, solo laptop sets. In collaboration, however, he and Bernhard have created a unique side project that is wholly centered around locked grooves. In performance they play together under the moniker "The Bareback Show," a name that connotes the perilousness (and also the freedom) of performing with such minimal materials. Each musician uses two turntables and his own mixer, while a third mixer controls the combined output. The entire performance consists of locked grooves, some composed by other musicians and some by Phon.o and/or Bernhard. I observed and filmed one such performance at the club Maria in Berlin on July 9, 2005. I then interviewed Phon.o and Bernhard on July 20, 2005 about the event and their approaches to performance and production.

The process of composing and recording locked grooves began with Bernhard, who produced three locked-groove records as part of a diploma project in art school, a conceptually oriented event at which he and two other musicians played his grooves using six turntables.[51] The sounds on the records consisted entirely of samples from his personal record collection. He subsequently decided to continue this process, planning a series of thirteen records in all, the sides of which would be labeled A–B, C–D, and so on, continuing through the rest of the alphabet. For each record he chose a restricted and quite particular sample set: one, called *Sounds of Death and Horror*, was derived entirely from soundtracks for Super 8 horror films;

---

[50] For discussion of "techno" as a genre, see Butler (2006, 41–43 and 45–47).

[51] Moosbauer is a visual artist by profession, active primarily in photography but also in media art. In the latter capacity he has worked under the name "exsample" (www.exsample.org; accessed May 1, 2011), and in the former he has founded galleries such as compact/space (originally based in Berlin, but now located in Los Angeles and Geneva).

compact/tool

Vinyl-Endlosloopplatten-Serie.
Geplant sind insgesamt 13 Vinylplatten, jeweils in einer limitierten Auflage von 500 Stück. Auf jeder Plattenseite sind 50 1,8-Sekunden lange Soundloops.
Die Serie wird Veröffentlicht auf dem Label „normoton".
Mittlerweile gibt es 5 verschiedene Platten.

Auflage: jeweils 500
Preis pro Platte: 25,-

FIGURE 4.6. Locked-groove records by Bernhard and Phon.o, from a catalog for compact/space Berlin

another, called *Fieber* ("fever"), took its samples from a Polish Elvis impersonator. After hearing some of Phon.o's music, Bernhard invited him to contribute to the series. In contrast to Bernhard's sample-driven approach, Phon.o composed his own grooves, using traditional EDM production methods. Figure 4.6 shows the five records that had been released as of 2007.

Although Bernhard and Phon.o did not collaborate during the production of these records, they soon began to do so within performance. Each instance of "The Bareback Show" is almost entirely improvised, as the two musicians explained when I asked them about the planning and coordination of their performances:

> MARK BUTLER: I want to ask about how the planning worked, because you were playing both on two turntables, and I was wondering how you were coordinating that.
>
> PHON.O: I would say that we don't have a special order of records. And we have really just a few combinations of records, for better loops, because there are…a lot of loops on one record. But normally we try to avoid a special order of loops or something. So [in this way we] keep it…
>
> BERNHARD: …keep it live. The most important thing about it is, every performance is very, very different. We just, maybe before the show, discuss the direction, something like "start with dub, then go on with house, and then stop with techno stuff," or something. But this is the only thing we…
>
> PHON.O: …decide, really, in the beginning, inside the club.

Needless to say, the simultaneous control of four turntables is an extremely complex task. Moreover, one of the chief technical aids of the standard DJ set—the ability to pre-listen to a mix through headphones before making it audible to the audience—is in this case severely handicapped (each musician can pre-listen to his own pair of turntables, but not to the overall sound). Working to the musicians' advantage, however, is a difference unique to an all locked-groove show: there is no need to beat match, because every groove has the same tempo. It is still necessary to align the loops in a pleasing way, however. For instance, playing the downbeat of one groove against beat 2 of another would be a serious mistake. More generally, Phon.o and Bernhard strive to make effective combinations of sounds. The texture must be balanced, and neither too thin or too thick. On the one hand, it would be problematic for both musicians to be digging in the crates for a new loop at the same time; this could lead to an overly minimal texture as well as a lack of dynamism in the mix. On the other hand, it would be poor to have two leading melodies playing at the same time. Phon.o and Bernhard noted that they sometimes avoid such situations by using hand gestures to indicate that they are about to bring in a

new loop. In general, however, they structure their interaction through spontaneous responses that are guided by knowledge of the other player's style, as Bernhard
explained in this interchange:

MARK BUTLER: Do you have any kind of plan for who's going to put a record
on when? Or are you both just going independently?

BERNHARD: It's more like a session tool, you know? We are right at the beginning, in the moment, you can say. And from each session to each session, we
get to know each other better. So actually it's like a chess session, too, you
know? Everybody has his instrument, or a range of instruments, and you
have to know how the other one thinks.

In describing locked grooves as "tools," Bernhard makes it quite clear that he imagines
these musical entities as a kind of technology that facilitates improvised performance.
The paragraphs below address the musical properties that I observed in their grooves,
through analysis of eleven grooves found on a record given to me by the two musicians at the time of the interview. The sounds on this record were composed by
Phon.o; each of its two sides (which are labeled "I" and "K," respectively) contains
fifty grooves. I listened to each groove, made written observations of its interesting
features, and assigned it a number (I1–50 or K1–50). I then produced detailed transcriptions of eleven grooves (Fig. 4.7), which were selected for their representative
range of properties. These will serve as a reference point for my discussion.

In order to understand the operation of these repetitive technologies, one must
keep in mind how they are implemented both physically and temporally. First, what
is produced in the creation of a locked groove is not simply a four-beat pattern (as
shown in the transcriptions) but also a specific kind of material object. This object is
a "groove" in the strictest possible sense, and in geometric terms it is a circle—as we
have seen, the shape that creeps up again and again in numerous characterizations of
repetition. The circular groove gives no clues about its temporal design; one cannot
find the downbeat (or any other beat) from a visual examination. Geometry must
therefore give way to process. The DJ's interaction with the groove is a technologically mediated process of entrainment. The first step in this process is to place the
needle on the record's surface, an action that sets the groove in motion at a randomly
chosen point. The downbeat—the most important source of the DJ's orientation to
the groove—can only be found by listening. Moreover, orientation to the regulari-
ties of the downbeat and its subsidiary beats ("entrainment") arises specifically
through the technology of looping. The groove is a kind of self-stabilizing system: it
begins to repeat and then the listener (in this case the DJ) "finds" a downbeat to
entrain to. In this way, the process becomes the point.

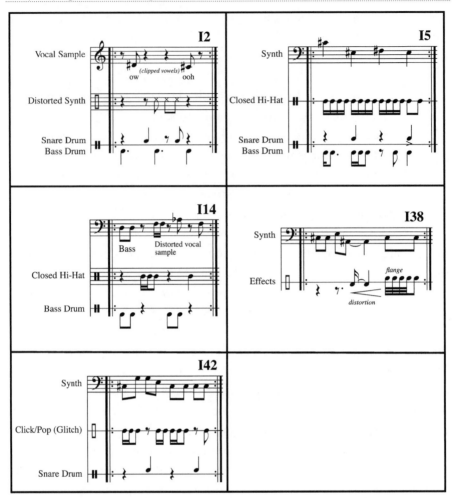

FIGURE 4.7. Locked grooves from record *I-K* by Phon.o

Not surprisingly, all of the grooves shown in Figure 4.7 feature some sort of clear articulation on beat 1. The majority also further mark the downbeat with a bass-drum attack (the three exceptions are I38, I42, and K3). I14 doubles the bass drum's eighth notes at the beginning of the measure, thus creating a low-end convergence. At times defined pitch plays an additional role in marking the downbeat, as with the high C♯ in I5. In general, however, pitch is used sparingly within these groove-based designs. Although pitch does retain a significant perceptual salience when it occurs, its presence is so restricted that it remains subsidiary to the overall repetitive structure. It is treated not as the core of the music but rather as one of its many effects.[52]

---

[52] The salience of pitch as an orienting factor is also reduced by the surprisingly frequent use of diminished triads within these grooves (although it is unclear whether this effect was intentional). Such triads, which resist functioning as tonics, appear in the synth lines of I14, I38, and I48.

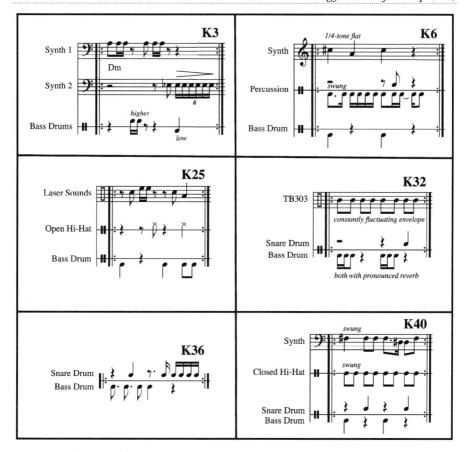

FIGURE 4.7. (*Continued*)

Second in importance to beat 1—yet clearly a place where very interesting things happen—is beat 4. This primary upbeat is a powerful locus of musical dynamism; its thrust propels the teleology forward. Beat 4 is almost always implicated in some kind of change or contrast within the pattern. In some cases the change is relatively simple, as in I5, in which beat 4 is marked through a dynamic accent and a reduction in bass-drum activity. K32 takes this simplicity to a much greater extreme, as the snare-drum attack on 4 is really the only departure from rhythmic evenness within the entire pattern. More typical are I38 and K3, which feature clusters of change around the upbeat. In K6, meanwhile, beat 4 is defined by the absence of an attack, producing a kind of negative space within the ongoing flow of sixteenths and eighths.

A subcategory of this emphasis on beat 4 appears in several patterns that feature a strong 3+3+2 division of the measure. I previously discussed this pattern as one of a distinct subclass of "diatonic" rhythms (Butler 2006, 82–89). When the 3+3+2 organization spans a full measure, it places its last attack squarely on beat 4, creating the upbeat emphasis noted above. Also significant is the way in which 3+3+2 begins on beat 1, "departs" to an offbeat (beat 2.5), and then returns to alignment on beat 4. In Figure 4.7, 3+3+2 patterning appears in I2 (very clear, thanks to its presence in the bass drum) and K3. K36 contains 3+3+2 over a half-note span, which accordingly emphasizes beat 3 and its eighth-note upbeat.

As an upbeat rather than an afterbeat, beat 4 has the energetic quality of leading *to* beat 1. This tendency is often made more explicit through increases in rhythmic activity that push toward the downbeat and then diminish. Such patterns are most noticeable in K25 and K36 but are also evident in I38 and K3. (Note that these grooves generate this dynamism with little or no involvement from pitch.) Moreover, beat 4 often has a companion on beat 2; the snare-drum offbeats that appear in I2, I5, I42, and K40 serve an orienting role that is nearly as important as that of the strong-beat articulations.

Considered collectively, these grooves clearly exemplify the autotelic properties discussed earlier. This is evident first in the way in which each groove leads forward to its own beginning. The strong emphasis on beat 4 is a key technology leading forward in momentum to 1. There is one possible exception to this trend, however. A small number of Phon.o's locked grooves—generally, those that feature mostly even rhythms—exhibit ambiguity regarding the location of the downbeat. More specifically, this is an either/or type of ambiguity involving beats 1 and 3, in which either location may be heard as the downbeat. In Figure 4.7, I42 and K40 are representative of this type. Whereas Phon.o generally uses many syncopated and uneven rhythm patterns (indeed, it is striking that none of the grooves in Fig. 4.7 contains a four-on-the-floor bass drum), the rhythms within these two patterns are mostly even, and pitch and other factors are insufficient to disambiguate between beats 1 and 3 as potential downbeats. This type of ambiguity is not uncommon in electronic dance music,[53] and within the specific context of locked grooves it should not be regarded as a deficiency. Nevertheless, it does mean that the teleology of these grooves is flatter. Though they might be mixed more easily with other patterns (because of the dual downbeat possibilities), their configuration of musical energy is also less particular.

Like other autotelic grooves, the patterns shown in Figure 4.7 are also not complete in themselves. None would feel resolved if the pattern stopped at the end of the measure; each needs the resolution that the downbeat provides. Related to this point, the downbeat within each groove works simultaneously as both arrival and departure. The locus of energy for this resolution-that-gets-the-groove-going-again is both the beginning of the pattern proper (that is, the specific pitches, attacks, and timbres that constitute it) and the downbeat more broadly as an ener-

---

[53] For a discussion of ambiguity in electronic dance music, see Butler (2006, chap. 3).

getic field. Or, to express this from a slightly different perspective, one might also say that the whole process that sets up beat 4 (the tensional peak) is also needed to resolve it. When the downbeat functions as both departure and arrival, it not only generates its own teleology but also resolves it—and this process is constantly renewing itself.

The locked grooves that Phon.o and Bernhard compose—and the live musical events in which they perform them—function as a kind of laboratory for testing the effects of repetition. The conditions are tightly constrained, and consistent across all subjects. During our interview Phon.o and Bernhard explained that the next record in the series, for which each musician would contribute one side, would be called *The Most Wanted*—because after performing together in "The Bareback Show," they had formed much more precise opinions about the qualities that constitute an effective loop, and they wished to produce a record that embodied these attributes. Indeed, they frequently spoke of the perfect loop, an entity that could be repeated for exceptionally long periods of time without diminishing the listener's interest. Phon.o refers to that ideal in this passage:

> It should be such a good loop that it could run an hour and you [do] not feel bored of it. Because there are loops—for example, if you listen to Maurizio or somebody like this, they did tracks which are very repetitive, but they could run a year and you wouldn't feel really bored. And that's the perfect loop.[54]

In a similar fashion the two musicians explained that their goal for their next two records was to make a set of loops so useful that "you really could play, just with these two records, a two hour set or something." In such remarks the musicians reveal an attitude in which repetition is not downplayed or apologized for, but rather treated as the standard against which their experiment is evaluated. The best possible groove is the one that can be repeated for the longest possible time. For Phon.o and Bernhard, the perfect loop is the ultimate musical technology.

Riding

To introduce the next theme, "riding," I would like to return to a quotation from Robert Henke that I first presented in Chapter 2, and from which I ultimately derived the title of this book:

---

[54] The German term for locked groove, *Endlosloopplatte* or "endless loop record," is also evocative in this regard. See the text of Figure 4.6 for a usage of this term.

I think the main difference is, in electronic music, there's a lot of ways to create something that runs—that is static, but nevertheless, it's creating something. Take a drum computer: you turn it on and it plays a pattern. And you cannot turn on a drummer. A drummer always has to do something in order to work. And the drum computer, you turn it on and the pattern is there, but the action of the person who is playing the drum computer is changing the pattern.

Henke's remarks clearly invoke a product/process dialectic: on the one hand, he speaks of stasis and a sound with an ambient, almost objectlike presence ("the pattern is there"); on the other hand, this sound runs, creates, and invites dynamic action on the part of the performer. In addition, the process in which the sound is imbricated is technologized. By this I mean not only that technology facilitates the process, but also more precisely that it is conceptualized in technological terms. This is evident in the way Henke configures the agency of the performer: the "person who is playing the drum computer" is able to stand outside the process and reflect on it as it proceeds, yet she or he is also controlling its overall direction.

It is precisely this distinctive relationship between musical experience and technologized process that I refer to with "riding." Riding denotes a quality of feeling that arises through these highly mediated formal processes, and it also references a common set of ways in which they are described. Note that riding, in its everyday sense, is an inherently mediated experience: whatever one rides is always external to the self. In modern times, moreover, the objects that humans spend the most time riding are our own mechanical inventions (trains, bicycles, cars, etc.), in most cases independently powered. Riding is also inherently processual and continuous. It involves motion, which is often but not necessarily goal-oriented.

In a DJ or laptop performance, what is ridden is the sound itself. The sound offers itself as a vessel for such an engagement because it flows continuously; its motion is presented without interruption or cessation.[55] Herein lies one of the chief liberative potentials of prerecorded sound. For musicians who have learned how to marshal this capacity, technology that "captures" sound becomes a crucial source of freedom in performance. It fosters the distinctive attitude of listener orientation, described in Chapter 2, in which the musician's position is simultaneously performative and interpretive. Moreover, the *musical* technologies described in this chapter also support riding as a mode of engagement. The performer rides not only the continuous flow of sound but also the repeating constituents that form it. Cycles and grooves work

---

[55] Although I am speaking at a broad aesthetic level here, one should not forget that this continuity is the direct result of the musician's skill. In an EDM performance one produces a continuous flow of sound from discrete objects.

well within continuous, improvised performance in part because they provide consistent horizons of expectation. In addition, they offer a quite particular *kind* of expectation. One does not anticipate a stand-alone dissipation of tension (as with a full cadence, for instance) but rather a resolution that will simultaneously initiate a new series of dynamic events.

As these last remarks suggest, riding also has a special relationship to teleology. Clearly one must "travel" in a particular direction. This does not mean, however, that the end result of such movement is specified or known at the outset. In other words, even though riding is certainly compatible with motion toward a predefined goal, it is not inherently goal-directed. In an earlier work I evoked these qualities through the image of a certain kind of journey by train:

> In a set,… form is not derived from an object-like model, in which coherence can be viewed within a complete musical structure just as one would perceive the unity of a sculpture (all at once), but rather on a sense of a continuous development through time. This approach to form is more perceptually than structurally based: it is like a journey on a train in which the destination is unknown to the rider, but one can see out the window the whole time. We end up in a completely different place than we started, but our route made sense; the coherence is that of the trip itself, not its components.
>
> (Butler 2006, 242)

At the time my goal was to describe the coherence and unity of a DJ set, and to do so in terms that would be process- rather than object-based. Within the current project, my interest lies more with the experiential dimensions of this kind of formal approach, and also with the technologized terms in which it is conceived. (In retrospect I am struck by my choice of a technological image, as this was not a deliberate goal at the time.) Consider, then, the perspective of a listener experiencing a performance in this way. Within grooves and other small-scale spans, he or she will sense a clear and specific goal ahead. The listener will also feel strong growth processes and climaxes over midlevel spans, especially the sections of increasing intensity known as "buildups."[56] The specific point at which the buildup will peak, however, is not defined and in most cases is difficult to anticipate precisely. (Indeed, DJs frequently tease audiences by delaying the arrival of the climax.) Over the course of an entire performance things become even harder to predict; it is here that the train simile becomes most apt. The audience members have no way of knowing where the performance will end up; they have to place their trust in the DJ.

---

[56] See Butler (2006, 223–24), for a definition.

For a DJ or laptop performer the perspective is somewhat different, as he or she is the engineer directing this train. In contrast to an actual train journey, however, the route and destination of the trip are not known at the outset. Prior to beginning, the performer may have some idea about the overall direction of the set, but the details are deliberately left open in order to allow flexible responses to the contingencies of the live event. For performers, the idea of riding a technological entity is more germane to the freedoms engendered by listener orientation, especially as concerns the practice of delegating a certain portion of sound-production responsibility to machines. In this way, the performer directs the energy of "something that runs."

Considering the teleological dimensions of this formal approach also raises questions of agency. The prevalent paradigms of teleology in current music scholarship center on ideas of an individual subjectivity striving toward a goal. In EDM performance, however, the relationship between subjectivity and growth is differently configured. One does not imagine a subject striving, nor seek to identify with such a subject. Rather, growth is technologized. The person who is "riding" has chosen to be propelled by some force or conveyance more powerful than him- or herself. Although it is important to realize that forward momentum and growth *are* important parts of this musical practice, one feels its growth through riding its processes.

Technologized process as a formal principle may also be conceptualized through concepts of *algorithm*. Though musical algorithms have structural and organizational effects, they are exemplars of process as well. In essence they are sets of formal instructions that "run" on their own once set in motion.[57] In contemporary art music, "algorithmic composition" is a well-established practice. In EDM, algorithms are important to the technical dimensions of production, although musicians rarely work with them directly.[58] In particular, EDM incorporates algorithms into production software in a number of ways. Within sequencing programs they are used to generate various profiles of "swing," for instance, as well as to control many other features. This aspect of musical infrastructure thus informs the means through which music is made.

---

[57] It is worth noting that algorithms are not inherently technological; they are essentially mathematical in origin and long predate the kinds of mechanical and electronic technologies discussed in this book. In describing them as technologized processes, I am therefore extending a concept in a manner comparable to the move that produces "musical technologies." This viewpoint also reflects the strong associations between algorithms and computer technology that have developed in recent decades.

[58] This statement is arguably less true for those musicians who employ the program Max (described in Chapter 2). These individuals are a minority, but the group includes highly prominent producers such as Aphex Twin, Kit Clayton, Matmos, and Monolake. Recently, the company behind Max has introduced "Max for Live," which lists among its features the ability to "create algorithmic composition tools" (http://cycling74.com/products/; accessed September 2, 2010).

A related concept that ties together questions of agency and technologized process is *automation*. Performers routinely initiate patterns and processes that continue of their own accord, as Henke's comments point out. In Live, automation is the subject of an entire chapter in the manual as well as an in-program tutorial. In practice automation is frequently applied to effects and other means of modulating the stereo signal; for example, the left/right panning of the bass line might change regularly within a track, or the envelope of a synth loop might be varied through numerous tiny changes that imbue the sound with texture or "grain." Henke specifically mentioned "applying envelopes which are not repeating with the loop lengths but with a different period" in order to generate "permutation within the loop." The musical effects of such changes are subtle: although the listener may not consciously notice them, they add interest and depth to the composition.

Automation within performance is also discernible in a broader sense, one that involves the issue of improvisational constraints. As discussed in Chapter 3, musicians often seek to relinquish their agency during performance by "losing themselves" in optimal flow states. In some cases this release of intentionality also has strong technological associations.[59] Musicians frequently express a desire to enter a kind of automatic state while performing (and often while composing as well). For instance, Daniel Bell—a "minimal techno" musician whose style of DJing is noticeably restrained—characterized the flow he achieves in his best sets as "moving into auto-pilot." In such statements performers articulate a wish to merge with machines, even as they more obviously seek to master them as well. This merger effect, which increases as musicians begin to achieve the ideal of technological fluency, can sometimes be so strong as to seem visually apparent to the audience. We might imagine these musicians as *automating* performance, turning their bodies and decisions into their own self-perpetuating technologies.

Transitioning; Flowing

The last two musical technologies under consideration, which I have placed together because of their interrelatedness, are *transitioning* and *flowing*. Transitioning is important because it operates as a fundamental formal principle within EDM performance. As such, forming the term from the gerund assumes particular significance: whereas a "transition" is a delimited formal section, "transitioning" denotes an ongoing musical

---

[59] The brain-as-computer metaphor, pervasive within cognitive-science writing such as that of Pressing (1998, cited above) and evident in phrases such as "processing capacity" and "processing resources," may trigger additional associations of this kind for some readers.

strategy. Let us begin with the first sense. The most common musical context in which EDM performers generate transitions is the DJ mix. The passages in which the DJ begins to move from one record to the next, in which both records audibly overlap, is a type of transition: it begins with one clearly defined musical entity (record A) and then moves into an unstable passage (the overlap), which in turn leads to a second clearly defined musical entity (record B). Laptop sets that feature clearly defined tracks work in the same manner, though the technical means of producing the transition differs. This kind of transition is conceptually similar to the formal paradigms of transitions delineated by music theorists, the major difference being that EDM does not need tonality to effect a formal shift.

Transitions in this conventional formal sense exhibit certain qualities: they are inherently goal-directed (they get us from one place to another), they are functional, they are less integral to the identity of a composition than the surrounding expository or thematic material, they are not complete in themselves, they are unstable, and when we hear them we know that they must end—they cannot be sustained forever. The aesthetics of EDM praxis, however, generate a mode of transitioning that is more independent and more complex. In an expertly executed DJ or laptop performance, transitioning is not a means to an end but rather a goal in itself. The ideal of the "third record" informs performance at every moment. A poor DJ set would consist of short transitions that are clearly audible as such, with long stretches of single tracks in between. One can easily hear such performances in many a second-rate club. In an ideal performance, by contrast, transitional states are drawn out for as long as possible, and it is difficult to tell where one record ends and another begins. One often senses change retroactively, several repetitions after it has actually begun. This applies both to the introduction of new sounds or tracks and to their removal: in the majority of cases we realize only gradually that we have arrived in a new place.

Therefore, rather than transitory connections between stable states, this aesthetic of transitioning produces a sense of constant flux. The way in which the performer aims to keep the transition going in the face of certain obvious constraints—the transitional state is still unstable, particularly in comparison to the solidity of each individual track—is reminiscent perhaps of juggling, or more aptly, surfing. The performer is riding a wave and it cannot last forever, but no matter: the activity itself is the goal.

In saying this, however, it is important to realize that teleology is still a part of the equation. When the music is transitioning, it continues to push forward. It cannot be described as "circular," therefore—but neither is it "linear" in the sense of progressing toward a clearly defined and anticipated goal. As with riding, we know that we are going somewhere, but our precise destination and point of arrival emerge flexibly and contingently. Transitioning obviously differs from the immediate repetition that characterizes cycling, but it is not its forward-striving opposite either. Instead, transitioning produces a constant, self-renewing teleology. The image that best captures this idea is that of a fountain. During an ideal EDM performance, the forward motion of transitioning keeps on bubbling up. In this sense, transitioning is not so much unstable as *dynamic*.

Of course, as discussed in previous chapters, performers *do* employ recognizable tracks at certain moments within their performances. For example, in a 2007 mix entitled "Crossfaded and Turned Tabled" (released as a free download), Phon.o frequently introduced short passages from well-known hip-hop tracks. As with the non-EDM samples used by Henrik Schwarz (see discussion in Chapter 2), these moments stand out in comparison to the more abstract sounds that constitute the overall fabric of the set. In the novel context of performance, their effect is one of defamiliarization. At the same time, however, they foster pleasurable recognition, inviting participation and gestural identification through actions such as singing along. In some cases—as for instance when Jeff Mills plays his famous track "The Bells" in a DJ set (as discussed in Chapter 3)—they may even mark peak moments. Nevertheless, because they can have such a strong effect on the audience, moments of recognizability are used sparingly. This strategy can be harnessed to positive ends, but it will quickly lose its power and become a ploy if used repeatedly and incessantly. If there are too many distinct tracks, the performance will not take the audience to the place that the aesthetics of the event demand. Instead, the majority of sounds must assume relatively neutral musical identities; they must avoid repeatedly coalescing into "songs." As a technology, transitioning effectively subverts this tendency.[60]

Closely related to transitioning is *flowing*, which I use to describe a particular quality of technologized process. The noun form ("flow") is important as well, and I will use the two words interchangeably. "Flow" in particular has cropped up in several distinct branches of scholarship. The first of these is African American studies. As early as 1981, James Snead wrote, "In black culture, repetition means that the thing *circulates* (exactly in the manner of any flow, including capital flows) there in an equilibrium" (149–50). Snead's focus, however, was clearly on repetition. The first

---

[60] For particularly intense examples of the breakdown of individual track identity in favor of an aesthetic of transitioning, see the *DE9* series of recordings by Richie Hawtin: *Decks, EFX, & 909* (Mute minus4cd, 1999), *DE9: Closer to the Edit* (Mute 3064-2, 2001), and the appropriately titled *DE9: Transitions* (Mute 3087-2, 2005). Each is a continuous mix lasting less than ninety minutes. The first recording mixes elements from twenty-eight tracks and the second from more than seventy. The third recording is broken down into twenty-eight sections, with the number of tracks in each section ranging from four to ten. (Because of the continuous nature of the mix, some tracks overlap from one section to the next.)

work in this field to address flow directly was Tricia Rose's monograph on rap, *Black Noise* (1994). Rose uses "flow" to describe the creation and sustainment of motion, continuity, and circularity within African American expressive practices, including cultural and social processes as well as rhythm.[61] "Flow" is also widely used within hip-hop vernacular as a term to describe the rhythmic qualities of a rapper's delivery; scholars such as Miyakawa (2005) and Krims (2000) have developed and extended this more specifically musical sense.

Also writing extensively about flow is psychologist Mihaly Csikszentmihalyi, who claims that people use this word more than any other to describe the feelings experienced during states of maximal happiness. Terming such episodes "optimal experiences," he claims that they are characterized by extreme absorption in the task at hand, a feeling that the demands of the activity are challenging yet well-matched to the participant's skill level, and a sense that the activity itself is intrinsically rewarding (Csikszentmihalyi 1990, 48–70).[62] More recently, Robert Fink has used concepts of flow to draw connections between the temporal structure of contemporary media experiences and that of minimalist music. He focuses particularly on the experience of watching television, emphasizing how short bursts of ads, along with intervening programmed material, combine to form a seemingly endless flow of the "media sublime" over the course of an evening's viewing.[63] As mentioned in the previous discussion of listener orientation (Chapter 2), Fink notes (and promulgates) the recurrence of water images as a metaphor for this phenomenon. In addition to flow itself, related metaphors that I have used in this chapter include references to the bubbling up of a fountain and to transitioning as riding a wave.

The appearance of "flow" in such disparate contexts is striking. What might these authors' concepts of flow have in common, and what might they contribute to an understanding of flow in electronic dance music? First, their descriptions reveal (with varying degrees of explicitness) the *continuity* and *indefiniteness* of flow, two aspects that are essential to the flowing qualities of EDM. Within EDM, flow arises first from the continuity that characterizes performance. When sound unfolds for hours without a pause or break, it is natural to experience it as a flow. Within certain experiences, moreover, continuity may stretch across multiple performances.

---

[61] Although "flow" is one of three keywords appearing in the title of Rose's chapter 2, her discussion of the term is actually very brief (it occurs mainly on pp. 38–39, with short appearances on 40 and 59). Nevertheless, her formulation of the concept has been influential.

[62] Csikszentmihalyi describes intrinsically rewarding activities as "autotelic," thus opening a potential connection to the autotelic grooves discussed earlier in this chapter.

[63] Fink (2005); see esp. chap. 3. Fink attributes his use of flow to the scholar of television Raymond Williams, who defines it as a new type of media experience that is "the defining characteristic of broadcasting, simultaneously as a technology and as a cultural form" (1975, 86).

A dancer spending the evening in a particular club is likely to encounter perfor- mances by several musicians. These are also presented without breaks: the musicians change, but the sound goes on.

In addition, this continuity is indefinite. There is no way to know with any cer- tainty when a performance will end. In an ideal context, this is also true for the club night. In locations such as Berlin, this paradigm has been put into practice: clubs have no legally defined closing times, and the most intense after-hours scenes continue well past Saturday night into Sunday afternoon and beyond. For listen- ers involved in moment-to-moment experience, indefinite continuation necessi- tates a certain letting-go of expectation. If attending is characteristically about tuning in to expectations and their confirmation or denial, then highly repetitive, infinitely continuous music demands that one radically readjust these behaviors. This does not mean that expectation is not involved, but rather that listeners must recalibrate the time scales that they bring to the experience.[64] At the same time, precise attending over shorter time spans is supported by the twin technologies of periodicity and pulse, which provide tools for structuring expectation by articu- lating and dividing spans.

Despite their diversity, the accounts of Rose, Csikszentmihalyi, and Fink reveal a second significant shared feature, as a kind of *techné* facilitates each instance of flow. This is most obvious in Fink, who speaks of a "clear technological impetus" behind repetitive listening (2005, 175). In hip-hop, the continuous, technologically facili- tated groove provides the means through which the rapper develops flow. At a broader level, Rose carefully highlights the complex relationship between rap music as cultural expression and its technologically mediated means of production. For Csikszentmihalyi, technology is not a focus, but its sibling, "technique," is ubiqui- tous. The word that Csikszentmihalyi uses is *skill*. Skill, broadly defined, is essential to flow states, which must challenge but not overwhelm the abilities of the person involved. In the ideal state, when the participant's skills are perfectly matched to the challenges of the task, action and awareness merge (1990, 53–54). One of Csikszent- mihalyi's research subjects, a rock climber, explains that "you are so involved in what you are doing [that] you aren't thinking of yourself as separate from the immediate activity" (ibid.). This merger often involves a more specific sense of union between subject and environment; notably, the "environment" is typically the physical medium through which the activity is enacted. "The solitary sailor begins to feel that

---

[64] Fink makes a related point in a discussion of how minimalism fosters a mode of attending that differs from the paradigm demanded by current classical-music ideals. He cites music critic Andrew Porter, who speaks of a kind of wall that successful listeners break through in order to "relax into" the music's expanded scale (Fink 2005, 198–200).

that the boat is an extension of himself," Csikszentmihalyi writes, and the climber develops a "sense of kinship...between fingers and rock" (64).

In the context of EDM performance, this physical medium is none other than the interface itself, and the union between subject and environment is precisely the ideal merger between performer and instrument detailed in the previous descriptions of liveness (Chapter 2) and automation. Moreover, the interplay between control and subjectivity highlighted in Chapter 3 (with reference to improvisational constraints) also proves to be a central component of flow. Csikszentmihalyi, in a section entitled "The Paradox of Control," notes that individuals experiencing flow states feel perfectly in control of their activities, without the sense of anxiety or struggle so often associated with maintaining control (1990, 59–62). This occurs because the ego's self-critical monitoring has receded, allowing participants to become fully absorbed in the experience. Csikszentmihalyi's observations add significant nuance to the descriptions of "losing one's self" that often follow such states: it is not the self per se that is obliterated, nor consciousness, but rather consciousness *of* the self.

Finally, flow is an essential component of improvisation. Indeed, it may be regarded as the ultimate technology of improvisation, for the effortless momentum that develops within an ideal improvisation is none other than flow itself. As with grooving, riding, and transitioning before it, flow—or *flowing*, to revisit its most active sense—is best understood through the lens of technologized process. These dimensions of improvisational performance are not only facilitated through technology in a conventional sense (and in some cases, through subverting and surpassing the conventional limits of technology). Above and beyond this, the ways in which they grow, develop, and otherwise proceed through musical time are also conceptualized in technological terms. Moreover, the improvisations that develop through such processes depend on repetition—or, more precisely, on musical designs that are perpetually repeating. Repeating, as a musical technology, sponsors the special relationship between musical creation and time that characterizes improvised performance. In transcending the physical and temporal limitations of recorded objects, EDM performers shed the cultural baggage that repetition has accumulated, engendering musical experiences that are not bounded, closed, or static, but rather flowing constantly forward into new, unknown directions.

Afterword

Looking Back

When I first began to conceptualize this book, I imagined it as a continuation of the work begun in *Unlocking the Groove*. Detailed musical analysis was at the core of that project, although ethnography was also an essential methodological component. My goal was to come to a detailed understanding of the rhythmic and metrical organization of electronic dance music. Because there were no systematic or in-depth treatments of the subject, methodologies had to be developed from the ground up. This necessitated a focus on the clearest possible analytical object: the individual record, as heard on its own. In performance, however—as any reader who has made it this far will be acutely aware—recordings are not experienced in isolated or stable forms, but rather combined with other recordings and significantly reworked.[1] Even while researching and writing *Unlocking*, I envisioned a second book

---

[1] *Unlocking the Groove* also makes this point, explicitly and repeatedly. That work often comments on the ways in which the properties of a particular track might inform its incorporation into a DJ set, and the final chapter addresses formal and aesthetic criteria guiding the shaping of sets. However, *Unlocking* does not attempt close readings of *actual performances*; the ethnography involved was almost entirely interview-based. In addition, its account of performance focuses largely on DJ sets; laptop sets were still emerging during the years in which it was researched.

that would bring the lens of close musical analysis to bear on this real-world experiential context. The methodologies developed in the first phase of research would lay the foundation for the complexities inherent in the second.

The book that I imagined at that time, however, was a simpler and more straightforward project than the one it has become. The primary conceptual binaries that I initially had in mind were product/process and fixed/fluid. The former of these was already a prominent theme in scholarship on improvisation and an issue I had been thinking about for some time. It was clear that this dichotomy bifurcated scholarly conceptualizations of improvisation, and I wanted to challenge this polarization through a consideration of the challenges and possibilities introduced by technological mediation. The remaining oppositions—prerecorded/live, work/performance, static/dynamic, material/immaterial, permanent/ephemeral, technological/human— emerged and became more vivid over the course of my research. Furthermore, it became apparent that these pairs were interconnected, sometimes unexpectedly. Although the interplay of product and process retained its foundational status, it became an increasingly rich optic through its interaction with these related lenses.

Performance has remained the central focus throughout, although it took some time for its relationship to recording, composition, and improvisation to coalesce into the specific chapter foci of ontology, interface design and liveness, improvisation in relation to preexistent elements, and musical technologies. Each focus, meanwhile, turned out to be a very large theme in itself. At the same time, other themes emerged that cut across the chapters. One of the most apparent of these has been an emphasis on possibility, potentiality, and antideterminism, whether applied to technologies, texts, or preexistent elements. Affordance relates to this emphasis, but also invokes its opposite: the importance of creative or productive constraints. Multiplicity is another property that has emerged in various domains, and especially within ontological realms. I have theorized the ontology of electronic dance music as manifold, modeling it in terms of webs, networks, or constellations of musical identity. These constellations, I have suggested, constitute fields of possibility that musicians navigate, just as the assemblages of hardware and software used in performance constitute environments that they flexibly traverse. The nodes and pathways of these networks are formed by multiple creative agents, and they change and grow over time.

I have conceptualized technology in both the traditional sense of the term and in a broader sense encompassing aspects of sonic organization that facilitate fluid, improvised performances involving recordings. Both musical and physical technologies afford a wide range of creative interaction. Interaction between performers and audiences, filtered through expectations of liveness, has implications for both the ways in which performances are fashioned and the ways in which they are experienced. As musicians and dancers work together to heighten perceptions of immediacy and co-presence, they must negotiate tensions between the ways in which the senses come together in an event and the tendency of certain technologies to separate them. The roles of producer and consumer bleed into each other: DJs perform consumption through creative media play, while the audience (performatively) consumes both music and performance. Experience itself is technologized, whether through the listener consciousness that increasingly characterizes the epistemology of performance or through the metaphors used to imagine its teleology (riding, transitioning, flowing). And finally: all of this happens, crucially, in time. By consistently emphasizing temporality in relation to the core themes of recording, performance, composition, and improvisation, I have called attention to the importance of change, dynamism, attending, and unfolding to the technologically mediated contexts of DJ and laptop sets.

This book, like much of my previous work, might be described as empirical in orientation. I have engaged closely with individual musicians, specific musical texts, technologies used in composition and performance, and most importantly, with actual performances. To a large extent, the issues that I have chosen to explore emerged from these engagements. Many incredibly creative and generous musicians gave me close access to their work; they invited me into their home recording studios, spent hours talking with me, and allowed me to film their performances. Originally I had planned to focus primarily on DJ sets, but it soon became clear that laptop sets were becoming ever more prevalent over the course of the 2000s. When I first started to film these performances, I found myself staring at computer screens full of small colored blocks, with little understanding of what the musicians were doing. However, the knowledge that they shared with me shed a great deal of light on their creative practices, revealing common strategies as well as individualized approaches.

I conceived of the project as interdisciplinary from the beginning. As in *Unlocking*, I intended to use ethnographic methodology as a means to get at music-theoretical questions. The issues that emerged from my objects of study, however, led me in many additional directions. One of the most rewarding (and unexpected) intellectual areas with which I began to find myself affiliated was sound studies. When I first began to explore the questions that led to this book, sound studies was still rather new as a field of inquiry—in 2004, as cited in the introduction, Pinch and Bijsterveld defined it as "an emerging interdisciplinary area" (636)—but its growth has accelerated quite significantly over the intervening years. Music studies disciplines have increasingly become a part of this trend. Within the humanities more generally, sound studies is part of a larger "material turn," and my increasing awareness of this project as a kind of materially based music theory intersects with this development.

The questions I have asked here, and the kinds of objects I have studied, have taken me well beyond the borders of music theory as it has conventionally been practiced; the initial idea of analyzing live performance has expanded to include analysis of interfaces and interaction, ontological networks, improvisation based on pre-recorded elements, and other related phenomena. All the same, I still regard the work as having a music-theoretical core, exemplified by its interests in the technical means of musical production and close readings.

Looking Forward (and Outward)

In the introduction to this book I framed electronic dance music as a case study, one that foregrounds the interplay of recording and performance in particularly vivid ways. As one of the first popular styles to make recordings central to the creative practices of performance, club music was at the forefront of a trend that has only increased in recent decades. If, as I have argued, the issues that emerge from its technologically mediated creative practices are also present to varying degrees in an increasingly broad swathe of the world's music, then it may be useful to briefly expand our view to consider several contemporary musical phenomena that also configure recording/performance relationships in interesting ways. In the spirit of looking forward, these examples are meant to be suggestive of some possible directions in which mediated music-making may proceed in the future. My remarks are necessarily speculative rather than definitive, however. As this project concludes, I wish to open up lines of inquiry rather than close them off.

Turning on the television in the United States of 2013, one immediately encounters a plethora of singing-based competitions. Although the rise of such shows can obviously be understood in relation to the emergence of "reality"-based television, their most direct precedent is the *Idol* phenomenon that has swept much of the globe. *American Idol* is ostensibly all about singing, yet it is striking that the contestants' repertoire consists almost entirely of previously recorded songs.[2] The same is true of the immensely popular show *Glee*. Although real Glee clubs have traditionally sung a wide range of music, their fictional TV counterpart features songs from the American Top 40 (past and present) and popular musicals. The premise is usually that the Glee Club or various of its members are performing the song. At a deeper level, however, these performances enact an emotionally heightened version of singing along with recorded song (and of performatively identifying with recorded singers).

---

[2] During the finale the two remaining contestants sing a "coronation song." In contrast to the rest of the show, these are usually new compositions that are then released commercially.

As with karaoke—an obvious predecessor for such practices—these phenomena depend on an epistemology of popular song as fundamentally recorded.[3]

In recent Top 40 R & B and rap, it has become very common to build a song, in an obviously referential way, on another quite familiar song. Some very clear examples include Jason Derulo's "Whatcha Say" (2009), which samples "Hide and Seek" (2006) by the indie electronic singer-songwriter Imogen Heap; Kanye West's "Stronger" (2007), built over the Daft Punk song "Harder Better Faster Stronger" (2001); and Rihanna's "Don't Stop the Music" (2007), which samples parts of the Michael Jackson hit "Wanna Be Startin' Somethin'" (1983).[4] Each of these six songs was a major chart success. In "Whatcha Say" the sampling occurs in the chorus; in fact, *most* of the singing in the chorus is done by Heap rather than Derulo (who sings responses to her calls in a kind of cyber-duet). In "Stronger" the borrowed materials underlie nearly all of the track. In "Don't Stop the Music" the sample begins to fade in starting around one minute into the track, becoming loudest during the climactic release of the chorus. Near the end of the track Rihanna begins to sing the signature phrase "Mama-say, mama-sa, ma-ma-ko-ssa."[5] Since the song's lyrics are about dancing to recorded music (and the video is set in a club), the clear implication is that Rihanna is listening to and enjoying the sampled song as the narrative of her own song unfolds. These songs obviously participate in the intertextuality that characterizes popular music more generally, and they can also be understood more specifically in relation to the foundational rap practice of building a "beat" (the instrumentals underlying a rap) from previous recordings.[6] What seems intensified in these more recent cases is the direct and obvious use of songs from the contemporary pop media sphere; this amplifies the pop referentiality of the final result.[7]

Mashups, another contemporary genre, are especially recording-centric: they are formed by combining two or more recordings—often with radically different semiotic, cultural, or genre associations—into a single track. Most paradigmatically, mashups overlay *a cappella* vocals from one record over backing tracks or instrumentals

---

[3] In karaoke, I would argue, one is not just singing the song, or singing along with the song; one is inserting oneself into the recording.

[4] Another Rihanna song partaking in the trend described above is "SOS" (2006), which is built over instrumentals from Soft Cell's "Tainted Love" (1981).

[5] This phrase, which also appears near the end of the Jackson song, can be traced back to the 1972 Manu Dibango track "Soul Makossa."

[6] The definitive treatment of this practice appears in Schloss (2004). In contrast to the pop examples cited here, Schloss describes a tradition in which samples are brief, from rare or older sources, and not meant to be recognized.

[7] In 2007, the year in which "Stronger" was released, the original Daft Punk song was also the basis for a series of highly viewed YouTube memes, the most popular of which were "Daft Hands" and "Daft Bodies."

from another.[8] However, it is not at all uncommon for more than two tracks to be involved—recordings by Girl Talk may involve as many as twenty or thirty—and there are many approaches to track combination and arrangement.[9] Regardless of the style of the songs involved, the producer expects his or her intended audience to recognize them; this is crucial to a track's creative success. The mashup, like DJing, is an intense form of media play. Mashups, however, are not invested in real-time performance in the same way; by and large, they are a studio genre.[10] For this reason, they do not deconstruct the recording/performance binary in the same manner (or to the same extent).

The related phenomena known variously as "silent discos," "silent raves," and "flash mob" raves bring together the practices of personal, private listening and public, collective dancing in novel ways. In a silent disco (or "silent rave"), the audience listens to the DJ through wireless headphones instead of speakers. As with club music more generally, collective listening and dancing within such events would seem to privilege the idea of music and the beat as vehicles for group synchrony. Frequently, however, silent discos allow DJs to "compete" by performing simultaneously, with individual audience members choosing which stream they wish to tune into at any given moment. In such cases, in a radical departure from club music conventions, there is no single musical core binding the audience together. In flash mob raves, the soundtrack is even more individualized and private; dancers listen to music on their own personal playback devices, without any form of wireless synchronization.[11] At the same time, such events amplify the performative dimensions of public dancing; unlike typical club events, the spectacle they create is meant to be witnessed by non-participants. For all of these "silent" performances, however, continuity with club-cultural traditions is evident in the privileging of site-specificity, co-presence, and event, and in the performative consumption of recorded music.[12]

As these examples reveal, the technologies used to create and perform music are changing rapidly, and they will continue to do so. The same is true of musicians' practices. What new forms of musical identity will emerge in the coming years?

---

[8] For example, this is the technique behind DJ Danger Mouse's *The Grey Album* (2004), which famously combined vocals from *The Black Album* by Jay-Z with instrumental portions from the Beatles' *White Album*.

[9] For an extended discussion of these matters, see Boone (2011).

[10] With respect to one of the previous examples, however, it is interesting to note that sung mashups have been featured frequently on *Glee*. As with the show's more straightforward pop song renditions, these performances should be understood to refer back to a recording—in this case a mashup that may or may not actually exist.

[11] As with other kinds of flash mobs, these events are organized via social media, take place in public spaces, and dissipate quickly. The effect is of a large group of people descending on a space and beginning to dance for no apparent reason.

[12] One might also see these phenomena as playing with the affordances of headphones, which have long been central to EDM performance but have received much less attention than the other technologies involved.

How will their interrelated forms of existence be configured? Will liveness persist as a criterion for evaluating performance, and if so, how will it be articulated? What new kinds of interfaces will become important? Which features of currently used interfaces will remain? What novel epistemologies will coalesce around musical performance? How will preexistent recordings enter into the dynamic realm of improvisation? Which musical technologies will facilitate these improvisational interventions? The answers to these questions are yet to be determined. Regardless of what happens, however, I expect to be surprised.

Bibliography

Abbate, Carolyn. 2004. "Music—Drastic or gnostic?" *Critical Inquiry 30*: 505–36.

Adorno, Theodor W. 2002 [1941]. On popular music. In *Essays on music: Theodor W. Adorno*, ed. Susan H. Gillespie and Richard D. Leppert, 437–69. Berkeley: University of California Press.

———. 2006 [1958]. *Philosophy of new music*. Trans. Robert Hullot-Kentor. Minneapolis: University of Minnesota Press.

Albiez, Sean. 2005. "Post soul futurama: African American cultural politics and early Detroit techno." *European Journal of American Culture 24*(2): 131–52.

Alperson, Philip. 1984. "On musical improvisation." *Journal of Aesthetics and Art Criticism 43*: 17–43.

Andersen, Tue Haste. 2003. Mixxx: Towards novel DJ interfaces. In *Proceedings of the 2003 International Conference on New Interfaces for Musical Expression*, ed. François Thibault, 30–35. Montreal: Faculty of Music, McGill University. http://www.informatik.uni-trier.de/~ley/db/conf/nime/nime2003.html.

Appleton, Jon. 1984. "Live and in concert: Composer/performer views of real-time performance systems." *Computer Music Journal 8*(1): 48–51.

Attali, Jacques. 1985 [1977]. *Noise: The political economy of music*. Trans. Brian Massumi. Minneapolis: University of Minnesota Press.

Auslander, Philip. 1999. *Liveness: Performance in a mediatized culture*. New York: Routledge.

Austin, J. L. 1962. *How to do things with words*. William James lectures 1955. Cambridge, MA: Harvard University Press.

Bailey, Derek. 1992. *Improvisation: Its nature and practice in music*. New York: Da Capo Press.

Barthes, Roland. 1977. *Image-Music-Text*. New York: Hill and Wang.

Benadon, Fernando. 2007. "A circular plot for rhythm visualization and analysis." *Music Theory Online 13*(3). http://mto.societymusictheory.org/issues/mto.07.13.3/mto.07.13.3.benadon.html.

Benjamin, Walter. 1969 [1936]. The work of art in the age of mechanical reproduction. In *Illuminations*, ed. Hannah Arendt, 217–52. New York: Schocken.

Berliner, Paul. 1994. *Thinking in jazz: The infinite art of improvisation*. Chicago: University of Chicago Press.

Bernard, David. 2002. Experimental controllers for live electronic music performance (vs. copyright). In *Proceedings of the 2002 International Conference on New Interfaces for Musical Expression*, ed. Eoin Brazil, 189–90. Dublin: Media Lab Europe. http://informatik.uni-trier.de/~ley/db/conf/nime/nime2002.html.

Berry, Wallace. 1989. *Musical structure and performance*. New Haven: Yale University Press.

Blum, Stephen. 1998. Recognizing improvisation. In *In the course of performance: Studies in the world of musical improvisation*, ed. Bruno Nettl and Melinda Russell, 27–45. Chicago: University of Chicago Press.

Bohlman, Phillip. 1999. Ontologies of music. In *Rethinking music*, ed. Nicholas Cook and Mark Everist, 17–34. Oxford: Oxford University Press.

Boone, Christine. 2011. "Mashups: History, legality, and aesthetics." Ph.D. dissertation, University of Texas at Austin.

Borgo, David. 2005. *Sync or swarm: Improvising music in a complex age*. New York: Continuum.

Born, Georgina. 1995. *Rationalizing culture: IRCAM, Boulez, and the institutionalization of the musical avant-garde*. Berkeley: University of California Press.

———. 2005. "On musical mediation: Ontology, technology, and creativity." *Twentieth-Century Music 2*(1): 7–36.

Bowers, John. 2002. Improvising machines: Ethnographically informed design for improvised electro-acoustic music. M.A. thesis, University of East Anglia.

Bradby, Barbara. 1993. "Sampling sexuality: Gender, technology, and the body in dance music." *Popular Music 12*(2): 155–76.

Brewster, Bill, and Frank Broughton. 2000. *Last night a DJ saved my life: The history of the disc jockey*. New York: Grove Press.

———. 2002. *How to DJ (properly): The art and science of playing records*. London: Bantam.

Brothers, Thomas. 1994. "Solo and cycle in African-American jazz." *Musical Quarterly 78*(3): 479–509.

Brownell, John. 1994. "Analytical models of jazz improvisation." *Jazzforschung/Jazz Research 26*: 9–30.

Buckland, Fiona. 2002. *Impossible dance: Club culture and queer world-making*. Middletown, CT: Wesleyan University Press.

Bull, Michael. 2000. *Sounding out the city: Personal stereos and the management of everyday life*. New York: Berg.

Burtner, Matthew. 2004. A theory of modulated objects for new shamanic controller design. In *Proceedings of the 2004 International Conference on New Interfaces for Musical Expression*, ed. Yoichi Nagashima and Michael J. Lyons, 193–96. Hamamatsu, Japan: Shizuoka University of Art and Culture. http://www.informatik.uni-trier.de/~ley/db/conf/nime/nime2004.html.

Butler, Judith. 1990. *Gender trouble: Feminism and the subversion of identity*. Thinking gender. New York: Routledge.

Butler, Mark J. 2000. Music as action: Techno and the perception of agency. In *Semiotics 1999: Proceedings of the Twenty-Fourth Annual Meeting of the Semiotic Society of America*, ed. Scott Simpkins, C. W. Spinks, and John Deely, 303–14. New York: Peter Lang.

———. 2001. "Turning the beat around: Reinterpretation, metrical dissonance, and asymmetry in electronic dance music." *Music Theory Online* 7(6). http://www.societymusictheory.org/mto/01.7.6/toc.7.6.html.

———. 2006. *Unlocking the groove: Rhythm, meter, and musical design in electronic dance music.* Profiles in popular music. Bloomington: Indiana University Press.

———, ed. 2012. *Electronica, dance and club music.* The Library of Essays on Popular Music. Farnham, Surrey, UK: Ashgate.

———. Forthcoming. (In)visible mediators: Interface design and the disappearing computer in Berlin-based laptop performances. In *The Oxford handbook of mobile music studies*, vol. 2, ed. Sumanth Gopinath and Jason Stanyek. New York: Oxford University Press.

Butterfield, Matthew W. 2006. "The power of anacrusis: Engendered feeling in groove-based musics." *Music Theory Online* 12(4).

———. 2007. "Response to Fernando Benadon." *Music Theory Online* 13(3).

Byrnside, Ronald. 1975. The performer as creator: Jazz improvisation. In *Contemporary music and music cultures*, ed. Charles Hamm, Bruno Nettl, and Ronald Byrnside, 223–52. Englewood Cliffs, NJ: Prentice-Hall.

Chabot, Xavier. 1990. "Gesture interfaces and a software toolkit for performance with electronics." *Computer Music Journal* 14(2): 15–27.

Chamblee, Catherine Burnette. 2008. Cognitive processes of improvisation: Performers and listeners in the organ tradition and contemporary gospel styles. Ph.D. dissertation, University of Pennsylvania.

Chanan, Michael. 1995. *Repeated takes: A short history of recording and its effects on music.* New York: Verso.

Chernoff, John Miller. 1979. *African rhythm and African sensibility: Aesthetics and social action in African musical idioms.* Chicago: University of Chicago Press.

Clarke, Eric. 1992. Improvisation, cognition, and education. In *The companion to contemporary musical thought*, ed. John Paynter, Tim Howell, Richard Orton, and Peter Seymour, vol. 2, 787–802. New York: Routledge.

———. 2007. "The impact of recording on listening." *Twentieth-Century Music* 4(1): 47–70.

Collins, Nick. 2003. "Generative music and laptop performance." *Contemporary Music Review* 22(4): 67–79.

Collins, Nicolas. 1999. "Ubiquitous electronics—Technology and live performance 1966–1996." *Leonardo Music Journal* 8: 27–32.

Cone, Edward. 1968. *Musical form and musical performance.* New York: Norton.

Cook, Nicholas. 1995a. "Music minus one: Rock, theory, and performance." *New formations* 27: 23–41.

———. 1995b. The conductor and the theorist: Furtwängler, Schenker and the first movement of Beethoven's Ninth Symphony. In *The practice of performance: Studies in musical interpretation*, ed. John Rink, 105–25. Cambridge: Cambridge University Press.

———. 1999a. Analysing performance and performing analysis. In *Rethinking music*, ed. Nicholas Cook and Mark Everist, 239–61. Oxford: Oxford University Press.

———. 1999b. Words about music, or analysis versus performance. In *Theory into practice: Composition, performance, and the listening experience*, ed. Peter Dejans and Frank Absteribbe, 9–52. Leuven, Belgium: Leuven University Press.

———. 2003. "Review-essay: Improvisation [Review of *In the course of performance: Studies in the world of musical improvisation*, ed. Bruno Nettl with Melinda Russell (Chicago: University of Chicago Press, 1998)]." *The World of Music* 45(2): 154–61.

———. 2004. "Making music together, or improvisation and its others." *The Source: Challenging Jazz Improvisation* 1: 5–25.

Corbett, John. 1990. "Free, single, and disengaged: Listening pleasure and the popular music object." *October* 54: 79–101.

Crawford, Richard. 1993. *The American musical landscape*. Berkeley: University of California Press.

Csikszentmihalyi, Mihaly. 1990. *Flow: The psychology of optimal experience*. New York: Harper & Row.

Cumming, Naomi. 1997. "The horrors of identification: Reich's 'Different Trains.'" *Perspectives of New Music* 35(1): 129–52.

D'Arcangelo, Gideon. 2001. Creating contexts of creativity: Musical composition with modular components. In *Proceedings of the 2001 International Conference on New Interfaces for Musical Expression*, ed. Ivan Poupyrev, Michael J. Lyons, Sidney Fels, and Tina Blaine. Seattle. http://www.informatik.uni-trier.de/~ley/db/conf/nime/nime2001.html.

Danielsen, Anne. 2006. *Presence and pleasure: The funk grooves of James Brown*. Middletown, CT: Wesleyan University Press.

Davies, Stephen. 1991. *Definitions of art*. Ithaca, NY: Cornell University Press.

Deleuze, Gilles. 1994 [1968]. *Difference and repetition*. Trans. Paul Patton. New York: Columbia University Press.

DeNora, Tia. 1999. "Music as a technology of the self." *Poetics* 27: 31–56.

———. 2000. *Music in everyday life*. Cambridge: Cambridge University Press.

Dunn-Newton, Henry, Hiroaki Nakano, and James Gibson. 2003. "Block jam: A tangible interface for interactive music." *Journal of New Music Research* 32(4): 383–93.

Emmerson, Simon, and Denis Smalley. 2007. Electro-acoustic music. *Grove Music Online*.

Erlmann, Veit. 2000. Communities of styles: Musical figures of black diasporic identity. In *The African diaspora: A musical perspective*, ed. Ingrid T. Monson, 83–100. New York: Garland.

Everett, Walter. 1995. The Beatles as composers: The genesis of Abbey Road, side two. In *Concert music, rock, and jazz since 1945: Essays and analytical studies*, ed. Elizabeth West Marvin and Richard Hermann, 172–228. Rochester: University of Rochester Press.

Fabian, Johannes. 2002 [1983]. *Time and the Other: How anthropology makes its object*. Reprint. New York: Columbia University Press.

Ferand, Ernst. 1938. *Die Improvisation in der Musik: Eine Entwicklungsgeschichte und psychologische Untersuchung*. Zurich: Rhein Verlag.

Ferreira, Pedro Peixoto. 2008. "When sound meets movement: Performance in electronic dance music." *Leonardo Music Journal* 18: 17–20.

Fikentscher, Kai. 2000. *"You better work!" Underground dance music in New York City*. Middletown, CT: Wesleyan University Press.

Fink, Robert. 2005. *Repeating ourselves: American minimal music as cultural practice*. Berkeley: University of California Press.

Folio, Cynthia. 1995. An analysis of polyrhythm in selected improvised jazz solos. In *Concert music, rock, and jazz since 1945: Essays and analytical studies*, ed. Elizabeth West Marvin and Richard Hermann, 103–34. Rochester: University of Rochester Press.

Foster, Susan Leigh. 2010. *Choreographing empathy: Kinesthesia in performance*. London: Routledge.

Foucault, Michel. 1988. *The care of the self*. Trans. Robert Hurley. 1st ed. The History of Sexuality. New York: Vintage Books.

———. 1997a [1981]. Technologies of the self. In *Ethics, subjectivity, and truth*, ed. Paul Rabinow, 223–51. New York: New Press.

———. 1997b [1982]. Sexuality and solitude. In *Ethics, Subjectivity, and Truth*, ed. Paul Rabinow, 175–84. New York: New Press.

Freud, Sigmund. 1961 [1920]. *Beyond the pleasure principle*. Ed. J. Strachey. Trans. J. Strachey. New York: Liveright.

Frith, Simon. 1996. *Performing rites: On the value of popular music*. Cambridge, MA: Harvard University Press.

Garcia, Luis-Manuel. 2005. "On and on: Repetition as process and pleasure in electronic dance music." *Music Theory Online* 11(4). http://www.societymusictheory.org/mto/issues/mto.05.11.4/toc.11.4.html.

Gates, Henry Louis, Jr. 1988. *The signifying monkey: A theory of Afro-American literary criticism*. Oxford: Oxford University Press.

Gell, Alfred. 1998. *Art and agency: An anthropological theory*. Oxford: Oxford University Press.

Gibson, James J. 1977. The theory of affordances. In *Perceiving, acting, and knowing: Toward an ecological psychology*, ed. Robert Shaw and John Bransford, 67–82. Hillsdale, NJ: Erlbaum.

———. 1979. *The ecological approach to visual perception*. Boston: Houghton Mifflin.

Gilbert, Jeremy, and Ewan Pearson. 1999. *Discographies: Dance music, culture and the politics of sound*. New York: Routledge.

Godøy, Rolf Inge, and Marc Leman, eds. 2010. *Musical gestures: Sound, movement, and meaning*. New York: Routledge.

Goehr, Lydia. 1992. *The imaginary museum of musical works: An essay in the philosophy of music*. Oxford: Clarendon Press.

———. 2007. Introductory essay: His master's choice. In *The imaginary museum of musical works: An essay in the philosophy of music*, xvii–lii. Rev. ed. New York: Oxford University Press.

Goldsworthy, David. 2005. "Cyclic properties of Indonesian music." *Journal of Musicological Research* 24: 309–33.

Goodman, Nelson. 1968. *Languages of art*. Indianapolis: Bobbs-Merrill.

Gracyk, Theodore. 1996. *Rhythm and noise: An aesthetics of rock*. Durham, NC: Duke University Press.

Grant, Roger Mathew. 2010. Four hundred years of meter: Theories, ideologies, and technologies of musical periodicity since 1611. Ph.D. dissertation, University of Pennsylvania.

Gumbrecht, Hans Ulrich. 2004. *Production of presence: What meaning cannot convey*. Palo Alto, CA: Stanford University Press.

Gumbrecht, Hans Ulrich, and Michael Marrinan, eds. 2003. *Mapping Benjamin: The work of art in the digital age*. Writing Science. Palo Alto, CA: Stanford University Press.

Gunther, Eric, and Sile O'Modhrain. 2003. "Cutaneous grooves: Composing for the sense of touch." *Journal of New Music Research* 32(4): 369–81.

Hadley, Daniel. 1993. "'Ride the rhythm': Two approaches to DJ practice." *Popular Music Studies* 5: 58–67.

Haraway, Donna J. 1991. *Simians, cyborgs, and women: The reinvention of nature.* 1st ed. New York: Routledge.

Hasty, Christopher. 1997. *Meter as rhythm.* New York: Oxford University Press.

Hatten, Robert S. 2004. *Interpreting musical gestures, topics, and tropes: Mozart, Beethoven, Schubert.* Musical meaning and interpretation. Bloomington: Indiana University Press.

Hayles, N. Katherine. 1999. *How we became posthuman: Virtual bodies in cybernetics, literature, and informatics.* Chicago: University of Chicago Press.

Headlam, Dave. 1995. Does the song remain the same? Questions of authorship and identification in the music of Led Zeppelin. In *Concert music, rock, and jazz since 1945: Essays and analytical studies*, ed. Elizabeth West Marvin and Richard Hermann, 313–64. Rochester: University of Rochester Press.

Henke, Robert. 2007. "Live performance in the age of supercomputing." *Textura.* http://www.monolake.de/interviews/supercomputing.html.

Hennion, Antoine. 2003. Music and mediation: Toward a new sociology of music. In *The cultural study of music: A critical introduction*, ed. Martin Clayton, Trevor Herbert, and Richard Middleton, 80–91. New York: Routledge.

Horlacher, Gretchen. 1992. "The rhythms of reiteration: Formal development in Stravinsky's ostinati." *Music Theory Spectrum 14*: 171–87.

———. 1995. "Metric irregularity in 'Les Noces': The problem of periodicity." *Journal of Music Theory 39*(2): 285–309.

———. 2000. "Multiple meters and metrical processes in the music of Steve Reich." *Intégral 14*(15): 265–97.

———. 2001. "Bartók's 'Change of time': Coming unfixed." *Music Theory Online 7*(1). http://www.societymusictheory.org/mto/issues/mto.01.7.1/toc.7.1.html.

Hughes, Timothy. 2003. Groove and flow: Six analytical essays on the music of Stevie Wonder. Ph.D. dissertation, University of Washington.

Ives, Charles. 1970. *Essays before a sonata, the majority, and other writings.* Ed. Howard Boatwright. New York: Norton.

Johnson, Mark L., and Steve Larson. 2003. "'Something in the way she moves': Metaphors of musical motion." *Metaphor and Symbol 18*(2): 63–84.

Jones, Mari Riess, Heather Moynihan Johnston, and Jennifer Puente. 2006. "Effects of auditory pattern structure on anticipatory and reactive attending." *Cognitive Psychology 53*(1): 59–96.

Jones, Mari Riess, Heather Moynihan, Noah MacKenzie, and Jennifer Puente. 2002. "Temporal aspects of stimulus-driven attending in dynamic arrays." *Psychological Science 13*(4): 313–19.

Kaltenbrunner, Martin, Günther Geiger, and Sergi Jordà. 2004. Dynamic patches for live musical performance. In *Proceedings of the 2004 International Conference on New Interfaces for Musical Expression*, ed. Yoichi Nagashima and Michael J. Lyons, 19–22. Hamamatsu, Japan: Shizuoka University of Art and Culture. http://www.informatik.uni-trier.de/~ley/db/conf/nime/nime2004.html.

Kassabian, Anahid. 2002. Ubiquitous listening. In *Popular music studies*, ed. David Hesmondhalgh and Keith Negus, 131–42. New York: Oxford University Press.

Katz, Mark. 2004. *Capturing sound: How technology has changed music.* Los Angeles: University of California Press.

Keil, Charles. 1966. "Motion and feeling through music." *Journal of Aesthetics and Art Criticism* 24(3): 337–49.

———. 1987. "Participatory discrepancies and the power of music." *Cultural Anthropology* 2(3): 275–83.

Keil, Charles, and Stephen Feld. 1994. *Music grooves: Essays and dialogues.* Chicago: University of Chicago Press.

Kingsbury, Henry. 1988. *Music, talent, and performance: A conservatory cultural system.* Philadelphia: Temple University Press.

Kirschenbaum, Matthew G. 2004. "Extreme inscription: Towards a grammatology of the hard drive." *TEXT Technology 2:* 91–125.

Kiser, Spencer. 2006. SpinCycle: A color-tracking turntable sequencer. In *Proceedings of the 2006 International Conference on New Interfaces for Musical Expression*, ed. Norbert Schnell, Frédéric Bevilacqua, Michael J. Lyons, and Atau Tanaka, 75–76. Paris: IRCAM and Centre Pompidou in collaboration with Sorbonne University. http://www.informatik.uni-trier.de/~ley/db/conf/nime/nime2006.html.

Kivy, Peter. 1993. *The fine art of repetition: Essays in the philosophy of music.* Cambridge: Cambridge University Press.

Krebs, Harald. 1999. *Fantasy pieces: Metrical dissonance in the music of Robert Schumann.* New York: Oxford University Press.

Krims, Adam. 2000. *Rap music and the poetics of identity.* Cambridge: Cambridge University Press.

Kvifte, Tellef, and Alexander Refsum Jensenius. 2006. Towards a coherent terminology and model of instrument description and design. In *Proceedings of the 2006 International Conference on New Interfaces for Musical Expression*, ed. Norbert Schnell, Frédéric Bevilacqua, Michael J. Lyons, and Atau Tanaka, 220–25. Paris: IRCAM and Centre Pompidou in collaboration with Sorbonne University. http://www.informatik.uni-trier.de/~ley/db/conf/nime/nime2006.html.

Large, Edward W., and Mari Riess Jones. 1999. "The dynamics of attending: How people track time-varying events." *Psychological Review 106*(1): 119–59.

Larson, Steve. 1987. Schenkerian analysis of modern jazz. Ph.D. dissertation, University of Michigan.

———. 1998. "Schenkerian analysis of modern jazz: Questions about method." *Music Theory Spectrum 20*(2): 209–41.

———. 1999. "Swing and motive in three performances by Oscar Peterson." *Journal of Music Theory 43*(2): 283–314.

———. 2006. Rhythmic displacement in the music of Bill Evans. In *Structure and meaning in tonal music: A Festschrift for Carl Schachter*, ed. Poundie Burstein and David Gagné, 103–22. Hillsdale, NJ: Pendragon Press.

Leman, Marc. 2007. *Embodied music cognition and mediation technology.* Cambridge, MA: MIT Press.

Lerdahl, Fred, and Ray Jackendoff. 1983. *A generative theory of tonal music.* Cambridge, MA: MIT Press.

Lester, Joel. 1995. Performance and analysis: Interaction and interpretation. In *The practice of performance: Studies in musical interpretation*, ed. John Rink, 197–216. Cambridge: Cambridge University Press.

Levinson, Jerrold. 1980. "What a musical work is." *Journal of Philosophy 77*: 5–28.

———. 1990. *Music, art, & metaphysics*. Ithaca: Cornell University Press.

Lewis, George. 1996. "Improvised music after 1950: Afrological and Eurological perspectives." *Black Music Research Journal 16*(1): 91–122.

———. 2000. "Too many notes: Computers, complexity, and culture in Voyager." *Leonardo Music Journal 10*: 33–39.

Leydon, Rebecca. 2002. "Towards a typology of minimalist tropes." *Music Theory Online 8*(4).

Lidov, David. 1979. "Structure and function in musical repetition." *Journal of the Canadian Association of University Schools of Music 8*(1): 1–32.

Lippit, Takuro Mizuta. 2004. Realtime sampling system for the turntablist version 2: 16 padjoy-stickcontroller. In *Proceedings of the 2004 International Conference on New Interfaces for Musical Expression*, ed. Yoichi Nagashima and Michael J. Lyons, 211–12. Hamamatsu, Japan: Shizuoka University of Art and Culture. http://www.informatik.uni-trier.de/~ley/db/conf/nime/nime2004.html.

———. 2006. Turntable music in the digital era: Designing alternative tools for new turntable expression. In *Proceedings of the 2006 International Conference on New Interfaces for Musical Expression*, ed. Norbert Schnell, Frédéric Bevilacqua, Michael J. Lyons, and Atau Tanaka, 71–74. Paris: IRCAM and Centre Pompidou in collaboration with Sorbonne University. http://www.informatik.uni-trier.de/~ley/db/conf/nime/nime2006.html.

Locke, David. 1982. "Principles of offbeat timing and cross-rhythm in southern Eve dance drumming." *Ethnomusicology 26*(2): 217–46.

London, Justin. 2004. *Hearing in time: Psychological aspects of musical meter*. Oxford: Oxford University Press.

Lord, Albert. 1960. *The singer of tales*. Cambridge, MA: Harvard University Press.

Loubet, Emmanuelle. 2000. "Laptop performers, compact disc designers, and no-beat techno artists in Japan: Music from nowhere." *Computer Music Journal 24*(4): 19–32.

Lowe, Bethany. 2005. "On the relationship between analysis and performance: The mediatory role of the interpretation." *Indiana Theory Review 24*: 47–106.

Lysloff, René T. A., and Leslie C. Gay, Jr., eds. 2003. *Music and technoculture*. Middletown, CT: Wesleyan University Press.

MacDonald, Alistair. 1995. "Performance practice in the presentation of electroacoustic music." *Computer Music Journal 19*(4): 88–92.

Machover, Tod. 2002. Instruments, interactivity, and inevitability. In *Proceedings of the 2002 International Conference on New Interfaces for Musical Expression*, ed. Eoin Brazil, 196. Dublin: Media Lab Europe. http://www.informatik.uni-trier.de/~ley/db/conf/nime/nime2002.html.

Madrid, Alejandro L. 2008. *Nor-tec rifa!: Electronic dance music from Tijuana to the world*. New York: Oxford University Press.

Magnusson, Thor, and Enrike Hurtado Mendieta. 2007. The acoustic, the digital, and the body: A survey on musical instruments. In *Proceedings of the 2007 International Conference on New Interfaces for Musical Expression*, ed. Langdon Crawford, 94–99. New York: New York University. http://portal.acm.org/portal.cfm.

Malbon, Ben. 1999. *Clubbing: dancing, ecstasy, and vitality*. New York: Routledge.

Marsh, Charity. 2005. Raving cyborgs, queering practices, and discourses of freedom: The search for meaning in Toronto's rave culture. Ph.D. dissertation, York University.

Martin, Henry. 1996. *Charlie Parker and thematic improvisation*. Lanham, MD: Scarecrow Press.

———. 2006. "We remember Clifford: Variation technique at the middleground." *Dutch Journal of Music Theory 11*(1): 1–8.

Martin, John Joseph. 1936. *America dancing: The background and personalities of the modern dance.* New York: Dodge.

Maus, Fred Everett. 1988. "Music as drama." *Music Theory Spectrum 10:* 56–73.

McClary, Susan. 2007. Cycles of repetition: Chacona, ciaccona, chaconne, and the chaconne. In *Reading music: Selected essays,* 317–42. Aldershot, UK: Ashgate.

McClelland, Ryan. 2005. "Performance and analysis studies: An overview and bibliography." *Indiana Theory Review 24:* 95–106.

McRae, Chris. 2009. Becoming a bass player: Embodiment in music performance. In *Music auto-ethnographies: Making autoethnography sing/Making music personal,* ed. Brydie-Leigh Bartleet and Carolyn Ellis, 136–52. Sydney: Australian Academic Press.

Middleton, Richard. 1983. "'Play it again, Sam': Some notes on the productivity of repetition in popular music." *Popular Music 3:* 235–70.

———. 1990. *Studying popular music.* Milton Keynes, UK: Open University Press.

Miyakawa, Felicia M. 2005. *Five Percenter rap: God hop's music, message, and Black Muslim mission.* Profiles in popular music. Bloomington: Indiana University Press.

Monson, Ingrid T. 1996. *Saying something: Jazz improvisation and interaction.* Chicago: University of Chicago Press.

———. 1999. "Riffs, repetition, and theories of globalization." *Ethnomusicology 43:* 31–65.

Montague, Eugene. 2001. Moving to music: A theory of sound and physical action. Ph.D. dissertation, University of Pennsylvania.

Moore, Allan F. 2001. *Rock: The primary text: Developing a musicology of rock.* 2nd ed. Burlington, VT: Ashgate.

Neill, Ben. 2002. "Pleasure beats: Rhythm and the aesthetics of current electronic music." *Leonardo Music Journal 12:* 3–6.

Nettl, Bruno. 1974. "Thoughts on improvisation: A comparative approach." *Musical Quarterly 60*(1): 1–19.

———. 1992. *The radif of Persian music: Studies of structure and cultural context in classical music of Iran.* Revised. Champaign, IL: Elephant and Cat.

———. 1998. An art neglected in scholarship. In *In the course of performance: Studies in the world of musical improvisation,* ed. Bruno Nettl and Melinda Russell, 1–23. Chicago: University of Chicago Press.

Nettl, Bruno, and Melinda Russell, eds. 1998. *In the course of performance: Studies in the world of musical improvisation.* Chicago: University of Chicago Press.

Norman, Donald A. 2002 [1988]. *The design of everyday things [The psychology of everyday things].* New York: Basic Books.

Nye, Sean. 2009. "'Love Parade, please not again': A Berlin cultural history." *Echo: A Music-Centered Journal 9*(1). http://www.echo.ucla.edu/Volume9-Issue1/table-of-contents.html.

Oore, Sageev. 2005. Learning advanced skills on new instruments; or, practising scales and arpeggios on your NIME. In *Proceedings of the 2005 International Conference on New Interfaces for Musical Expression,* ed. Sidney Fels and Tina Blaine, 60–65. Vancouver: University of British Columbia, Media and Graphics Interdisciplinary Center. http://www.informatik.uni-trier.de/~ley/db/conf/nime/nime2005.html.

Ostertag, Bob. 2002. "Human bodies, computer music." *Leonardo Music Journal 12:* 11–14.

Overy, Katie, and Istvan Molnar-Szakacs. 2009. "Being together in time: Musical experience and the mirror neuron system." *Music Perception 26*(5): 489–504.

Paradiso, Joseph A., and Sile O'Modhrain. 2003. "Current trends in electronic music interfaces." *Journal of New Music Research 32*(4): 345–349.

di Pellegrino, G., L. Fadiga, L. Fogassi, V. Gallese, and G. Rizzolatti. 1992. "Understanding motor events: a neurophysiological study." *Experimental Brain Research 91*(1): 176–80.

Peraino, Judith Ann. 2006. *Listening to the sirens: Musical technologies of queer identity from Homer to "Hedwig."* Berkeley: University of California Press.

Phelan, Peggy. 1993. *Unmarked: The politics of performance.* London: Routledge.

Pike, Alfred. 1975. "A phenomenology of jazz." *Journal of Jazz Studies 2*(1): 88–94.

Pinch, Trevor, and Karin Bijsterveld. 2004. "Sound Studies: New technologies and music." *Social Studies of Science 34*(5): 635–48.

Pinch, Trevor, and Frank Trocco. 2002. *Analog days: The invention and impact of the Moog synthesizer.* Cambridge, MA: Harvard University Press.

Pini, Maria. 1997. Cyborgs, nomads and the raving feminine. In *Dance in the city*, ed. Helen Thomas, 111–29. London: Macmillan UK.

———. 2001. *Club cultures and female subjectivity: The move from home to house.* New York: Palgrave.

Porter, Lewis. 1985. "John Coltrane's *A Love Supreme*: Jazz improvisation as composition." *Journal of the American Musicological Society 38*(3): 593–621.

Potter, Gary. 1990. "Analyzing improvised jazz." *College Music Symposium 30*(1): 64–74.

Potter, Russell. 1998. Not the same: Race, repetition, and difference in hip-hop and dance music. In *Mapping the beat: Popular music and contemporary theory*, ed. Thomas Swiss, John Sloop, and Andrew Herman, 31–46. Oxford: Blackwell.

Povel, Dirk-Jan, and Peter Essens. 1985. "Perception of temporal patterns." *Music Perception 2*(4): 411–40.

Pressing, Jeff. 1987. "The micro- and macrostructural design of improvised music." *Music Perception 5*(2): 133–72.

———. 1988. Improvisation: Methods and models. In *Generative processes in music: The psychology of performance, improvisation, and composition*, ed. John Sloboda, 129–78. Oxford: Oxford University Press.

———. 1990. "Cybernetic issues in interactive performance systems." *Computer Music Journal 14*(1): 12–25.

———. 1993. "Relations between musical and scientific properties of time." *Contemporary Music Review 7*: 105–22.

———. 1998. Psychological constraints on improvisational expertise and communication. In *In the course of performance: Studies in the world of musical improvisation*, ed. Bruno Nettl and Melinda Russell, 47–68. Chicago: University of Chicago Press.

Rahn, Jay. 1996. "Turning the analysis around: African-derived rhythms and Europe-derived music theory." *Black Music Research Journal 16*(1): 71–89.

Rahn, John. 1993. "Repetition." *Contemporary Music Review 7*: 49–57.

Rapp, Tobias. 2009. *Lost and sound: Berlin, techno, und der Easyjetset.* Frankfurt am Main: Suhrkamp.

Rietveld, Hillegonda C. 1998. *This is our house: House music, cultural spaces, and technologies.* Brookfield, VT: Ashgate.

———. 2004. Ephemeral spirit: Sacrificial cyborg and soulful community. In *Rave and religion*, ed. Graham St. John, 45–60. New York: Routledge.

Rink, John, ed. 1995. *The practice of performance: Studies in musical interpretation*. Cambridge: Cambridge University Press.

Rink, John. 1999. Translating musical meaning: The nineteenth-century performer as narrator. In *Rethinking music*, ed. Nicholas Cook and Mark Everist, 217–38. Oxford: Oxford University Press.

Rose, Tricia. 1994. *Black noise: Rap music and black culture in contemporary America*. Hanover, NH: Wesleyan University Press.

Rosenwald, Lawrence. 1993. "Theory, text-setting, and performance." *Journal of Musicology 11*(1): 52–63.

Rothstein, William. 1995. Analysis and the act of performance. In *The practice of performance: Studies in musical interpretation*, ed. John Rink, 217–40. New York: Cambridge University Press.

Rowe, Robert. 2001. *Machine musicianship*. Cambridge, MA: MIT Press.

———. 2003. *Interactive music systems: Machine listening and composing*. Cambridge, MA: MIT Press.

Sarath, Ed. 1996. "A new look at improvisation." *Journal of Music Theory 40*(1): 1–38.

Sawyer, R. Keith. 1996. "The semiotics of improvisation: The pragmatics of musical and verbal performance." *Semiotica 108*: 269–306.

———. 2003. *Group creativity: Music, theater, collaboration*. Mahwah, NJ: Erlbaum.

Schafer, R. Murray. 1977. *The tuning of the world*. 1st ed. New York: Knopf.

Schechner, Richard. 1977. *Essays on performance theory, 1970–1976*. 1st ed. New York: Drama Book Specialists.

Schloss, Joseph. 2004. *Making beats: The art of sample-based hip-hop*. Middletown, CT: Wesleyan University Press.

Schmalfeldt, Janet. 1985. "On the relation of analysis to performance: Beethoven's bagatelles Op. 126, Nos. 2 and 5." *Journal of Music Theory 29*(1): 1–31.

Schnell, Norbert, and Marc Battier. 2002. Introducing composed instruments: Technical and musicological implications. In *Proceedings of the 2002 International Conference on New Interfaces for Musical Expression*, ed. Eoin Brazil, 138–42. Dublin: Media Lab Europe. http://www.informatik.uni-trier.de/~ley/db/conf/nime/nime2002.html.

Schoenberg, Arnold. 1984 [1950]. Brahms the progressive. In *Style and idea: The writings of Arnold Schoenberg*, ed. Leonard Stein, trans. Leo Black, 398–441. London: Faber & Faber.

Schwarz, David. 1993. "Listening subjects: Semiotics, psychoanalysis, and the music of John Adams and Steve Reich." *Perspectives of New Music 31*(2): 24.

Scruton, Roger. 1983. *The aesthetic understanding*. New York: Methuen.

Sellin, Yara. 2005. DJ: Performer, cyborg, dominatrix. Ph.D. dissertation, University of California, Los Angeles.

Sharon, Michael Eyal. 2004. The stranglophone: Enhancing expressiveness in live electronic music. In *Proceedings of the 2004 International Conference on New Interfaces for Musical Expression*, 213–14. Hamamatsu, Japan: Shizuoka University of Art and Culture. http://www.informatik.uni-trier.de/~ley/db/conf/nime/nime2004.html.

Sicko, Dan. 1999. *Techno rebels: The renegades of electronic funk*. New York: Billboard Books.

Sklar, Deidre. 1994. "Can bodylore be brought to its senses?" *Journal of American Folklore 107*(423): 9–22.

Slawek, Stephen. 1998. Keeping it going: Terms, practices, and processes of improvisation in Hindustani instrumental music. In *In the course of performance: Studies in the world of musical improvisation*, ed. Bruno Nettl and Melinda Russell, 335–68. Chicago: University of Chicago Press.

Small, Christopher. 1998. *Musicking: The meanings of performing and listening*. Music/culture. Hanover: University Press of New England.

Smith, Gregory. 1983. Homer, Gregory, and Bill Evans? The theory of formulaic composition in the context of jazz piano improvisation. Ph.D. dissertation, Harvard University.

Snead, James. 1981. "On repetition in black culture." *Black American Literature Forum* 15(4): 146–54.

Spicer, Mark. 2001. British pop-rock music in the post-Beatles era: Three analytical studies. Ph.D. dissertation, Yale University.

Sterne, Jonathan. 2003. *The audible past: Cultural origins of sound reproduction*. Durham, NC: Duke University Press.

Stockhausen, Karlheinz, Aphex Twin, Scanner, and Daniel Pemberton. 2004. Stockhausen vs. the "Technocrats." In *Audio culture: Readings in modern music*, ed. Christoph Cox and Daniel Warner, 381–85. New York: Continuum Books.

Strunk, Steven. 1979. "The harmony of early bop: A layered approach." *Journal of Jazz Studies* 6(1): 4–53.

Sudnow, David. 1978. *Ways of the hand: The organization of improvised conduct*. Cambridge, MA: Harvard University Press.

Tagg, Philip. 1994. "From refrain to rave: The decline of figure and the rise of ground." *Popular Music* 13(2): 209–22.

Taylor, Timothy. 2001. *Strange sounds: Music, technology, and culture*. New York: Routledge.

Temperley, David. 2001. *The cognition of basic musical structures*. Cambridge, MA: MIT Press.

Théberge, Paul. 1997. *Any sound you can imagine: Making music/consuming technology*. Hanover, NH: Wesleyan University Press.

Thompson, Emily. 2002. *The soundscape of modernity: Architectural acoustics and the culture of listening in America, 1900–1933*. Cambridge, MA: MIT Press.

Thornton, Sarah. 1996. *Club cultures: Music, media, and subcultural capital*. Hanover, NH: Wesleyan University Press.

Tirro, Frank. 1974. "Constructive elements in jazz improvisation." *Journal of the American Musicological Society* 27(2): 285–305.

Titon, Jeff Todd. 1978. "Every day I have the blues: Improvisation and daily life." *Southern Folklore Quarterly* 42(1): 85–98.

Toussaint, Godfried. 2003. Classification and phylogenetic analysis of African ternary rhythm timelines. In *Proceedings of BRIDGES: Mathematical connections in art, music and science*, 25–36. Granada, Spain: University of Granada.

Toynbee, Jason. 2000. *Making popular music: Musicians, creativity and institutions*. London: Bloomsbury Academic.

Treitler, Leo. 1974. "Homer and Gregory: The transmission of epic poetry and plainchant." *Musical Quarterly* 9: 333–72.

Veal, Michael. 2007. *Dub: Soundscapes and shattered songs in Jamaican reggae*. Middletown, CT: Wesleyan University Press.

Villar, Nicolas, Hans Gellersen, Matt Jervis, and Alexander Lang. 2007. The ColorDex DJ System: A new interface for live music mixing. In *Proceedings of the 2007 International*

Conference on New Interfaces for Musical Expression, ed. Langdon Crawford, 264–69. New York: New York University Press. http://portal.acm.org.

Waksman, Steve. 2003. "Reading the instrument: An introduction." *Popular Music and Society 26*(3): 251–61.

Walser, Robert. 1995. "Rhythm, rhyme, and rhetoric in the music of Public Enemy." *Ethnomusicology 39*(2): 193–217.

Waterman, Richard Alan. 1952. African influence on the music of the Americas. In *Acculturation in the Americas: Proceedings and selected papers of the XXIXth International Congress of Americanists*, ed. Sol Tax, 207–18. Chicago: University of Chicago Press.

Waters, Keith. 1996. "Blurring the barline: Metric displacement in the piano solos of Herbie Hancock." *Annual Review of Jazz Studies 8*: 19–37.

Williams, Raymond. 1975. *Television: Technology and cultural form*. New York: Schocken.

Winkler, Todd. 1998. *Composing interactive music: Techniques and ideas using Max*. Cambridge, MA: MIT Press.

Wise, M. Norton. 1993. Mediations: Enlightenment balancing acts, or the technologies of rationalism. In *World changes: Thomas Kuhn and the nature of science*, ed. Paul Horwich, 207–56. Cambridge, MA: MIT Press.

Wurtzler, Steve. 1992. "She sang live, but the microphone was turned off": The live, the recorded, and the subject of representation. In *Sound theory/sound practice*, ed. Rick Altman, 87–103. New York: Routledge.

Yeston, Maury. 1976. *The stratification of musical rhythm*. New Haven, CT: Yale University Press.

Zadel, Mark, and Gary Scavone. 2006. Different strokes: A prototype software system for laptop performance and improvisation. In *Proceedings of the 2006 International Conference on New Interfaces for Musical Expression*, ed. Norbert Schnell, Frédéric Bevilacqua, Michael J. Lyons, and Atau Tanaka, 168–71. Paris: IRCAM and Centre Pompidou in collaboration with Sorbonne University. http://www.informatik.uni-trier.de/~ley/db/conf/nime/nime2006.html.

Zak, Albin J. 2001. *The poetics of rock: Cutting tracks, making records*. Berkeley: University of California Press.

Zbikowski, Lawrence. 2002. Cultural knowledge and musical ontology. In *Conceptualizing music: Cognitive structure, theory, and analysis*, 201–42. Oxford: Oxford University Press.

———. 2004. "Modelling the groove: Conceptual structure and popular music." *Journal of the Royal Musical Association 129*(2): 272–97.

Index